ROMA SACRA

ROMA SACRA
ESSAYS ON CHRISTIAN ROME

BY

WILLIAM BARRY, D.D.

Essay Index Reprint Series

Originally published by:

LONGMANS, GREEN AND CO.

BOOKS FOR LIBRARIES PRESS, INC.
FREEPORT, NEW YORK

First Published 1927
Reprinted 1968

LIBRARY OF CONGRESS CATALOG NUMBER:

68-14896

PRINTED IN THE UNITED STATES OF AMERICA

PREFACE

These nine essays, dealing with one great chapter in History which unites and explains them, are taken from the *Dublin Review*, by kind permission of its proprietors. I wish to return them sincere thanks for this and other gracious acts during our association of now more than half a century. And let me name among those who have passed away my friend Wilfrid Ward, editor of the *Dublin Review* as his father had been, and Dom Férotin, O.S.B., whose discovery of the lost 'Liber Ordinum' of Toledo gives a title to my essay on that subject. Dom Férotin and I were bound to each other by strong ties of study and sympathy which, please God, will never be sundered.

To Mr. Wilfrid Meynell, acting for the *Dublin Review* while these articles were submitted to it, I owe a debt of gratitude, nor can I overlook the approval they received from that woman of rare poetic genius, his wife, Mrs. Alice Meynell.

With regard to the epoch-making work of Professor Asin, which demonstrates beyond question how much in the structure and conduct of the 'Divine Comedy' was derived from Islamic sources, I might have added not a little, thanks to my own observation of a similar ground-plan in the Sufi poets (Jelal Eddin Rumi and Farid Eddin Attar, for example) as well as in their spiritual guides. But I have simply affirmed my conviction that Dante's unique worth, as the supreme Christian and Catholic poet, remains unaffected by the disclosure of any possible sources upon which he drew. In this, as in so much else, he resembles Shakespeare.

Lastly, I thank my Rev. Censor for his kind care in reading through these pages.

WILLIAM BARRY.

ST. PETER'S,
   LEAMINGTON.
     June 29, 1927.

CONTENTS

' His ego nec metas rerum nec tempora pono ;
Imperium sine fine dedi.'

ÆNEID, I. 278–9.

ROMA SACRA

I

THE UNKNOWN PLOT— A FRAGMENT

AMONG the slighter pieces of Molière one has always taken my fancy, not only by its gay and brilliant conduct of situation and scene, in themselves just nothing of consequence, or by the quality of its language, so firm as to appear struck out with a chisel, yet natural as everyday talk ; but especially by its foreshadowing of a deeper theme in title and handling than the author had in mind—I mean, ' L'Impromptu de Versailles.' This little sketch, a play that seems to be no play, has been termed ' the comedy of a comedy,' and with reason. It might also have gone by the name of ' A Rehearsal Interrupted ' ; but ' The Impromptu ' is better. Molière calls his company together that they may practise for an entertainment commanded by the King. He has had no time to write the book ; the actors are not well up in their parts ; and some do not even know what characters will be given them. Others grumble at having unsuitable rôles in which they are sure to fail. And so the play must be made as the rehearsal goes along. But one cross incident after another is continually throwing it off the lines. Molière himself talks too

B

much, though well, of the rivals he is taking off ; the
women have their say, leading him into more disqui-
sition and more waste of time ; an idle ' impertinent '
strolls in—we say in English an ' impertinent idler,'
but the French is good—and drives the actor-manager
almost crazy by questions at random. What has
become of the original plot ? It is hanging loose in
the air, while conversation holds the stage. A first
and second messenger announce that the King is
coming ; the actors must begin at once ; but in dis-
may the women cry out that they cannot possibly
appear ; they have forgotten everything they knew ;
and Molière, in an agony, screams back to them, ' Do
the best you can.' At that moment a third herald
enters and puts them out of their fright : His Majesty
has been told that they are not quite ready, and he
graciously remits the performance till another day.

Very simple, is it not ? And how ingenious and
diverting ! Yes, of course, for Molière is the author
and in happy vein. But I need not tell my reader that
this ' Rehearsal Interrupted ' was, in fact, the play.
His Majesty was there all the time, looking on from
the royal box ; he had not adjourned the performance ;
and the supposed original plot would never be acted.
Now, if instead of ' The Impromptu of Versailles ' I
write ' The Impromptu of Life,' perhaps my drift in
this Fragment will be sufficiently obvious. I think,
indeed, that were Shakespeare on the boards during
that bright French encounter of wits and smiles he
would have uttered an aside or two like his own
melancholy Jacques, hinting at the application to our
human stage of every line spoken, nay, of the invention
as a whole. For so it is that in the seven ages of man
we play our parts.   The book is not put into our hands ;

we fancy what we should like to be, and act up to that ; we believe, or at least imagine, that it is mere chance when our favourite character (in which we should be undoubtedly great) is thwarted in its fulfilment by one hindrance after another—by want of friends, want of pence, sickness, public events, private fallings out, our own folly, laziness, ignorance—and then we are too old ; we shall never realise that character for ourselves in this world. We intended to become that which we never were, never shall be. The dreaming idealist of our youth is at length a commonplace way-worn pilgrim, dragging behind him a caravan of cares and sorrows for which he did not bargain. He has acted a part thrust upon him bit by bit, while he thought another would have suited him infinitely better ; and he supposed even that he was not shaping the very details and binding them into a chain, which must make this grander thing impossible to him for ever. Dante remarks (' Paradiso,' viii) on this possible divergence of choice and calling from another point of view ; and Sir Thomas Browne, in his ' Vulgar Errors,' drives the argument home : ' The wisdom of God,' he says, ' hath divided the genius of men according to the different affairs of the world . . . which they who consider not, rudely rushing upon professions and ways of life unequal to their natures, dishonour not only themselves and their functions, but pervert the harmony of the whole world.'

To be used to a situation may, and commonly does, blunt our sense of its strangeness, but cannot change its true quality. Were we not familiar at every turn with what is surely in itself a most remarkable fact, namely, that life is an improvisation, should we be able to endure the thought ? ' I so run,' says the

Apostle, ' not as at an uncertainty.' But all we run
at is uncertain to us. Time brings no assurance
whatsoever. If there is a plot in the life of each we do
not know it. Our days, viewed from the outside, as
they come and go, seem to be mere contingency.
The French proverb means this when it observes,
' Les jours se suivent et ne se ressemblent pas.' For
even in lives where little or nothing seems to happen
there will be thought ; and the associations of thought
on which our judgments depend are beyond reckoning.
Events like earthquake or war visibly shake the play
we have been acting out of its order, and fling it into
the heart of the unknown. But apart from such
catastrophes, there is the endless change of persons, of
opinions, of likings and dislikings, of bodily and mental
states in general, which we have scarcely any means of
controlling before it is upon us ; and always it is liable
to a complete revolution brought in by Chance or
Fate. By which, then, since not by ourselves ? That
is the question. But here we are driven to repeat after
Aristotle (whom I find myself quoting lately more
than for years was my custom), and to repeat with
sadness, that ' there is no science of the individual.'
To science the individual is an unknown quantity.
And as little is the Ego known to art. For if science
deals in laws, art deals in types ; and both are pre-
cluded by their necessary conventions from taking you
or me as their subject. I have seen it written that ' the
supreme art is the art to live.' But there is no such
art. And for an overpowering reason which I will
name, under due reserve, the infinitude of the Ego.

Carlyle was fond of reminding his generation,
judged by the seer to be rather frivolous and to move
on the surface of things, that we live ' in the conflux of

eternities and immensities.' In words not so terror-
striking, the point where we stand is connected with
every point in space ; the moment in which we
breathe comes out of a past eternity, and, while I note
its presence, is fleeting, is gone, before an eternal
future advancing to meet that past. I use the figure
of a procession ; but if in mood more profound we
declare that eternity is here and now, that it must be
the *Nunc Stans* of metaphysicians, it will not alter my
argument. As the Mystery character Time is shown
upon our boards, he is ever in motion, and we along
with him. Our ship of Life has constant connected
parts, or it could not be at all ; those parts are at rest
relatively to one another. But the ship is moving
over a moving sea ; and the earth is a wandering
planet ; and the sun is no more fixed than any other
star ; and the whole universe seen or photographed by
astronomers is, they would affirm, in never-ending
flight ; and the imagined ether, though adamant
impenetrable, can be strained in countless directions.
To these changes in time and space the Ego most
certainly responds ; and to others far more subtle in
a realm which time and space figure darkly enough,
being themselves but the tarnished and cloudy mirror
of the soul. This may help me towards the next
point to which I was coming : that the Ego is a
meeting-place of innumerable forces, ideas, volitions,
actions. It has no dimensions ; but looking into it
we scan abysmal depths. 'All grows and dies,' says
Carlyle again, 'each by its own wondrous laws, in
wondrous fashion of its own ; spiritual things most
wondrously of all. Inscrutable, to the wisest, are
these latter ; not to be prophesied of, or understood.'
I have been told that the problem of three bodies

in motion acting on one another is not yet reduced
to a general expression by mathematicians ; and I
can well believe it. Who, then, would attempt to
resolve what is humorously known as the ' Triangle '
of one lady and two lovers ? It has furnished epics,
tragedies, comedies, and romances since Trojan Paris
ran away with Helen of Sparta ; but next season will
bring more ; and, however inept most of them, the
circumstances will be varied in some particular, not
without significance, in every one.

I watch the white water as it comes tumbling,
foaming, shining, over the weir at Day's Lock, on the
Thames, where I used so often to pause and reflect in
old times. What endless change, baffling the science
of the modern, the fancy of the poet who heard
melodious birds singing madrigals to these shallow
lapses of the stream, the calculation of the geologist
counting ages since the river first made a turn at
Sinodun ! But the soul has had its foaming water-
falls ever since it was capable of impressions ; and
how far back did that begin ? Our experience
is a crowded palimpsest, ' scribbled, crossed, and
crammed ' with adventures half-done, abandoned at
stages the most diverse, forgotten, yet surely legible
still to some deciphering angel. Daniel the prophet
warns us, ' The books were opened.' Those are the
volumes in which a man makes of his own soul day-
book and ledger, with none of the items, debit or
credit, slurred over ; an automatic register—for every
touch of the spirit will have had its effect. However,
what cannot fail to strike a reflective mind in old age
is the immense number of possible stories begun, but
left half-told ; mere shreds and ribands hanging out
of dramas that might have come to something, which

floated up to the ship's side and drifted past, in the years that the locust hath eaten.

These débris of possibilities, on which the Impressionist leaps with delight, cannot be held of no moment because nothing apparently came of them. We owe to their unfinished reality one of the master-thoughts which, in our Catholic schools, have won adherents and inflamed controversy, the *Scientia Media* of Jesuit theologians. On this theory, associated with Molina and Suarez, the Divine foreknowledge extends to every possible state in which every created and creatable being could be found in any ' difference of time ' ; and thereby the mystery of election to grace would attain (if not a perfect, yet) a comparatively reasonable solution. I am not minded to lose myself in this Cretan labyrinth without an Ariadne clue ; but, as things seem to befall us, we cannot deny that our thought and our action at any given moment might, so far as we can perceive, have been other than they were. A million of million accidents might, without logical absurdity, often with no violent improbability, have changed our course. The soul is the meeting-place of contingencies to which we can assign no limit. And if this be true of a single individual, it must be granted for all. The infinite series, then, which would simply result from our being in contact, though we ourselves were stable and fixed in character, with all that there is, must now be multiplied by the infinite series of each in connexion with all. The mind faints before these appalling hierarchies of Pythagorean numbers, reaching from creation to consummation of the worlds which God has made. Yet I am powerless to deny that so it must be. Granting that the possible orders of being and their activities do, by cancelling

opposite contingent facts, reduce what would otherwise be a chaos to bounds and harmony, still the
' numbers numberless ' of chances exceed our faculty
to such a degree that dwelling on them seriously
would perhaps disorder the mind ; ' that way madness lies.'   But even in taking a hasty glance at the
' infinitesimals of the universe,' we cannot fail to see
how unlike are things behind the veil to our com-
fortable ordered existence on this side of it.

Ordered, yet, strictly speaking, liable to immediate
and irremediable ruin.   No calculus of probabilities,
however finely drawn, but must leave a corner for the
improbable which defies calculation.   And, in particular, who would say that it is given to us by ordinary
knowledge to forecast with certainty so much as the
outline of any single life ?   To enunciate this truism
may seem ridiculous ; for can we possibly deny it ?
Yet the thing itself is wonderful.   That multitudes
of rational beings should, during untold ages, have to
begin life without learning its direction or its end, but
by sheer painful experience have to make out path
and goal, is a mystery indeed.   The tribal instinct, we
will say, needs no explanation ; for the race necessarily
aims at its own continuance.   But man the individual
has talents and faculties which look to other ideals
than the tribal.   Yet they are, it would appear, sown
haphazard in a world of chance, where the odds
against their success may be safely taken.   The tribal
forces prevail because they must.   These hidden,
spiritual powers appeal to the tribe only so far as they
serve its purpose.   And, on that subject, a great deal
might be said which would throw a light on popular
science, art, literature, and even religion, were not my
intention leading me a different way.

The conclusion suggested is this, that not by social aims and needs can we clear up the problem of the rational Ego. The preservation of the Tribe is no secret at all ; therefore we shall not discover in it a clue to the ' Unknown Plot,' which individually we are helping forward while we act and suffer. In very superficial, because political, terms, we might ask whether the individual exists for the sake of the State, or the State for the sake of the individual. When, however, we identify the State and the Tribe, as in the last analysis reason demands that we should, and have put both aside, we open a gate into worlds unrealised, where each individual is, in some high significance, his own aim and ideal. The word of freedom here is ' Character.' Those powers of genius that in the eyes of the Materialist are only by-products, and of the politician, waste, reveal now the sphere for which they were created.

Amid the flux and reflux of contingencies, Character abides. It is the Man himself, existing at the centre of his being, and thence reacting on the forces of every kind, physical and metaphysical, that are brought to bear within his compass. It is an energy, and more than energy, latent at first, never perhaps rising into perfect self-knowledge because ' this muddy vesture of decay doth grossly close it in ' ; but controlling the mind and the senses by deep intimations, of which the truth is shown by the success that follows on obeying them. It knows what has to be done and how to do it. From the crowd it will choose fast friends, sure helpers ; it perceives at a flash and judges in the twinkling of an eye. It is not infallible ; but its misgivings rarely prove to be unfounded. It has first sight for love, hate, danger, opportunity ;

and second sight of the future which it intends to
realise.   It need not be selfish in its motives ; it can
be thrown off its balance only by some serious malady
or shock of intense agitation.   It refuses—on principle
I would say, but the word is too slight—rather by an
invincible repugnance, as though tempted to suicide,
it declines to be made a mere tool of any man or
company of men.   And it demands the consideration
which is due to the image of the Supreme within it.
Nothing is more evident in real Character, such as I
am here describing, than its ordered and habitual self-
control.   Therefore it has a certain loftiness akin to
the Stoic tranquillity ; and amid the storms of life it
is calm.   It begins to make its mark at an early age ;
it will survive the loss of health, decay of memory
and vigour of the senses.   Character, thus understood,
is that one thing which we were seeking to bind
and master chance, however multiplied.   And such
Character makes the play.

For while the ostensible drama is unfolding, with
chatter and impertinence on every side, and each
wants to rehearse a favourite part, the hidden intention is the trial of the actors.   Theatre, stage, story,
decorations, audience, the ostensible drama, the interruptions and asides, are all means, none of them the
end, but an ' unsubstantial pageant,' doomed to fade
when it has served its hour.   But, note well, that the
actors being the play, it is of a most peculiar kind,
is indeed unique.   It has unities of its own, not in
time, space, or incident ; far deeper than all that—
unities of which the beauty and truth are fully visible
only from the height where the actors live and move,
not from stalls or floors.   Its mere ' business ' can be im-
provised, in any matter at hand, high or low ; in cottage,

palace, prison, with endless variety of circumstance ; but the acting is the test, and wins or loses the meed of applause as the curtain falls ; *Vos valete et plaudite.*

And is that all ? By no means. The ' Impromptu of Versailles ' affords me another and still more elevated platform from which to survey the drama, worthy now to change its name and be called ' The Actor and Prompter,' or ' He Plays Two Parts.' Any sharp reader (and who is not sharp in our advanced era ?) will have admired the art which doubles Molière's office in this symbolic performance. He is an actor with his company in the ostensible business to execute which they are practising. But he knows all along what they have really come to do ; and the interruptions, the ' idle impertinent,' the messengers, the royal message, are of his contriving. He has learnt the King's mind ; he is an interpreter of the same, while never showing more acquaintance with it than the other persons cast for the piece have dreamt of. He is cunning, if not deceitful ; and without dissimulation his end would not be reached. The analogy is already clear. While to our empirical selves hazard seems the only word to describe experience ; while our own *scientia media* points at every parting of the ways to innumerable other lines of thought or action we might have followed ; there comes to the aged who have moved through so many scenes, and to the biographers of world-famous men, a sense, nay, we must allow it to be a conviction, that in the lives of individuals a plan may be detected, from first to last. They hear gladly the word of Plotinus the Alexandrian, who does not hesitate to declare that ' in life there is no such thing as chance, but simply one order and harmony.' [1]

---

[1] *Enneads,* iv. 4, 35.

In Plotinus, whom the French would smilingly call *un idéaliste enragé*, it is good from time to time that a man read to collect himself out of the fragmentary world in which our lot is cast. But this quotation serves like a text in front of Schopenhauer's thoughtful essay on 'The Apparent Plan in the Fate of the Individual.' You may disagree violently with the sage of Frankfort ; as in many things I do, being a Catholic believer ; but he is never dull, and rarely quite the unmixed German who cannot tell you what he means in less than a quarto volume. Taking over from Kant the distinction, since elaborated by psychical research, between the empirical and the subconscious self, this keen philosopher would give up to hazard the sensible, or surface dimensions of experience, at least as it shows to our ordinary work-a-day vision. That is the 'Impromptu' which disconcerts Molière's company. Nevertheless, men have always held that Chance was bound to the Wheel of Fate, which, under the ambiguous name of Fortune, includes both elements. The Greeks had their Anangke and Eimarmene ; the millions of Moslemin say devoutly, 'It is written' ; the disciples of Calvin, who scorn free-will as a heresy, work out their predestined doom of joy or woe in accordance with 'fixed fate' and 'foreknowledge absolute.' Among ourselves—but Schopenhauer, I think, did not know much about the Catholic schools—while Pelagius stands condemned, the most eminent Saints and Doctors, St. Augustine, St. Thomas Aquinas, and their multitude of followers, would be held to a system of absolute 'Divine decrees,' by the letter if not the spirit of their teaching. But leaving the religious problem unmolested, we find in these considerations that the idea of a plan, a 'plot,' known or unknown, has been at all times familiar to the human conscience ; that it is, in fact, the prevalent ' philosophy of history ' which, in spite of all the talk of ' Chance,' wins most suffrages among the learned and the crowd.   I was much struck when Dr. Newman in his reply to W. E. Gladstone, quoted, as at once obvious and devout, ' the grand lines ' of Aeschylus :

Οὔποτε τὰν Διὸς ἁρμονίαν
θνατῶν παρεξίασι βουλαί.

The wills and ways of men never did, never should, turn out of its course the ' settled rule ' of Zeus. When we reflect on the positions ascribed in the tragedy to Prometheus, the friend of man, and to the Deity who has had him chained to the Caucasian rock, such an application becomes the more remarkable, as bringing out the sense of a Supreme Disposer of events to whom all men bear witness.   Once more we hear, as in Plotinus, ' In life there is no such thing as Chance, but simply one order and harmony.'

In an earlier page we granted that none of us, relying on his everyday faculties, would pretend to sketch his own future, even in outline.   Yet some small gift of calculation will not be denied, such as Warwick, in the ' Second Part of Henry IV,' allows :

> There is a history in all men's lives,
> Figuring the nature of the times deceased ;
> The which observed, a man may prophesy,
> With a near aim, of the main chance of things
> As yet not come to life, which in their seeds
> And weak beginnings lie intreasurèd ;
> Such things become the hatch and brood of time.

Neither science nor common sense would quarrel with a lucid connection thus adequately set up between cause and effect. This philosophy of Warwick's is not less rational than the inference from seed-time itself to harvest. But in Schopenhauer's essay, and in the strong belief of not a few, there exists quite a different, as well as a really transcendent faculty, by virtue of which the future (and its equivalent the distant) may be seen in direct vision. Many are the names bestowed on this inexplicable power— clairvoyance, second sight, divination, soothsaying, prophecy ; and it is everywhere accepted as more than probable, as attaching itself to certain persons, places, and even processes which anyone may attempt, at his peril. Inference holds of reason ; but second sight and the rest are forms of intuition. The empirical Self calculates ; the subliminal Self perceives.

At this turn in the road we catch sight of Schopenhauer, marching along by himself towards the Hill Difficulty, where since his time explorers have discovered, as they assert, the phenomena called tele-pathic, and whence they gaze upon a land hidden from materialistic science. Schopenhauer held that view of Time on which Kant has set his mark, although it is common to many mystics, and is implied in the Dantean phrase, ' One moment seems a longer lethargy than five and twenty ages had appeared '—the view that Time is a form of our minds, not a substance or reality outside them ; that it is a necessary illusion, not a delusion, in our present stage of being. It was, therefore, easy in Schopenhauer's philosophy to expand life on the empirical plane, as we all do and must, into days and years ; or to contract and focus it in one luminous point, somewhat after the fashion of a Greek tragedy, which in the happenings of a single twenty-four hours recapitulates and sums up the story of many

years, making past and future present.   To this power
of ideal construction we must add, in the sage's
opinion, that which he judges to be the fact, namely,
that no 'universals' are real, because reality ever is
singular and individual.   Lastly, we know, and he
repeats in this speculative essay, that his Absolute, the
Primary Will, was by him supposed to exist whole and
entire in every such living singular.   The efficient
cause, therefore, of the seeming 'plot' which makes
life resemble a drama, is also the agent which, of its
own knowledge, communicates to the empirical Self
warnings, visions, intimations, presentiments, signs
and omens and portents, of what in the Time series
we call Future or Past.   That very Absolute is the
Molière who has contrived the play ; and when it
chooses, it can reveal the coming scenes.   Accidents
and errors it weaves into its all-encompassing web.
For to speak with Seneca, *Ducunt volentem fata,
nolentem trahunt.*

I hope that my exposition is fairly intelligible.
Schopenhauer obeys his own logic, in which, granting
the premises, I do not find any serious flaw, despite the
inward contradiction I shall notice later.   That, techni-
cally speaking, this doctrine spells Monism will hardly
be disputed ; yet, by insisting on the individual as the
only real, it takes a seductive appearance of almost
tangible fact.   This, too, gives many of his observations a value quite without reference to the theory by
which he would justify them.   He maintains that the
Ego emerges from conditions seemingly fortuitous by
metaphysical necessity, with a character so framed that
all the events of this particular human course are
already folded up in it, and their unfolding is due to
the inevitable nature of their antecedents.   But when

and how was that inevitable established ? In a former existence, from which one vast Religion, the Buddhist, appears to derive its chief dogma, the famous Karma ? Or was it, as the Vision tells us that concludes Plato's ' Republic,' by the soul's free choice of its future lot, before descending into the mortal body ? And is the true demon, guide, angel, star, of the individual man nothing but himself in his metaphysical form, which these ' mythologies ' (according to Schopenhauer) all recognise ? He quotes Horace,[1] whose delineation of the ' guide ' is beautiful :

> Genius, natale comes qui temperat astrum,
> Naturæ deus humanæ, mortalis in unum—
> Quodque caput, vultu mutabilis, albus et ater.

But while Schopenhauer grants the ' apparent plan ' or ' seeming intention,' by which life puts on the regularity of an ordered play, he never concedes that ' Providence,' foreseeing and designing, is the cause of such harmony. His metaphysical necessity turns out to be a blind, even a furiously blind, instinct, the Will to Live, which rushes forth in all possible directions and strikes on every side. This conception of a tele-ology achieved without choice, not by intellect, is thoroughly Darwinian, yet was already affirmed in Schopenhauer's masterpiece, ' The World as Will and Idea,' not later than 1819. Darwin arrived by the toilsome collocation of monographs on every province of biology at the conclusion—profoundly irrational as we hold it to be—which the philosopher of Frankfort had reached forty years earlier, by deduction from Kant's doctrine of the ' categories of the under-standing.' To Darwin it came as an unwelcome, but

[1] Ep., ii. 2, 187.

also undeniable, certitude that the struggle for existence
was a battle of forces, not of ideas, except in a secondary
and subsidiary way when the world of man had been
evolved.

In Schopenhauer's view, intellect and all its works
were a production of the brain, creating that sort of
play which I have termed the 'ostensible drama';
but something far more primeval than intellect had
created by sheer inward impulse the true tragedy—for
comedy it was not, and could not be—of the ill-fated
race of men. This wholly impersonal author, prompter,
manager, trainer, of his company of actors, went upon
a wave of energy, driving Fate itself before him. So
we could talk of freedom, since this Absolute was not
bound by force, law, idea. But we, the creatures of a
day, moving on that stage, having only senses which
were limited in time and space, with a mind serving
them, *we* were bound. From time to time, in ex-
tremity of danger, when otherwise death was upon us,
the hidden Power would signal a warning; or yet
again, our destruction was part of his will, and oracles
would lead us astray, or the means we took at his
hinting to ward off misfortune would turn and play us
false; for in the Absolute there was neither love nor
hate, but the stony indifference of a Power bent on
making all possible experiments to fill its aching void,
which yet could never be satisfied.

So much for Schopenhauer. He is fantastic, inhuman, yet strangely touched with pity, and most
modern in that he combines with a belief in the essential
Unreason of things a passion for scientific analysis and
connection. His significance for me in this Fragment
may be reckoned thus. For the extreme simplicity of
the surface presentation of the Ego, brought in after

the decay of scholasticism, he gives us a depth of
virtual distinctions which we may or must name otherwise than he did, but which corresponds more closely
to facts than the old Wolfian diagram of 'faculties.'
He reinstates genius and leaves room for inspiration.
His acceptance of the distinction between intuitive
perception and Locke's poor housemaid called Reflection, diligently sweeping up what the senses have
left, enables us to restore the whole wide range of
powers anterior to reasoning, and so not dependent
upon it, which gave St. Thomas after St. Augustine
that rich treasury of truths *per se nota*—seen, not
merely inferred—upon whose virtue the beauty and
strength of enthusiasm will ever be nourished. That
he was not ashamed to hunt round for evidence of
second sight and prophecy, with all they involve, when
the German universities were caught in the meshes of
Hegelian formalism, gave him an advance of some half-
century in the direction pursued by an inductive,
observant psychology to which no state of the spirit
was anathema or taboo. This affirmation of plan and
prevision, though so difficult to reconcile with his blind
aboriginal impulse, leads us towards a path of escape
from the poverty-stricken worship of Humanity on the
empirical, Positivist, or secular level of being to that
which Myers has well denominated 'planetary'; and
the grander cosmic horizons begin to dawn in our
sight with radiance of an unexpected morning. We
may hope to know a little now of the thought which
created all the universe of matter, but which made us
something utterly beyond it in faculty and aspiration.

In the grim philosopher whose work I have been
turning to our own good purpose, we can distinguish
two conflicting moods. He stands with Mephisto-

pheles when he denies the Primal Light ; but he passes over to Aristotle when he maintains that reality is individual and is in us capable of transcending time and space by its own power ; is, in short, not physical but metaphysical. From elder German mystics he drew the belief which we find clear and fierce in Mephisto's account of himself after Faust has called to him, ' Thy name ? ' Let us hear the reply, significant, as I will show in an instant, of much that concerns the century past. Thus, then, the Tempter :

> Part of the part am I, which at the first was all ;
> A part of darkness which gave birth to Light—
> Proud Light who now his Mother would enthral,
> Contesting space and ancient rank with Night.

Of all heresies none is like to this in destructive power and potency—the creed which affirms that Man and the Universe are products, by Fate or Chance, of Unreason. And, among contradictions, where shall we strike across a greater one than that of ' science,' as we have known it in the seats of the mighty, winning new conquests every day by sheer activity of mind, yet arguing without pause or pity to an Absolute Nescience presiding at the birth of worlds and holding sway through the ages ? Irreligion, established on Unreason, has pulled down the fair creations of light, until now we behold it in the shape of perfect mechanical art, inspired by hatred, laying waste our whole civilization. The great Anarch triumphs ; it is surely his hour and the power of darkness.

Most lamentable, indeed. Nevertheless, we are confident that the hour will pass. The other mood of Schopenhauer, which led him to the Hill Difficulty, when it had taken him there flung him as from a high

cliff into the fourth dimension, not of space but of
spirit. To normal science what had the soul become ?
I have said it already—a by-product or a waste-
product ; in the later talk of the lecture-hall an ' epi-
phenomenon.' All things went on as if it did not
exist ; for it could make no difference to weights or
scales, however delicate. Now, then, certain watchers
of phenomena declared that in cases tested by severe
observation something which was not merely physical
or ethereal did intervene to convey knowledge, to
hinder or to accelerate or to produce results, by means
which scorned distances, showed the past, anticipated
events to come in their exact setting, but were not the
ordinary channels of action and cognition. The soul,
denied or treated as a negligible effect, if not simply an
abstract summation of strong or faint feelings, vindi-
cated its claim to be a real efficient cause, yet not as one
more added to the physical chain, but as above and
outside it. Religion did not need to be taught a truth
which was the first article of its belief. Mankind,
told haughtily to have done with anthropomorphic
fancies, knew at all times how close was the spirit-
world to the world of sense ; and its very superstitions
now appeared to have a foundation more solid than the
agnostic refusal to see what there was to be seen.

A higher key gave a fresh reading of the code.
Powers, admitted as existing in every period and phase
of human experience, had always implied that there
was a sphere of reality (in modern jargon, an ' environ-
ment ') to which they corresponded, and into which
they gave entrance. Nor was it a question chiefly of
hypnotism, trance, faith-healing, premonitions, and
such-like ; far from it. The most rare and sacred of
gifts enjoyed by man, not known to physical science at

all, religious and ethical ideals, works of genius in its
whole range, the affinities and affections by which we
are most truly ourselves, found their sure defence here,
and this world beyond the world was perceived to be
their home.   I do not say—Heaven keep me from such
profanity !—that Faith or Genius was in doubt before
Psychical Research came to their assistance.   But to
each disease its remedy ; and unbelieving yet dogmatic
science, as held by great professors, was compelled
by its own methods to grant the active presence of
powers which it could not measure or control.

Enough for this once.   We will not now throw the
lists open where champions of the soul's pre-existence,
of reincarnations and Platonic reminiscence, would fain
tilt against the armed Knight of Christendom.   Another
day will perhaps be set for that strange tourney.   But
we have yet to thank Molière for his ' Impromptu,'
and to give its final scene as I figure it might take
place on the Greek stage, if not the Shakespearean.
For there is something hitherto left unsaid.   Suppose,
then, the third and last of the King's messengers, who
brings the company of actors their release, had been
charged to reveal the secret knot by which all threads of
a play so seemingly incoherent were bound together.
Let him stand aloft, as a god in his chariot, clad in
shimmering raiment, now sable as a night without
stars, and again delicately glancing as with a thousand
tints and tones of soft colours, dreamlike in their
evanescence.   Amid a great stillness he speaks ; and
his voice is like the sound of a breaking sea thunder-
ing over wide wastes of sand.   To every soul there he
brings a word, delivered into the heart.   And thus he
addresses them :

' Men and women, ye company of players, brought

hither as to a Rehearsal—and thou, Molière, poet, teacher, choragus, to all these—hear my message. The play for which ye were practising is ended and not ended. Ye too have been caught in a net of illusion, while ye were making ready to illude others for their entertainment and your profit. Did this company imagine that the drama, whereof certain imperfect readings were given out to be learnt, was all written in the poet's book, fit to be taught even to the fall of the curtain? But it was not so. And thou, poet, shall I inquire of thee, standing there with eyes downcast, if more than this " Impromptu " itself was in thy mind, except perchance at moments when something too great for apprehension flashed by and was gone? No, all were taken in, all made to move in the Unknown Plot, company and choragus alike. On these boards it could only be rehearsed in snatches, by subtle devices of a master-hand, mightier than poet or teacher. It is the King's own Secret. So vast are its dimensions that to stage it would rend the walls and bring down the roof of your theatre in ruin. Its scenery is all the romance of landscape, and beauty of life, that have ever been. It must clothe itself in a glory exceeding Solomon's, yet gracious and tender as the lilies of the field. Its language excels all prose and verse that genius has uttered ; yet no child could whisper more lovingly-simple. Its innermost meaning is the contest between Fate and Free Will—man tempted by sin, tried by suffering, shown his infinite weakness and passion for the abyss, with great heights to climb and the sun offered him as recompense. Its music is the still sad music of humanity, with chords triumphant swelling out at last over a sea of sorrow. And could ye venture to rehearse the acts of such a drama, yet live until the consummation ? Not one, neither poet nor player. In pity, then, his royal Majesty has permitted that, by trivial situation and aimless talk and jest, fancying ye were loitering between scenes half-practised, ye should make proof and trial of the faculties that each one possessed. The King, whom ye did not see, has watched your behaviour and judged your performance. He throws open his royal palace to be your stage and spectacle for the play itself. Come, then, and give it at last in his sight.'

This third of the heralds, clad in sables and wearing the device of a night without stars, we know well, though I write not his name. The tired age through which we have passed was wont to declare that life is not worth living. The messenger has come ; and heroic youths, to whom life offered love, success, renown, have given it joyfully in the great battle where the soul affirms its supreme right to sacrifice all things, save justice and honour.

II

THE HOLY LATIN TONGUE [1]

A WELCOME addition has lately been made to our
liturgical treasures in the shape of the 'Liber Ordinum'
from Toledo, which was lost for centuries, and which
constituted, as it were, the centre of the so-called
Mozarabic rite. The story of its discovery in a
manuscript dating back to 1052—the time of Pope
Alexander II—and of the monastery at Silos where it
was found, reads like a romance. It is one more page
in the antiquarian quest which has made the last century famous ; and it reflects a fresh ray of splendour
on the sons of St. Benedict, who devote themselves to
studies so ecclesiastical, but, above all, on Dom Marius
Férotin, the modest and accomplished discoverer,
editor and critic, whose labours have been crowned
with such rare success.

On the transcription and bringing out of this
beautiful volume, Dom Férotin has spent fifteen years,
grande mortalis aevi spatium, as he pathetically observes.
It was time well given to a worthy object. The 'Liber
Ordinum' will henceforth figure among those jewels of
the Church that are as much her credentials as her

---

[1] (1) *Le Liber Ordinum en usage dans l'Église Wisigothique et Mozarabe
d'Espagne ;* publié pour la première fois par D. Marius Férotin, Bénédictin
de Farnborough. Paris : Firmin-Didot. 1904.

(2) *Liturgia Mozarabica :—Missale Mixtum : Breviarium Gothicum.*
Migne, *Patrol. Lat.* 85, 86. Paris. 1862.

adornment. For the history of dogma it is not without significance. It enhances the value even of that 'incomparable religious literature' which Spanish Catholics have inherited from time immemorial. It is a storehouse of prayers and supplications couched in language that we admire, perhaps envy, too, for its depth, vigour and unction : the perfect expression of Christian ideas in their purity, as little touched by age as our creed itself. We can desire no more persuasive apologetics than these public solemn acts, in which the everlasting truths of religion are displayed with a freedom from superstition, a direct and constant appeal to the Father through the Mediator, an affectionate remembrance of the words of Holy Writ, surprising, doubtless, to 'those without,' but deserving their closest attention. For this is the Catholic Faith in life and speech, as it was known to the orthodox Spaniard from the fifth to the eleventh century ; in other words, during the 'Dark Ages,' and in presence of Arians, Jews and Moslemin. It is our Faith still ; an argument from identity which cannot be broken.

However, we do not propose to handle this large tome from the expert's point of view, an undertaking for which the present writer would be slenderly equipped ; and if we dwell in passing on its apologetic excellence, we are yet more immediately concerned with it as literature, and that because it affords an admirable instance of the Latin which the Church has always used. Our object is to stir up younger men, especially among those who in charge of country missions have a certain degree of leisure, and who would find in the study of that immense library which we call the Fathers, the liturgies and the schoolmen, provinces by no means exhausted, suggestions for preaching of a kind far beyond the more modern authors, and a comfort to themselves in their austere solitude.

Now, to begin.   There is a passage in the second volume of Macaulay's ' History of England ' over which Catholic readers will have sometimes lingered with mixed feelings.   The story-teller is describing how a commission was set up in 1689 to revise the Book of Common Prayer, an attempt which he deprecates on literary grounds ; and he is led to observe as follows :

The English liturgy indeed gains by being compared even with those fine ancient liturgies from which it is to a great extent taken.   The essential qualities of devotional eloquence —concinesness, majestic simplicity, pathetic earnestness of suplication, sobered by a profound reverence, are common between the translations and the originals.   But in the subordinate graces of diction, the originals must be allowed to be far inferior to the translations.   And the reason is obvious.   The technical phraseology of Christianity did not become a part of the Latin language till that language had passed the age of maturity and was sinking into barbarism . . . The Latin of the Roman Catholic services, therefore, is Latin in the last stage of decay. The English of our services is English in all the vigour and suppleness of early youth.   To the great Latin writers, to Terence and Lucretius, to Cicero and Cæsar, to Tacitus and Quinctilian, the noblest compositions of Ambrose and Gregory would have seemed to be, not merely bad writing, but senseless gibberish.[1]

In these rolling periods we hear the accents of a scholar, widely read if not exquisite in judgment, who repeats, nothing doubting, the verdict which was passed by the lights of the Renaissance on Christian Latin and the Catholic liturgies.   Macaulay echoes, in his vigorous manner, the sentiments of Politian and

[1] *History of England*, ii. 114.

Bembo, Sannazzaro and Valla ; nay, of churchmen like Urban VIII, who gave to the Roman Breviary its last classic touch.   The standard by which, after the Council of Trent, its editors approve, reject, reform, is Ciceronian or Virgilian ; they count themselves happy when the matter on which they are operating does not turn restive under their hand.   Yet there is something which the true Catholic hardly welcomes in this deference to Horace, who wrote the ' Carmen Saeculare,' when our sacred odes are in question, or to Lucretius, with whose melancholy verses ' De Rerum Natura ' the Gospels do not tesselate easily into one mosaic.   Even Cicero, grave and elegant, a religious philosopher attached to the New Academy, seems wanting in the qualities of inspiration, reverence and simple faith, which ought to mark the ritual of believers.   Should we have gained if our liturgy had come down to us direct from the Augustan age, from Virgil's ' Aeneid,' Livy's majestic prose, or Tully's copious diction ?   To the mind of the Renaissance this could not appear disputable ; and in a vague, uncritical fashion the view still survives that Christian Latin is barbarous, or decadent, or a second best, for which we apologise, not having any better to show.

As precisely the same course of reasoning was applied to mediaeval architecture during more than three centuries, with consequences not now pleasant to look upon, we may ask leave to examine the things themselves before we give them up to the spoiler. ' Lex orandi lex credendi,' we say, and it is universally true.   A critic far more competent than Macaulay— we mean Walter Pater—has bidden us in his ' Marius the Epicurean ' to admire ' the wonderful liturgical spirit of the Church, her wholly unparalleled genius for

worship,' and her ritual-system which, ' as we see it in
historic retrospect, ranks as one of the great conjoint
and, so to term them, necessary products of human
mind.' That system, he continues, ' destined for ages
to come to direct with so deep a fascination men's
religious instincts, was then already recognisable '—in
the second Christian century, under the Antonines—
' as a new and precious fact in the sum of things.' And
again, ' In a generous eclecticism, within the bounds
of her liberty, and as by some providential power
within her, [the Church] gathers and serviceably
adopts, as in other matters so in ritual, one thing here,
another there, from various sources, Gnostic, Jewish,
Pagan, to adorn and beautify the greatest act of worship
the world has seen. It was thus the liturgy of the
Church came to be—full of consolations for the human
soul, and destined, surely ! one day, under the sanction
of so many ages of human experience, to take exclusive
possession of the religious consciousness.' [1]

Such is the verdict of a criticism at once literary
and spiritual, trained to discriminate between epochs of
creation, not hidebound in a scholarship which would
measure the Latin Psalms of Ascent by the *Gradus
ad Parnassum*. Walter Pater felt that our Christian
language, as we read it in the Fathers, the Mass, the
Sacramentaries, is not Latin in the last stage of decay,
but represents ' the dawning of a fresh order of experiences,' and ' the regenerate type of humanity.' In
the happy phrase of Mr. David Lewis, it is ' baptised '
Latin, the new dialect of faith, hope and charity. The
Church, as an original and independent association,
had in a sense everything to create—ideas, forms of
thought, rules of conduct, a discipline that should give

---

[1] Pater, *Marius the Epicurean*, ii. 134, 138.

strength while it made up for the loss of shows, feasts, sacrifices, and all the picturesque though not always innocent symbols which decorated the pagan world.[1] And she succeeded triumphantly. At this day men otherwise steeled against her charms, allow that in two lines of achievement she stands without a rival : she has wrought up into a noble art, grand in its principles, wise and effective in its practices, the *Vita Devota*, the life of the spirit unto God ; and she has given it full expression by means of rites and sacraments which crown the year with gladness. Of all institutions existing among civilised peoples the Catholic Church is, beyond question, at once the most concrete and the most satisfying to our poetic imagination. As a work of art she bears no parallel from the societies which have grown up beneath her shelter or have borrowed her maxims in their laws and usages. But the point to be observed (though too often not regarded by friends or foes) is this—that her spiritual training never sprang from a philosophy set out in abstract terms, nor did the ritual come into existence by deliberate choice. Both the one and the other grew up in commemoration of the crucified, risen, ascended Christ, who had gone away, yet was ever coming again to His little flock. ' Do this in remembrance of Me,' the Master said, leaving to all future ages the Great Charter of a service which was not less inward than outward, and which embraced the whole of life.

We cannot seek analogies for a conception so deep, or an energy so penetrating, in the dry recitatives which were all that Roman religion had known how to invent, binding the gods by spells of flamens, augurs and other

[1] Tertullian, *De Spectaculis, De Corona* ; Newman, *Callista*, 40, 113–115 ; Gibbon, xv. 182–189, Smith's ed.

legal functionaries, in whose chants and gestures no moral element was discoverable. The nearest resemblance may be sought among Greeks with their Eleusinian mysteries, and Orientals, to whom the tragic sufferings of a deity—Adonis, and far more ancient than the youth of Lebanon, Osiris—were familiar from of old. These dim, far-stretching backgrounds are not to be hastily overlooked. They hint a world of myths and allegories which was waiting, so to speak, until it could be taken up into what St. Augustine admirably calls the ' Apostolic and Evangelical light,' where ethics should give to religion its power for righteousness, and religion should transfigure the code of morals to a passionate worship of Jesus. Heathen converts would surely bring into the new company they joined an acquaintance with ' divine acts,' myths of Demeter and Iacchos, like yet unlike to the catechetical instruction they were receiving. The Christian baptism and, above all, the Holy Eucharist as it was celebrated from the earliest times, would awaken in them such memories as at Eleusis or Byblus they had stored up. Thus it came to pass that while the common people as well as the philosophers termed Christianity a superstition, a piece of witchcraft, and a lately trumped-up course of magic, believers themselves could not deny that it had its hidden rites ; its ' things done, said and shown,' as at the Great Dionysia ; its vows, fastings, processions, evocations of the divine ; and its *disciplina arcani*, which extended to the Sacred Books themselves.[1]

These aspects of the nascent Christian religion were long disregarded, if not simply denied, by the

----

[1] Older views on this subject in Dollinger, *Heidenthum u. Judenthum*, 156–178, ed. 1857 ; recent, to be carefully criticised, in J. G. Frazer, *The Golden Bough*.

Reformers, to whose position it seemed indispensable that all sacredness in material objects should be cast out, and that the sum of belief should find its expression in an open volume, to be read by everyone who chose to buy it. Revelation was a sort of philosophy, a study for the chamber, without priests, or rites, or divinely ordained actions, or symbolism other than the imagery preserved in the Bible. Its chief outward sign was the written Word. It could not inspire any of the fine arts, except perhaps music ; at the best, it claimed a rank as literature, though for many years the Scriptures received no literary handling, and became a mere dictionary of texts, all equivalent, however disparate. On this method a true understanding of Church history could never be gained. The first centuries were accordingly neglected by Protestants, who broke off their ecclesiastical studies with St. John's Apocalypse. In consequence, they failed to perceive that the New Testament itself was composed in view of a Liturgy which it reflects, while exhibiting in its *logia*, parables, incidents and general structure, the Life of Christ as present to His Church. But more accurate investigations have completely overthrown this unhistorical idea.

Not only then were the Sacred Books given canonical rank by the Society on whose behalf the Apostles and Evangelists wrote them, but they took their actual shape as destined to be read where Christians came together for worship. Their aim, in the new language so rapidly developed, was the edification of the faithful. They supposed the Church already in existence, with her undying memory of the Bridegroom, her creed in the heart, her Easter and Pentecost, her daily or weekly Eucharist, to which all other ceremonies converged.

Both Testaments furnished matter for recitation ; but the Old was interpreted as a shadow of the New, and the New abounded in references to the glorified Christ at His Father's right hand. He was not simply the Messiah of the Prophets, but the Lord of the Church. He it was who baptised, who anointed the sick, who broke the living bread of the Sacrament, who should raise up believers from the dead. Evidently we are here in presence, not of any philosophical theorem, though it were the Fatherhood of God ; we recognise a dedication of the whole man, which implies the taking of our Lord's humanity for an example, and the planting of ourselves into the likeness of His death.[1]

Scholars had long been familiar with St. Paul's insistence on these principles ; but, if Protestants, they were inclined to look on him as somehow distinct from the Twelve in so arguing, and his Epistles were set apart by themselves.   Now, however, the most careful students find that St. Paul's isolation is due to our own fancy ; it cannot be maintained. The synoptic Gospels are written from a point of view identical with the Pauline—ecclesiastical and, if the term may be allowed, transcendental. The parables in St. Matthew, the works of power in St. Mark, the discourses and hymns and catecheses in St. Luke, bear tokens on them of a purpose not less didactic than that which controlled the Letters to the Romans or the Ephesians. As regards the Fourth Gospel, nothing perhaps in recent criticism has been so generally approved as the contention that it is a treatise on the sacraments of Baptism and the Eucharist, mystically associated by the Apostle with his Lord's death on the

[1] Here is, in our opinion, the decisive argument against Prof. Harnack's *Essence of Christianity.*

cross, which he witnessed, and the piercing of the
sacred side.   We cannot indeed suffer ourselves to be
carried away into allegories ; but the fact of symbolic
Church meanings in St. John is undeniable, and it casts
a broad light upon the temper of mind, contemplative
in a high degree, which prevailed among Christians
when the second century was beginning.   That temper was one which threw into dramatic forms all it
had learnt concerning Jesus of Nazareth.   It dwelt
upon Him as the great High Priest, and it was already
substituting for the Temple which had passed away an
altar with its everlasting sacrifice, a calendar of its
own, a recited narrative leading up to Communion,
and the watchwords whereby Christians should know
one another.

Elements, therefore, of ritual, which we discern in
St. Paul, become elaborate when we open the Apocalypse, give its inward meaning to the Fourth Gospel,
and are accounted for systematically in the Epistle
to the Hebrews.   How striking is the resemblance
in this liturgical mood between St. John's Gospel
and another work not later than it—the ' Teaching of
the Apostles '—has been forcibly pointed out.   Both
documents employ a similar language ; both regard
Christ as ever present among His people.   The one
letter of St. Clement of Rome which is genuine
Dr. Lightfoot calls ' a great eucharistic psalm, which
gathers about its main practical aim, the restoration of
order at Corinth.'   Significantly enough, critics of the
older school disputed its authenticity on the ground
that hierarchical and sacramental features were too
manifest in a Christian tractate alleged to be of one
period with St. John.   But its long-lost ending has
been recovered, and this turns out to be more distinctly

D

of an hieratic nature than the chapters which we already possessed. Without supposing a fixed observance, we may still believe that the ' chief pastor of the Roman Church ' is here, in these antithetical forms and measured cadences, recalling the language that his ministrations had made familiar to him. The *ex tempore* utterances to which Justin Martyr, forty years afterwards, seems to allude in his ' First Apology,' ' He that presideth sends up prayers and thanksgivings also, as much as he is able,' would in Rome itself, sooner than elsewhere, have given way to fixed supplications. For the Roman love of order and authority, on which Pope Clement dwells with grave enthusiasm, did not tolerate free prophesyings at any period, as the Montanists found in that crisis when their Puritan efforts were defeated by the larger wisdom of the Pontifex Maximus.[1]

Moreover, the Eucharist became a symbol of union with the bishop, and the giving or withholding it a test of orthodoxy, in so marked a manner, that St. Ignatius can appeal to the one altar exactly as he does to the episcopal divine right, combining both in defence against current heresies.[2] When we read the Greek terms in Clement of Rome (see, for instance, section 41), which speak of ' eucharist,' ' canon,' ' liturgy,' and the like, our minds, acquainted with later epochs, are carried on insensibly to the day that stereotyped them as they are now in use. We seem to be present at the actual birth of our Church services. In St. Ignatius of Antioch the Johannine expressions concerning our Lord as ' God's bread,' and the flesh and blood received

[1] Lightfoot, *St. Clement Rom.* i. 382–393 ; for the liturgical ending, ii. 172–188. On the *Didache*, Batiffol, *Six Leçons*, 131.

[2] Ignat., Ephes., 4, 5, 20 ; Magnes., 3, 6, 7 ; Trall., 3, 7 ; Philadelph., i. 4, 7 ; Smyrn., 8.

as pledges of incorruption, though not perhaps derived from our written Fourth Gospel, bear witness to a tradition which the martyr could take for granted in the West as in his native Syria.   They need no change to find a place in our Roman Missal.   This continuity of eighteen centuries is so perfect that it leaves us not a little amazed.   But the most obstinate of critics cannot refuse Clement, or postdate the Johannine writings more than a few years, or get rid of the Ignatian Epistles.   All this literature is in its teaching highly sacramental, while in tone it anticipates the great public forms of worship, Syriac, Hellenic and Latin, which take us onward into the fifth century.   Whether we are able to date these precisely or not, certain it is that all their main elements and the laws of their combination may be studied in writings published before the year 150.   To sum up with St. Clement, ' The Apostles were sent by Christ, as Christ was sent by the Father.   Having received this commission, they preached the kingdom of God, and appointed presbyters and deacons in every place.' [1]   The one great permanent institution left to the Church by our Lord's Apostles is the Mass.   Baptism, called likewise ' Illumination,' gave the neophyte a claim to share in it ; the ordained ministers were set apart especially as consecrating the Eucharist ; and from the *synaxis*, or meeting, the elements were conveyed by deacons to the absent and the sick.

Statements to this effect are not inferences so much as quotations, which may be verified in documents of the sub-apostolic period.   Justin Martyr, in the ' Apology,' from which we took a sentence above, has described, with a Catholic feeling of its importance,

[1] Clem. Rom. Ep., sect. 42.

what his editor cannot help recognising as the ' first
Communion' of the convert who emerges from the
waters of baptism.   And in the following sections
Justin proceeds to give in outline a picture of the
Sunday celebration to which later times added nothing
essential.[1]   It has been reasonably argued that Christians, as regards the substance of public worship, would
naturally build upon the lines traced by their Jewish
predecessors ; that ' the common Prayer, the lessons
from the Law, the lessons from the Prophets, the
chanting of the Psalms or of hymns ; the exposition or
homily, all were there ready for adoption ' ; that ' the
Eucharistic celebration,' whereby our Lord's Passion
was commemorated and applied, furnished ' the new
and vivifying principle, the centre round which these
adopted elements ranged themselves.' [2]   But, while
we trace the development of the Synagogue into the
Catholic Church, that very passage of Justin which
illustrates it also brings home to us the mystery, not
found in Hebrew ritual, of a sacrifice wherein the
Deity became Himself the victim.   ' We take these
things,' says the Martyr, ' not as common bread or
common drink.   But, as through the Word of God
Jesus Christ took flesh and blood . . . so the nourish-
ment over which thanks have been recited in the word
of prayer ordained by Him—we have been taught—is
the Flesh and Blood of that incarnate Jesus.' [3]

We understand now why Christians, as the Pagans
knew or heard of them, fell into one category with
Oriental mystics ; why their rites were confounded in

---

[1] Justin M. i. *Apol.* 61, 65–67, edited by Otto ; see i. 154, quotation
from Augusti, *Christl. Archaeologie.*

[2] Lightfoot, *St. Clement Rom.* i. 393 ; Duchesne, *Orig. du Culte Chrétien,*
45 seq.

[3] Justin M., *ut supra,* 66, slightly compressed.

popular speech with those of Cybele, Isis and Mithras ;
why there was even talk of Thyestean banquets.   Nor
did our apologists deny the resemblance.   Justin dwells
upon it more than once ; Tertullian, following his
example, uses it as an *argumentum ad hominem* ;   and
Clement of Alexandria reiterates, in a cloud of learned
citations, the philosophy which ascribed to demonic
craft and Greek plagiarism a likeness, in itself unques-
tionable, between the new worship and the seemingly
more ancient laws of Crete, or the mysteries of Eleusis,
Mount Ida and Egypt.[1]   'Christianity,' observes
Cardinal Newman, ' came heralded and attended by
a cloud of shadows—shadows of itself—impotent and
monstrous as shadows are, but not at first sight dis-
tinguishable from it by common spectators.'   He
acknowledges even ' old traditions of the truth, embodied for ages in local or in national religions,' which
' gave to those attempts a doctrinal and ritual shape.'[2]
The fact, therefore, is abundantly clear, be its explanation what it may, that in our liturgy, which renewed,
as a sacred drama, Christ's suffering and death, while
offering to communicants the substance of His Body
and Blood, all alike perceived analogies to rites not
Hebrew in their origin, distinct from the ordinary
Greek and Roman public services, and known under
the special name of ' mysteries.'

Thirty years, perhaps, before Justin's ' Apology '
(dated 138), which contains the earliest account in any
detail of the Mass, Pliny opens its Latin history, so
to speak, in writing to Trajan from his government
of Pontus.[3]   He is shocked at the ' stubborn and

---

[1] Justin M. i. *Apol.* 21, 54, 66 ; on Dionysus, *contr. Tryphon.* 69 ;
Tertull. *Apol.* xxi. 85 ;   Clem. Alex. *Stromata*, i. 25, etc.

[2] Newman, *Development of Christian Doctr.* 211, 2nd ed.

[3] Pliny Junior, *Letters*, x. 97.

inflexible obstinacy' of these fanatics. He calls it madness, and their doctrine 'a bad and excessive superstition,' which, however, was emptying the temples of
their worshippers. From renegades he learnt that
'they were accustomed to meet before light on an
appointed day and to recite with one another an incan-
tation (*carmen*) to Christ as God, binding themselves
by oath (*sacramento*) not to do any crime, but rather not
to commit theft, robbery, adultery,' etc. What Greek
word is represented by these two Latin terms we can
scarcely conjecture.[1] Not until the second century
was drawing to an end do we read of Christian Latin.
But it comes before us in Tertullian and the Novatians
as passing already out of its first years. It had grown
and thriven unofficially in proportion as the Western
races, not merely slaves brought to the capital of the
world, but urban citizens, farmers and professional
men, had embraced the Gospel and created their own
clergy from among themselves. Rome had always a
mixed population, with Greek as its *lingua Franca* ;
but the aboriginal idiom was gaining the upper hand
between the days of St. Callistus, who still used Greek
(as we learn from the *Philosophumena*), and those of the
martyr Cornelius. This Pope's correspondence with
St. Cyprian, and the letters sent to Africa by the Roman
presbyters during the vacancy which preceded his
election, show that a new era had begun. From about
the year 250 we may take it for granted that the
Hellenistic dialect was no longer heard in the West
among believers.[2]

[1] Tertullian's variation of Pliny's language (*Apol.* ii. 8) is remarkable :
'allegans, praeter obstinationem non sacrificandi, nihil aliud se de sacra-
mentis eorum comperisse quam,' etc. Pliny's 'sacramentum' means an
oath ; Tertullian's plural is equivalent to our Church usage.

[2] Tertull. vol. iii. in Migne's collection.

St. Augustine, writing to Dioscorus in 410, throws
out an unexpected suggestion : ' Duae tantae urbes,
Latinarum litterarum artifices, Roma atque Carthago,'
he says, with a pride in his barbarian Africa somewhat disconcerting to the classical scholar.[1]   But our
Renaissance training blinds us to the highly artificial
character of the books we take up in school.   There
is a world of Latin beyond them, and there always
was.   The Roman classics are, on the whole, exotic, an
imitation of greater masters.   De Quincey, who had
looked far into this subject, concludes thus : ' A better
structure of Latinity, I will boldly affirm, does not
exist than that of Petronius Arbiter ; and, taken as
a body, the writers of what is denominated the silver
age are for diction no less Roman, and for thought much
more intensely Roman, than any other equal number
of writers from the preceding ages.[2]   Those who have
made the comparison will, it is probable, agree with
De Quincey.   The *Coena Trimalchionis*, for example,
to which he alludes, comes upon us at first reading as
a page torn from the liveliest and most natural of Italian
compositions.   Here is that *lingua vulgaris, lingua
rustica*, of which Pater says that it ' offered a thousand
chance-tost gems of racy or picturesque expression,
rejected, or at least ungathered, by what claimed to be
classical Latin.'[3]   The common dialect, spoken with
local differences in every part of Italy, in Gaul, Spain
and Africa, saw its happy moment arrive when
Christianity spread over those shores.   A literature
was in demand to which the standard authors might
lend occasional phrases and a certain air, as we will

---

[1] St. Aug. Ep. 118, sect. 9.
[2] De Quincey, Letter IV on *Education* ; Works, x. 59.
[3] *Marius the Epicurean*, i. 102.

immediately explain ; but in form and spirit they were
utterly alien from a movement so foreign to old Rome.

Let us distinguish carefully at this juncture. The
Roman religion was poorest in ideas and least affecting
in sentiment of any which civilised nations practised.
Janus himself, in Ovid's vision at the opening of the
'Fasti,' seems to blush for these rude conceptions,
multiplying prosaic epithets in a grammar of ritual ;
the god excuses them :

> Nomina ridebis ; modo namque Patulcius idem,
> Et modo sacrifico Clusius ore vocor ;
> Scilicet alterno voluit rudis illa vetustas
> Nomine diversas significare vices.[1]

When Cicero, in his ' De Legibus,' draws up a code
of laws for public and private worship, the quaint
idioms, lack of depth, and harsh accents, prove how
external a thing was the tradition which he followed.[2]
To his mind the service of the gods consisted in a
recitation of ancient formulas compelling them to
listen ; the priesthood was a department of law. Such
we find to be the religion of which he boasted that his
Romans excelled all other nations in their regard for
it.[3] Beyond this legal definition, Livy, who affected
a pious attitude, does not move. Concerning Numa
he writes :

> Virginesque Vestae legit, Alba oriundum sacerdotium, et
> gentis conditori haud alienum. His, ut assiduae templi anti-
> stites essent, stipendium de publico statuit ; virginitate aliisque
> caeremoniis venerabiles et sanctas fecit.[4]

The Vestals, who were thus chosen for an exalted

---

[1] Ovid, *Fasti*, i. 129–132 ; Döllinger, *ut supra*, 526–534, 540–548, on
the Roman year and its ritual.

[2] Cic. *De Legibus*, ii. 17–22.

[3] *De Haruspicum Responsis*, 9.   [4] Livy, i. 20.

state, nevertheless did not cultivate the *Vita Devota*, as
Christians conceive of it ; they were neither called to
be saints, nor bound to aspire towards ethical perfection. It is an often-quoted observation of Cicero that
no man dreamt of asking virtue from the gods ; a
truth which in every allusion to sacred rites and ceremonies among the Romans is clearly evident.[1] Virtue
was not in the bond ; the *religio*, whereby gods and
clients entered into partnership and rendered each
other services—*Deos homini quod conciliare valeret*, says
Ovid [2]—had no message for the conscience. Wealth,
success, victory over the foe, the turning away of evil
from house and field—*Di meliora piis, erroremque
hostibus illum*—such were the objects prayed for in
the solemn supplications, the *lectisternia*, the *vota* and
piacula, which fill so large a space in Roman history.
Auguries, sacrifices, inspection of victims, Saliarian
dances, the *dapes pontificum* which, originally a sort of
communion, degenerated into luxurious banquets, had
never borne a moral significance. It gave no offence
that adulterers should be supreme pontiffs. When
Clodius talked of religion being outraged, the Sena-
tors smiled, but did not think him unfit to occupy a
sacred function ; while Mark Antony, on ' the feast of
Lupercal,' was held capable of bestowing divine gifts,
ex opere operato, as he ran by naked with his wild company. These rites had not in them anything spiritual ;
they were charms and spells by which an inscrutable
Fate made the gods subject to men. Prayer, in the
sense of petition for grace to lead a good life, was
utterly unknown to the old Roman worship.[3]

Yet, as Roman law built a foundation on which

---

[1] *De Natura Deorum*, iii. 36.　　　　　　[2] *Fasti*, i. 337.
[3] Juvenal, vi. 385 ; Persius, ii. 3 ; Horace, Ep. i. 16.

the Institutes of Popes and Councils were afterwards reared, so the language, not indeed of those mechanical formulas we have touched upon, but of religious enactments and notices, had a certain majesty, an amplitude and decorum, which passed into the new Catholic tradition. Of that style Cicero is the consummate master ; Virgil adds to it a pensive grace ; and Livy becomes almost hieratic whenever the story calls for recitation of portents, omens, feasts brought in, and priesthoods established. We feel as we read that if ever this dialect should be transposed to a genuine religious key, the result would be admirable. Illustrations, for which we cannot allow room, are at hand in such examples as the *Somnium Scipionis*, at every tenth page in Livy, and all through Virgil. The Sixth Book of the 'Aeneid,' however, is undoubtedly coloured by reminiscences of the Eleusinian drama, so that from this point of sight we do not esteem it Latin. Neither did it exercise any influence on our liturgy, direct or indirect. But the 'Fourth Eclogue' is a fragment of Sibylline literature, derived by strange paths from Isaiah's prophesyings ; and its hexameters announce the *connubium* destined one day to take place between the Hebrew spirit and the *vates*, already associated with the Vatican Hill, to which he gave his name.[1]

Two large movements appear to have gone forward at the same time in the course of this transformation, both distinctly visible when we turn to the African Church. One was the anonymous rendering of the Septuagint and New Testament in the version which is known as the *Vetus Latina* ; the other was an adapta-

---

[1] Cic. *De Divinatione* ; Livy, i. 18–22 ; vii. 2 ; x. 6, 9, on the Ogulnian Law, may be consulted ; Ovid's *Fasti*, for mythology and folklore.

tion of dogmatic language, originally Greek, to the
ruder Western idiom.   Behind or beneath such a
double process the Church's ritual grew up in silence.
No small part of the old Latin Bible is yet recoverable.
It takes us back on many lines to the later second and
early third centuries.   Its dialect is the vernacular of
which Plautus in his ' Comic Plays,' Terence occa-
sionally, despite his love of Greek elegance, and the
shameless author of the ' Satyricon,' have left us invaluable fragments.   But we should bear in mind that
the epoch-making appearance of both Testaments in
Latin was due to individuals rather than to authority.
It was brought to pass without observation, so that we
can fix neither its date nor its place.   No single writer
is associated with it.   Recent scholars would allow
that it was produced ' under the auspices of the Roman
Church.' [1]   But Africa may well have taken a share
in the work, as it certainly did much to propagate
and preserve it.   For ' the most advanced classes in
Carthage, of Roman origin and Latin tongue, were the
most Christian.' [2]   At all events this original *Vetus
Latina* (if *Itala* be a false lection in St. Augustine)
determined the cast of speech ever after to be employed
in the Mass and the Ordinal.   It lives on, not only in
the Books of Maccabees, Wisdom, Ecclesiasticus, but,
what is far more important, in the Psalms which we
recite every day.   How daring was the enterprise thus
achieved by humble Christians we will point out when
speaking of St. Jerome's Vulgate, not unfitly termed
its second edition.

Tertullian is the great name of this creative era.
We have known scholars, and ripe ones, too, that could

[1] G. Ranke, *Fragmenta Versionis S. Script. Antehieronym.* 3.
[2] Benson, *Cyprian,* xxxv.

not read him without having their teeth set on edge ;
' they had come,' they would smilingly tell one, ' fresh
from the *Pro Milone* or the *Tusculan Disputations.*'   He
is, in fact, no more to be tamed by rules than Carlyle,
whom, in his savage temper and the felicity of coin-
ing satirical phrases, he recalls.   But no second Latin
Father, not even St. Augustine, excels or equals him
in his gift of retorting on pagans and heretics their own
arguments.   His ' Apologeticum ' remains the pattern
on which all succeeding works of this polemical sort
have been modelled ; it is much the most picturesque,
pregnant and forcible of its kind, now perhaps antiquated, but never surpassed.   The minor Tracts
which embroider on some of its themes are not only
learned but astonishingly alive.   But it is in such
treatises as the ' De Praescriptione,' the ' Adversus
Marcionem,' and the ' Contra Praxeam ' that we recognise the divine whose terminology gives the law to our
scholastic Latin, so precise and adequate does it constantly appear.   If on some points, even before his
lapse into Montanism, Tertullian needs to be corrected,
the fault is not in his language but rather in a certain
crudity of thought which he shared with various of
the earlier Christian schools.   He seldom repeats himself, is curiously original, yet keeps close to tradition.
However, it deserves notice that strong and lasting
as was the African master's influence on Western
theology, we do not trace it in our Church services.
Tertullian was wanting in the tender grace which
makes our prayers edifying ; he was more of a soldier
than a contemplative.   The tradition of fierceness
which he bequeathed is not altogether praiseworthy ;
and, however stainless in his own life, he encouraged
the mad Phrygian ecstasies which it is the especial

merit of the Catholic ordinal to have subdued by its healing rhythms.[1]

St. Cyprian, who called the sarcastic defender of the faith his master—*Da magistrum*, he would say when asking for a volume of Tertullian—was a rhetorician, not harsh and rugged, but somewhat declamatory, though earnest and often affecting. His Latin is cultivated, yet not classic. We become aware in his paragraphs of the ' Asiatic ' strain, redundant in words, and passing into a prose-poetry which offended the nicer taste of Rome, but for that reason was adapted to the movement of feeling apart from which the most refined liturgy would be dead and cold. His Anglican biographer, the late Archbishop Benson, credited him, fairly enough, with ' the condensation and lucid arrangement of a pleader ' in reproducing the sum of Minucius Felix, whose ' Octavius ' he has copied, and in rendering more accessible to average minds Tertullian's ' magnificent presentment of the Person of Christ.' ' Cyprian's merit,' he says again, ' was not limited to the turn of a phrase or the smoothing of a *Postremissimus* into an *Extremi et minimi,* or the inweaving of expressions as beautiful as his *Law of Innocence.*' St. Jerome, dwelling on the triumphs of the cross over literary converts, names Cyprian among those who lay aside their eloquence and ' content themselves with the majesty of Christian thoughts.' [2] To St. Augustine it appeared that Cyprian and Ambrose were models of Catholic speech, preferable before all others, though he found too great a richness in some places of the Carthaginian bishop. The letter which

[1] Some excellent remarks on Tertullian's mind and writing in Preface to the Oxford translation.

[2] Jerome *in Jonam,* c. 3.

that prelate sent to the Church at Thibaris,[1] and in which occurs the fine image of the Christian gladiator, is otherwise beautifully intimate, persuasive and touching. But, perhaps, the one best-known passage of St. Cyprian is also the most admirable as metaphor and argument—that which, in the fifth chapter *De Catholicae Ecclesiae Unitate*, tells us how the episcopate is a living organism, *cujus a singulis in solidum pars tenetur*. The sentences move upon a cadence such as after ages loved to repeat :

Avelle radium solis a corpore, divisionem lucis unitas non capit ; ab arbore frange ramum, fractus germinare non poterit ; a fonte praecide rivum, praecisus arescit. Sic et ecclesia Domini luce perfusa per orbem totum radios suos porrigit ; unum tamen lumen est quod ubique diffunditur, nec unitas corporis separatur.[2]

How far the Prophets and Apostles themselves deserve the praise of eloquence—in other words, of literary charm—St. Augustine has considered in the Fourth Book just quoted on Christian doctrine. He decides, with only the *Vetus Latina* before him, that they have a persuasiveness of their own, but that in the translation *illa musica disciplina*, which forms so large a part of style, is sometimes or often wanting. And he analyses with curious ingenuity the phrases of his Latin St. Paul. The principles to be observed in preaching and teaching, as Augustine lays them down, show that he was bent on one supreme purpose : so to speak as African ears, and those not learned or fastidious, should understand what was said. *Quid enim*

---

[1] Ep. 58.
[2] Benson, *Cyprian*, 9, 59, 258 ; Aug. *De Doctr. Christiana*, iv. 45–50 ; Cypr. *De Habitu Virginum*, 2, 3 ; *De Unitate*, 5. See also E. W. Watson, 'The Style and Language of St. Cyprian,' in *Studia Bibl. Ecclesiast.*, Oxford, 1896.

prodest locutionis integritas, he exclaims, *quam non sequitur intellectus audientis ?* And on another occasion : [1] ' Better that grammarians should blame us than that the people should not comprehend.' Was this, then, opening the flood-gates of decadence ? But Latin literature, in the select meaning of the term, had lived its day. The tradition of the classics, between 150 and 400, gave birth to no achievements which are still on record. If the Roman language was not doomed to disappear, its renewal could be expected only from contact with life in the people at large. And a second period was granted, not less eloquent than the first. *In istis autem nostris,* observes St. Augustine with profound literary insight, *omnia magna sunt quae dicimus.* To be popular as regarded style, but lofty and impressive in meaning, was surely to unite the conditions under which the truest language would find its appositeness and beauty. The saint who thus despised mere ornament and tinsel rhetoric had given his best years to the composition of works which will last as long as the Eternal City :

> dum Capitolium
> Scandet cum tacita virgine Pontifex.

Macaulay held that St. Augustine in his ' Confessions ' writes like a field-preacher. It is Wesley in a Latin garb to him. But others, among whom J. A. Symonds calls for recognition, have judged very differently of the marvellous periods in which every problem of the time is handled with so subtle and suggestive an apprehension. For sheer weight of thought Augustine beggars the classic writers of Rome; they are children in comparison, as we might anticipate,

---

[1] *Enarr. in Ps.* 138, 20.

for what had they not imported from the Greeks ? But
we should appraise a man's language by the demands
made upon it ; and the question is whether he who
planned and executed the ' De Trinitate ' no less than
the ' De Civitate Dei ' ; who was capable of dissecting
to the finest fibre every subterfuge of the Pelagians ;
who put forth apologetic treatises such as ' De Ordine,'
' De Utilitate Credendi,' and so many more ; who in
a never-ending correspondence was always equal to the
minds, young or old, that addressed him ; and whose
religious biography touched chords unheard till then in
his native literature ; whether, we say, one so various,
deep, tender, ardent, unconstrained and individual,
has known how to forge an instrument responsive to
his needs. There cannot be a doubt in the judgment
of those who are qualified by study of St. Augustine to
return an answer. Considered in this light he stands
alone among the Latins ; he is a world in himself. No
research can exhaust his abundance. Macaulay speaks
as though this mighty genius had a single style ; but he
had as many as his themes required. He created not
one manner but all those which we light upon when we
turn over his vast folios : the pleasant, severe, playful,
vehement, argumentative, hortatory, devout. Yet he
is everywhere the Augustine we know ; his thoughts
rise within, flow out of their own accord, pursue their
inimitable course, and have no concealment. Sin-
cerity, originality, and as a consequence *naïveté*—these
are the warp and woof in a texture that exhibits the
Christian spirit under almost every one of its possible
aspects.

Yet Augustine teaches simply by interrogating his
own mind. *Quid mihi videtur ?* he seems to say. But
as a fertile speculative intellect, obedient to orthodoxy

while throwing out lights from the source within, our teacher of the year 430 remains incomparable. He is found at the well-head of mediaeval thought wherever we pursue it. St. Gregory the Great offers a replica subdued to an ignorant and barbarous audience of his general system. When philosophy starts again in the eleventh century, St. Anselm takes up the broken thread from lines drawn in the Anti-Pelagian treatises. The Angelical Doctor quotes him incessantly. And who shall measure the part which he plays during the conflicts where Luther, Calvin, Jansenius have won a doubtful fame ? After the Vulgate, which deserves to be called the first of modern books—an indispensable prologue not only to all Romance languages but to English and German Christianity—come the writings of St. Augustine, his ideas and the form in which he shaped them, not only for men who were professed theologians, but for all who read and studied. That immense collection, ' The City of God,' was the commonplace book of Charlemagne and the Middle Ages. It foreshadowed the Holy Roman Empire ; it distinguished between the Imperium and the Sacerdotium ; its echoes may still be heard in every Encyclical which issues from the Vatican touching Church and State. We define it the Catholic Apocalypse.[1]

A new religious key, we have said, was wanting by which to quicken the Roman hierarchical and ritual terms with a doctrine and worship worthy of them. If we may judge by what happened in the period reaching from St. Ambrose to St. Leo the Great (340 to 460 in round numbers), which includes the labours of

---

[1] A robust archaic rendering by John Healey of *The City of God*, in three volumes, has been published among Dent's ' Temple Classics.'

St. Jerome as well as of St. Augustine, we shall perhaps
conclude that many of the sacerdotal usages had their
origin at Rome, but the literature took its inspiration
from sources outside.

Modes of 'impassioned prose' (to borrow De
Quincey's phrase) were not strange in the African
writings. *Pectus est quod facit disertum*, Quintilian had
said. It was that vehemence, the ground-tone whenever he speaks, which drove Tertullian into paradox
and at last into heresy. St. Augustine never loses it,
though in him it is mellowed by compassion for all
suffering, by a deep sense of life's perplexities, and by
remembrance of his own past. Vehemence, intensity
of thought and aim, heighten his rhetoric, which had
been at first an echo, graceful enough, of Tully's
phrasing ; but as the stronger genius learned its
powers, that large, penetrating, widely-glancing style
was elicited under whose touch every question took
on facets beyond number and meditation found a form
as concrete as the world of matter itself.

We enjoy Augustine's youthful essays in the familiar Ciceronian speech, knowing that they *are* essays,
not masterpieces such as he will produce in riper
years. The long succession of Tracts on Donatism,
the controversies about grace and free-will, belong
rather to science than to literature. The Sermons,
with no care for composition, short and crisp in their
sentences, antithetical, quaint, happy in single words,
give us a language understood of the people, seldom
classic, yet often surprisingly beautiful. We might
instance as a perfect exercise in this Christian manner
the lections read in our Breviary on St. John's Octave,
and better still those of the Wednesday in Whitsun
Week. Regretfully we deny ourselves the pleasure of

quoting them.[1]   But whoever will go over these
passages aloud can surely not help feeling in them a
movement, tender at once and passionate, joyous and
majestic, altogether fresh to Latin as we learn it from
the Pagan class-books.   It is an interior style ; the
heavens have opened, man speaks to his brethren in
the presence of his Maker ; ' Ecce,' cries St. Cyprian,
' agon sublimis et magnus et coronae caelestis premio
gloriosus, ut spectet nos certantes Deus, et super eos
quos filios facere dignatus est oculos suos pandens, cer-
taminis nostri spectaculo perfruatur.'[2]   The ancient
liturgy is written in this temper of martyrdom.

Passages of a new splendour abound in ' De Genesi
ad Litteram,' which often rises to sublime poetry, in
the books on the Trinity, and whenever in ' The City
of God ' Augustine dwells on Paradise and the angels.
This Dantean string always resounds joyfully even
amid the ' inspissated gloom ' which gathers about his
last writings.   But we return by instinct to the ' Confessions ' as yielding in small compass the fruit of
Christian Latin.   Their tone is certainly impassioned,
not once alone, as De Quincey argued, when the saint
mourns for his dead friend, but all through, in the story
of his lapse from innocence, his wanderings through
the mazes of speculation, his repentance and conversion.   He charms by that constant fellow-feeling
which gave us the word humanity, and which flows in
such unsigned pages as the ' Epistle to Diognetus,'
while it dictates the most exquisite prayers in the
unpolished language we can still construe on epitaphs
of the Catacombs.

The Saint's rhythmical invocations to his Maker

---

[1] Consult the fine version in Lord Bute's *Roman Breviary*.   The references are to Aug. on St. John, 36, 26.   [2] Cyprian, Ep. 58.

are exceedingly human : *Et laudare Te vult homo, aliqua portio creaturae tuae.* Perhaps there is no citation from mystic theology more affecting than Augustine's discourse at Ostia with the dying St. Monica, *de regno caelorum,* as the chapter is inscribed,—*Dicebamus ergo, Si cui sileat tumultus carnis,* with what follows and what precedes. These words exemplify in a transport of which the most careless reader will be sensible, how the Latin speech that was rhetorical, unsympathetic and hard, has been softened by emotion, lifted on the wings of prophecy, made something with a soul in it, and a sacred tongue. By the same stroke it is fitted to discuss the mysteries of man as of God. Consider the meditations in the Tenth Book on the wonders of memory, in the Eleventh on time, as the spirit measures it—a conception bringing us up to the threshold of modern schools. Is all this field-preaching ? Or must we not say rather that, as the ancient literature went down into its tomb, having spent the ideas on which it was nourished, the modern, called by its right name the Christian, rose above it, conquering and to conquer ?

Over against Cicero, then, representing a civilisation that could not now survive, stands Augustine, conscious that one Platonic year of the world is ended, another begun. And of the second, more glorious cycle, he knows himself to be the prophet. The great Pan is dead. On the place of his sepulture a fresh dynasty of Supreme Pontiffs will proclaim : *Christus vincit, Christus regnat, Christus imperat.* Laws, rites, language, the basilicas of justice, the marble columns which bore up shrine and temple, will be consecrated to an everlasting worship, a spiritual liturgy. No institution will ever deserve so truly the title of Catholic.

For it will have absorbed into its life the elements which lay scattered through all religions—prehistoric Nature-worship, Eastern psalms and visions, the mysteries of Egypt and Greece, the Roman or Etruscan hierarchies, sifting and combining until the outcome shall be a form so beautiful, a virtue so divine, that henceforth wherever men celebrate visible rites they cannot but imitate or envy the Mass and the sacramental system in which it is embodied.

III

OUR LATIN BIBLE [1]

FIRST of modern books, we said in our preceding chapter, is the Latin Vulgate. Under one form or another it has come down to us through seventeen centuries ; and at this day it is alive, studied, recited, newly edited, by Catholic priests and religious vowed to its unceasing commemoration in their offices ; by scholars, Anglican or merely scientific ; by historians and *literati*, who follow the Roman chronicles in their second or Christian course. Of all versions which reproduce the Holy Scriptures in a Western tongue it may be considered the prototype. None have altogether escaped its influence : not Luther's Bible, nor King James's, nor the Revised of these latter years. The Catholic nations, from Poland to South America, read it in their own dialects, and that in translations the sources of which go back beyond the Council of Trent, especially as regards the New Testament. But on all the world of volumes thus widely scattered one stamp is discernible ; one editor, whom in a very true sense M. Berger styles the author, must be owned as gathering up whatever of value the classical Latin could be-

[1] (1) *Histoire de la Vulgate pendant les premiers Siècles du Moyen Age.* Par Samuel Berger. Paris : Hachette. 1893.

(2) *Geschichte der Vulgata.* Von Dr. Fr. Kaulen. Mainz. 1870.

(3) *Handbuch zur Vulgata. Idem.* 1870.

(4) *Opera Sti. Hieronymi,* studio D. Vallarsi. Venice. 1766–71.

queath, and combining with it elements rich in life and
poetry from the rustic old Italian for this book of books.
It was rightly termed in the Middle Ages the Divine
Library of St. Jerome : *Bibliotheca Hieronymi*.[1] Linguist, critic, master of words, genius by nature inde-
fatigable and severe, not to be moulded on another
man's pattern, the Dalmatian Saint was given that he
might do for mediaeval and modern Europe that which
Origen had not succeeded in doing for the Greeks.
His Vulgate remains unique among translations.   If
we will not say with Dean Burgon that it is ' the best
commentary on the Bible,' at any rate we know it to be
the most interesting and authoritative.   It is, in fact,
the Church's Bible.   And St. Jerome's name will
stand, while Rome lasts, on its title page.

Hence the Benedictine editors opened their collection of the Saint's writings with his Vulgate ; and
Vallarsi, to whom we are indebted for a still better
recension, admirable in type as in the more serious care
of text and notes, decided by their example that he must
also reproduce it.   He made use for this end of the
celebrated Codex of Verona, his native city, which has
Psalms and Gospels in Old Latin.[2]   But how many
others he would now have to consult before he might
call his edition critical, students like M. Berger will
tell us.   It appears that some eight thousand manuscripts of the Latin Scriptures are known to exist.   On
collation of a few among these and early printed Bibles
our present text, the Clementine of 1592, is founded.
The lately attempted revisions, which do not travel
outside the New Testament, are associated with the
names of Tischendorf, Hetzenauer, Wordsworth and

---

[1] Codex S. Germani, ad calcem Ep. ad Hebr.
[2] See Preface to vol. ix. pp. vii. seq., in Venice edition, 1766–71.

White. Anything like a complete and satisfactory screening of the materials extant would include a study of quotations in mediaeval Latin literature from the fifth century down to the time of Stephen Langton and Roger Bacon. Clearly there is no lack of opportunity here for scholars who know not how to dispose of their mornings in the country ! But in proportion as we appreciate St. Jerome's labours, so much the more shall we be encouraged to make the fruits of them our own.

Rightly, however, to estimate the mingled skill and good fortune which were combined in this *Opus Maximum* of Catholic antiquity, we must begin with its Old Latin foundation. The story is not yet unravelled, perhaps never will be, since, like other famous origins, the Vulgate has its period of darkness. We are driven to conjecture when we reach beyond St. Cyprian's date (A.D. 250), or at all events that of Tertullian, half a century earlier. The scattered notices in St. Augustine and St. Jerome have been carefully examined, but they yield very little, or rather nothing, that comes up to our demand for evidence, as regards the circumstances under which a Latin Bible first appeared. St. Augustine, who probably means by his word ' interpretation ' the original rendering, and not merely a recension, had no materials except the manuscripts of his day from which to draw inferences. Therefore his statement implying a large number of separate Old Latin versions from the Greek, and ' an infinite variety of interpreters,' leaves the history where it was. St. Jerome's language is ambiguous and disputable. Zahn observes with much good sense that if these Fathers had a definite tradition to go upon which reported the time, place and authorship of their elder version, we should find them explicitly setting it down. This in particular is true of St. Jerome, who was curious about facts, though not always disinclined to colour them in transit, as we sometimes feel where he quotes Eusebius. It would seem, therefore, that our only way of arriving at a sound conclusion must be indirect, by comparison of texts and versions themselves.[1]

St. Cyprian, whose musical periods betray the rhetorician, and are frequently, as Benson points out, ' a softened echo of strong words,' adheres to one particular type of text, perhaps always, in quoting Scripture, though he did not as a literary critic prize that rustic Latin at its genuine worth. Nevertheless, he keeps to it ; and his *Testimonia* (which in Hartel's edition occupy one hundred and fifty pages) exhibit a catena the links of which are all citations from the same version. Was it not then ' authorised,' as we now speak, in Africa, by the year 250, so that a Bishop of Carthage might not disregard it any more than a modern Bishop the Tridentine Bible ? It has been so held by competent writers. This Cyprianic recension is nearly identical with our Codex Bobiensis (*k*) in the Gospels (recognised as the standard Old Latin text) and has affinities with the Palatine and the Claromontane. Hort designated the group ' African.' He found a second which circulated in Northern Italy, and this he called ' European ' ; while a third, the second revised, as it would appear, and much used by St. Augustine, he termed ' Italian.' These names, however, do not indicate the origin but only the character of the readings in question. No recent explorer has accepted the solution which Wiseman put forward in this *Review*,

---

[1] Aug. *De Doct. Christ.* ii. 11, 13 ; Jerome, *Praef. in Paralip. ; in Job ; in Proverb. ; Ep. ad Damasum* ; Ziegler, *Latin Bible Versions before Jerome* (Germ.), 6, 10, 13 ; Wiseman, older view, *Essays*, i. 24.

suggestive and learned as it was at the time, viz.
that our Old Latin Scriptures displayed their African
provenance by the idioms occurring in them. Studies
more profound have brought to light the wide range of
popular Latin. If the first Western Bible holds much
in common with Carthaginian usages, it contains also
numerous elements that we may observe in Petronius ;
in the lawyers, as Papinian, Ulpian and Paulus ; nay,
in Spanish and Gaulish remains, as well as in the *Corpus
Inscriptionum* ; all bearing witness to a dialect with
variations according to locality, which developed on its
own lines and did not obey the classic rules. In other
words, the Bible was cast into spoken Latin, familiar to
every rank of society though not countenanced in the
schoolroom ; and thus it foreshadowed the revolution
of ages whereby the Roman tongue expanded into what
we may label as Romance—those rich and varied sister-
languages that are now spread over Europe from the
Black Sea to the Atlantic Ocean. Their common
prelude is the Vulgate.[1]

Tertullian could perhaps have enlightened us with
regard to its unofficial stage. He is not like Cyprian,
consistent ; often he translates directly from the Greek,
or his citations drop on the paper by memory. That
he follows in part the same text which Cyprian had is
indubitable. More we cannot affirm. And what was
the state of the case before Tertullian ? The Roman
Church, during the second century and some decades
of the third, kept its Greek liturgy ; nevertheless, it
surely made use of Latin to instruct and exhort the
native converts whose household dialect could not be
foreign. At this point we are left in the dark. How
shall we kindle a ray for future guidance ?

[1] Bibliography in Kaulen, *Handbuch*, 6, 8.

The map tells us that our sacred writings would
penetrate into Christian Africa by one, or both, of two
routes : most easily by way of Rome, which was
hardly more than twenty-four hours' voyage ; but
likewise by the northern coast from Alexandria.
Then, too, the Latin versions, being traceable to some
particular Greek sources, should carry in their make
signs and tokens of the quarter whence they proceeded.
The clue thus thrown out has been followed up. It is
known that Greek MSS. of the New Testament fall
into strongly marked groups, one of which, tabulated
as the Western, may be studied in the long-paramount
Codex of Beza (D). That recension, from the time of
Erasmus, held its rank as the *textus receptus* of the
sacred volume. It has now given place to a skilful
blending of sources more relied upon. But when
stripped of its ' conflate ' interpolations, it yields a
result substantially in agreement with our Old Latin ;
hence ' Western ' is an apt name for the group. To
these considerations it must be added that, while our
Latin on one side resembles the Western Greek family,
so on the other does the Syriac in its several versions.
The Old Latin, the basis of the Peshitta, and the
Western Greek, had a common home.

Arguments for this fascinating theory come by distinct paths ; as a conclusion it has found advocates of
the *momenta* composing it in Kaulen, Chase, Rendel
Harris, Sanday and Kennedy.[1] A German writer,
Resch, would even hold that the archetype of Codex D,
i.e. of this whole group, existed in a Gospel canon
made about the year 140. Speaking broadly, we may
say that the original from which our Old Latin was
derived belongs to the period of Tatian's ' Diatessaron,'

[1] Hastings, *D. B.* iii. 54–56, a good compendium.

if not somewhat earlier. Dean Robinson thought a Latin version was in existence so far back as A.D. 177, and was circulated in Gaul. Supposing that we allow Dr. Sanday's remarkable hypothesis of a ' workshop of manuscripts ' in the second century at Antioch, we are brought to the luminous though still conjectural idea that Greek, Latin and Syriac, by reason of their affinities, had their starting-point in that capital of Christendom, which Newman somewhere calls ' the first Apostolic See.' The primitive associations of Antioch with Rome are significant. We sum them up in St. Peter and St. Paul, St. Luke and St. Ignatius. ' Peter the Apostle,' says St. Jerome, translating the ' Chronicon ' of Eusebius under A.D. 42 or 44, ' first pontiff of the Christians, when he had founded the Church of Antioch, sets out for Rome, where he preaches the Gospel and continues twenty-five years Bishop of the same city.' There follows immediately another suggestive entry : ' Mark the Evangelist, St. Peter's interpreter, announces Christ to Egypt and Alexandria.' Thus, on whatever line of country the Scriptures came into the West, we find at its beginning St. Peter the Apostle. Who the translators may have been, we cannot say. But their work, in Antioch or elsewhere, went forward under the eyes of the Bishop ; and without his approval it would not have been finally received. For us it remains anonymous ; until St. Jerome revised its now corrupt editions, it had so great a dignity that St. Augustine shrank from any tampering with it. And the consequence has been altogether that our present Bible in manner and substance bears, throughout the New Testament as well as frequently in the Old, a close likeness to the primitive Latin from which it comes down.

To the Roman province of Syria, then, we may hold ourselves indebted for the first Western Bible. It had great merits. Kaulen has proved the acquaintance of its authors with Hebrew or Aramaic. Alone among versions from the Greek, it contains a text which antedates Origen's Hexapla. And so, as the ' Encyclopaedia Biblica ' says, it ' occupies a unique position, and must be regarded as the chief authority for the restoration of the κοινὴ ἔκδοσις, or pre-Hexaplaric LXX.' Another light shows how it is related by anticipation to the text of Lucian the Antiochene presbyter, whose Septuagint has good ancient readings. But the old Latin remains an ' invaluable witness,' for it gives the true Greek Vulgate ' approximately pure.' We need scarcely observe that such a check on the Massoretic recension has its doctrinal no less than its critical value.[1]

What of its literary form ? Granting the high antiquity of these older Latin versions, we see also that they represent the original with punctilious care. ' They preserve,' says Hastings' ' Dictionary,' ' the late Latin renderings of an extant Greek original,' prior to any MSS. which now survive, and they use many varieties of synonyms, abnormal constructions, strange formations, ' all of which reveal the tendencies of the later language.'

' It is disputed,' observes Matthew Arnold, ' what aim a translator should propose to himself in dealing with his original.' There is a school which would sacrifice verbal precision ; ' the reader should forget that it is a translation and be lulled into the illusion that he is reading an original work.' On the other hand, Francis Newman, who would not tolerate this method,

[1] *E. Bibl.* ' Text and Versions,' 5022.

was desirous ' to retain every peculiarity of the original,'
and ' with the greater care the more foreign it might
happen to be.' In like manner Robert Browning, ' If,
because of the immense fame of the following tragedy
[the ' Agamemnon '], I wished to acquaint myself with
it, and could only do so by the help of a translator,
I should require him to be literal at every cost save that
of absolute violence to our language.' [1]   Now the men
who took in hand to give Rome and the West a
rendering of the Bible from Hellenistic Greek, below
which lay Hebrew ideas, were moved thereto, not by
the ' immense fame,' but by the divinely inspired character of the volumes they had before them. Verbal
accuracy to the degree of barbarism was what they
aimed at, even as the Jew Aquila when he turned into
almost unintelligible Greek the language of Zion. So
they invented new words, set grammar at defiance,
transplanted Hebrew idioms bodily, and fashioned a
prose with its accent or music hitherto not dreamt of
in Latin.

Translations from the Attic style, from Plato and
Demosthenes, were a holiday task for Cicero ; but no
one had been led to the seemingly impossible thought
of putting Hebrew into a Latin toga. The languages
were as disparate as the matter was barbarous to civilised minds. We know how seldom an Oriental book
has triumphed over difficulties such as these. Nor
would the Scriptures have been more fortunate did they
simply appeal to a learned or literary audience. Their
claim was that under symbols rude and exotic they contained the wisdom of God. Their ' barbarism,' i.e.
their non-Hellenic origin, thus became their justification, as appears so forcibly in Clement of Alexandria

[1] Arnold, *On Translating Homer*, 2 ; Browning, Pref. to *Agam.* v.

But the impact of a new life, with which they smote upon literature in decline, was mighty enough to call out a reaction which is not yet exhausted. Graceful classic renderings could never have wrought this miracle. They would have defeated the religious purpose by subduing to colours already familiar a doctrine most unlike the cold, hard discipline of Rome ; and no literary transformation would have followed. But modern Europe owes its character in a marked degree to the combination of Hebrew ethics and dogmas with what was least unspoilt in provincial or rustic Latin. That neither Pagan, Jew nor Christian quite understood the movement at large is merely an illustration of the laws which govern historical perspective. The thing was too great to be measured by one age or generation.

Moreover, its real significance lay hid beneath a mask of Puritanism, which, as Tertullian exemplifies, made this new people, termed Christian, alien to the social usages, and consequently to much of the language, current around them. The cultivated style had become a dead letter, taught in schools, imitated by pedants, when our Bible was done into a vigorous uncouth dialect by men without respect for Quintilian. How much they brought of daring innovation and an entirely fresh poetical sense to the Latin they so violently handled, we shall point out later. To them, rather than St. Jerome, is due the ground-tone of the Vulgate which we possess. And this again we must attribute to a principle, in itself not accepted by the Saint—he calls it often ' misdirected zeal '—which clung to the letter, was rigidly faithful, and took no account of the reader's embarrassment before a text that he could not make out. Our Latin Psalms, in

particular, still offer dark sayings, where meaning and
construction are anything but clear. Yet St. Jerome
was hardly allowed to touch them, so sacred in the ears
of the congregations did they sound. The whole of
our New Testament had thus grown to be stereotyped ;
and though skilfully amended wherever possible in the
Hieronymian revise, it could not be simply translated
afresh from the Greek for public service.

Local differences, nevertheless, made their way in,
or existed from the beginning ; and so we are brought
round to the distinction established by Westcott and
Hort between African, European and Italian families
of Old Latin MSS.

Taking the Gospels for our standard, we learn that
the African, represented as was said by the Codex
Bobiensis, have the most ancient texts, not revised
according to any Greek sources after St. Cyprian.
The so-called European had their course in the fourth
century, among Gauls, Italians and Spaniards. Some
association of this group with Eusebius of Vercelli
has been traced ; it is possible that the Latin Irenaeus
(of disputed age, but undeniable importance) comes
from the same school. Critics observe a smoothness,
or even a certain insipidity, in the ' European ' type,
which leads them to consider it as the old African
revised. Its MSS. are numerous, centred round the
Veronensis (*b*) and the Vercellensis (*a*). When we
arrive at the ' Italian ' group, we find ourselves on a
battlefield crowded with combatants. Is this the
edition called ' Itala ' by St. Augustine and strongly
recommended in the well-known words, ' *In ipsis
autem interpretationibus Itala ceteris praeferatur, nam est
verborum tenacior cum perspicuitate sententiae* ' ? Our
greatest English scholar, ' slashing ' Bentley, proposed

to read *illa* for *Itala* ; others have suggested *usitata*.
But Kenrick showed, in 1874, that *Italia* was the
regular name from the third century onward of the
political diocese which had Milan for its capital.
St. Augustine's ' Confessions ' narrate how intently the
Bible occupied his thoughts and studies when he became acquainted in that city with its Bishop, Ambrose,
the quotations in whose writings exhibit the text now
preserved in the Codex Brixianus (*f*) and the Frei-
singen Fragments (*r*) of St. Paul's Epistles. It would
seem, therefore, to be probable that this family is the
one intended. But, as St. Jerome's New Testament
approximates more closely to the Brescian type thus
singled out than to any other, we can see why, later on,
St. Isidore of Seville and Walafrid Strabo fixed the
epithet ' Italian ' upon our actual Vulgate. For clearness' sake it is advisable not to employ the term ' Vetus
Itala,' when we mean the Old Latin.[1]

Neither must we draw these lines of variation too
strictly. St. Jerome's dictum concerning editions, ' *tot
sunt paene quot codices*,' while it exaggerates differences,
also proves what modern learning has demonstrated,
that our groups pass easily into one another—perhaps
that ' every region of importance ecclesiastically had its
own recension.' Here the name of Priscillian, Spanish
bishop, scholar and heretic, has lately become important. Bible quotations in his works display resem-
blances to Late African, and very markedly indeed to
the type of Leon. Another intermediate section brings
us across Lucifer, Bishop of Cagliari in Sardinia, whose
meddling at Antioch perpetuated the schism that provoked St. Jerome's famous letter to Pope Damasus.[2]
In it we reach once more the great Bible workshop

---

[1] Hastings, *D. B.* iii. 57.   [2] *Opera*, i. Ep. 16.

whence our Latin was directly or remotely derived. The next stage takes us on to Bethlehem, with its monks, scriveners, devout women, and to the Doctor Maximus, busy day after day for more than thirty years (389–420) in toil as unceasing as Origen's, amid controversies beyond number, always intent upon the Bible, translating, revising, explaining it, for the centuries to come.

A training more adequate to the extent and difficulties of his enterprise, no Christian scholar until the latest modern period has enjoyed. Almost from infancy the Roman lad, born on the confines of Dalmatia and Pannonia (340, 342 ?) was learning how to be a man of letters. His father, Eusebius, taught him the elements. He was sent to Rome as his university, put under the celebrated Donatus, became an excellent classic in both languages, Greek and Latin ; ' Well-nigh from our cradle,' he says, ' we have been exercised among grammarians, rhetoricians, philosophers.' But he had no turn for abstruse speculations, and he teaches even the mystical doctrines of Christianity with a hard common sense. Very characteristic are the swift vehemence, blazing temper, trust in his own resources, and somewhat unrefined humour which did not spare man or woman who crossed his way of thinking. Rufinus, when they had quarrelled, thought his heathen accomplishments disgraceful in a monk, ' *dum totus Plautinae et Tullianae cupis eloquentiae sector videri.*' And Jerome confesses, in the singular Epistle to Eustochium which is a page of his autobiography, that when he was worn out with fasting and tears he took up Plautus for recreation. The comedian's hearty laugh is echoed in the divine's correspondence. Strength, not subtlety or Virgilian pathos, marks the soldier-saint, whose breeding was in the neighbourhood of camps, and his life upon earth a warfare. In disposition he resembles Cato rather than Cicero ; but he was a born linguist. For words and phrases he had a memory which bit them as into steel or copper. He recalled them after twenty years without book. His own writing was direct, sarcastic, fierce to his enemies, a little too florid when addressing friends, astonishingly pure in diction, but it never touched the heights where prose or rhyme kindles to inspired beauty. He is, almost by definition, matter of fact.

Those who judge history to be a science, learning a question of detail, and criticism the anatomy of words, will find St. Jerome always interesting. He is their man. A great man, undoubtedly ; conspicuous among the world's triumphant scholars, not to be superseded in this day of Eastern discoveries and textual abundance. His merits cannot be overdrawn. Perhaps the chief of them was that he knew Latin so thoroughly as to elicit from its unsuspected powers a new language, equal to the demands of religion, strikingly novel in its whole effect, firm and deep enough to withstand the wear and tear of centuries, fresh now as in his own time. Neither Tyndale nor Luther, whom their English and German votaries would compare with St. Jerome, need be mentioned here. Both, in a certain degree, are antiquated ; the Latin of the Vulgate remains unsubdued by years. It claims all the privileges of a dead language, while it lives on the lips of generations ever new.

At Treves it was, when less than thirty, that Jerome wrote out the 'Commentaries' of St. Hilary on the Psalms. His baptism had taken place not long before. But the turning point in his life, as he looked back upon it, occurred in 373 at Antioch, after a journey from the West by Thrace and Asia Minor. He gave up the study of profane authors, retired to the desert and set about learning Hebrew. Pleasantly, in reply to critics later on, he observes, ' *Latinus sermo utcumque nobis non deest.*' Hebrew to the multitude of Christians was not simply unknown, but held in slight consideration ; while the Greek of the Seventy, as most among their teachers believed, had come to its interpreters straight from heaven. To pass it by and take lessons from ' the Jew, Barabbas,' implied no ordinary courage. But Jerome had his answer ready. When those Jews glanced at that unhallowed Greek, they charged upon it interpolations and mistakes ; neither would they suffer it to be quoted against them. ' Out of their own book,' said the new apologist, ' we Christians ought to convince our opponents ; therefore we must acquire the truth as it is in Hebrew.' Take note how, on one side, he was rebuked for his knowledge of heathen Latin ; on the other, for attempting to master the language of Israel. These are heads of accusation which he dwells upon constantly, returning scorn for scorn.[1] ' I thrust my hand into the fire,' he exclaims, ' that Jews might no more insult the Church as ignorant.'

In 379 he was (much against his will) ordained priest by Paulinus, the Latin Bishop of Antioch ; but it is remarkable that he never afterwards said Mass. His calling, as he viewed it, was that of the cenobite and the scholar. St. Epiphanius, who greatly admired him, puts down this resolution to the monk's profound humility ; nothing, at all events, would persuade

---

[1] Opera, i. 426–430, *Ep. ad Magnum.*

Jerome, even in the crisis brought about by his dispute with John of Jerusalem concerning Origen, to celebrate the liturgical office. Writer and cenobite he remained until his death. True, he spent from 379 to 381 with St. Gregory Nazianzen at Constantinople ; and then comes the Roman episode, without which no Vulgate of his editing would have reached posterity. Yet a few short years (382–385) will cover it. The rest of his days he spent in Palestine, where he died on September 30, 420.

To the Spanish Pope Damasus, ' a great Pontiff ' in modern estimation, and to his care for the order of Church service, we owe it that St. Jerome was made something like official translator in Rome. The Papal mandate first had in view a revision of the New Testament, largely corrupted by multiplication of copies. That he dealt with all its books has been doubted, yet his own language is very clear. Liturgical reasons forbade his undertaking a version utterly *de novo* ; his emendations of the Gospels were cautious, and in St. Paul's Epistles they are not easy to trace. What Greek MSS. he followed in particular we have no means of determining ; but their quality was excellent, and we may associate them with our actual Sinaitic and Vatican texts, though others must have been consulted. Outside the Gospels Jerome did little more than polish the Old Latin readings into smoother forms. At all times he worked with amazing speed. His first instalment, the four Evangelists, appeared in 383, after little more than twelve months' labour. By the end of 385 he had gone over the remaining books.

He also revised in Rome the old Psalter from the LXX during this busy period, which has given rise to the painters' legend of him as a Cardinal in a red hat.

Certainly his influence with Pope Damasus, and his fame in the world, might have yielded him these honours, if they were then accessible. Such things belong to another epoch. Jerome did not covet places, titles, or money. There was no copyright in the Vulgate ; nor would his dearest friends have ventured on offering the scholar payment for a single sheet. Their alms went to the work itself, to buy materials, supply MSS., and reward the numerous scribes who set down the text which Jerome dictated. He thought no virtue so easy as the disdain of wealth : ' *Hoc enim et Crates fecit philosophus, et multi alii divitias contemperunt.*' But Pope Damascus died towards the winter of 384 ; and Siricius, who did not favour Jerome, reigned in his stead. The monk naturally glanced eastwards again. He set out for Palestine in August 385, when his New Testament was done, travelled through the Holy Land, then saw Egypt, and fixed his abode at Bethlehem, where a double monastery was established in 389, after the Oriental fashion. Some time during these journeys he completed from the LXX a second revision of the Psalms, long known as the Gallican Psalter, which under St. Pius V became official, and is the one we use. It will be found in the Clementine Bible.

Very few Catholics now trouble themselves about the Septuagint. It has become in our schools the shadow of a name. For the Christians, however, of East and West until the fifth century dawned, that complex and unequal series of translations, made we know not exactly when or by whom, had authority as quoted by the Apostles and even as literally inspired. St. Jerome held the Lucianic recension in some disfavour ; resolute opponent as he was, after slight early

leanings the other way, of Origen's theology, as a text
he preferred the Hexapla by which to be guided in
amending the Latin Old Testament. His efforts,
which, if we take what he tells us rigorously, extended
to a complete handling of this vast collection, were
unfortunate. The greater part of his work, he wrote
in 416 to St. Augustine, had been stolen from him, and
nothing of it except a few fragments is left. Of one
thing we may be sure : the lonely scholar, confronted
by a Greek Old Testament received everywhere, did
his utmost to find and translate a satisfactory text.
Living, however, among Orientals, and daily better
versed in the language, manners, topography of the
Holy Land, the conviction grew upon him that none
but a fresh rendering from the Jewish Bible would
meet the demands of experts. Approbation, such as
he had from Pope Damasus for an amendment of the
popular Latin Gospels, was not likely to be given.
His most venturesome work was undertaken at the
instance of private friends, without a plan, as if merely
to please the more learned and not for public use.
Yet, even so, many condemned it in the strongest
terms as not only superfluous but rash and unsound.

About fifteen years elapsed (390–405) ere this immortal enterprise saw its completion. Jerome began
it with Samuel and Kings, to which he prefixed, *more
suo*, a challenge known as the Prologus Galeatus.
The Psalms, Prophets and Job followed, and before
396 the books of Esdras (i.e. Ezra-Nehemiah) with
Chronicles. 'Broken by a long illness,' he did
nothing for at least a year. In 398 he gave out
Proverbs, Ecclesiastes and Canticles, done, though
it seems hardly credible, in three days. When the
Pentateuch appeared is uncertain, perhaps 401.

Joshua, Judges, Ruth and Esther belong to 405. The
reluctant as well as rapid oversight of Tobias, Judith
and the Greek Daniel and Esther brought Jerome's
translations to an end.

Our interest in the story is manifold. The never-
ceasing quarrel between custom and scholarship finds
here one of its most remarkable exhibitions. Jerome
repeats, but to little purpose at his day, that he intends
no censure of the ancients ; that he venerates the
Seventy ; that he had kept close to his Hebrew original,
and thereby cleared up doubtful places in the Greek and
Latin. He was called a forger, *falsarius*, charged with
sacrilege as laying hands on a God-given text, and, as
he says, ' run down in public though read in private '
by the very men who blamed in him what they approved
in others. He complains bitterly, ' Were I making
baskets of reeds or weaving palm-leaves together, and
so eating my bread in the sweat of my brow, not a
creature would rend or rebuke me.' But he was doing
an imperishable work, hence the accusation. ' *Tanta
est enim vetustatis consuetudo,*' he remarks, ' *ut etiam
confessa plerisque vitia placeant, dum magis pulchros
habere volunt codices, quam emendatos.*' Cheap and poor
though his ' papers ' might be, however, in comparison
with old vellum copies inscribed in purple and uncial
letters, they represented the Hebrew truth. On this
foundation, *Hebraica veritas*, he took his stand with
increasing confidence. We now read the Saint's victorious prologues at the head of our Bible, inserted by
Roman authority.[1] The word Vulgate itself, long
applied to the Greek Seventy, has been taken over in
triumph and carries the name of Jerome in its syllables.

[1] See above passages in *Biblia Sacra*, Paris, 1870, vi., ix., xv., xvi., xxi.,
etc.

How did such a change come about ? Scholarship
alone would never have won the day. So much is clear
from the failure of the Saint's last work on the Psalms,
an admirable version, which could not gain a footing
in Missal or Breviary. What combination of elements
was it, then, that overcame the prepossessions even
of an Augustine before he died, so that he accepted
Jerome's Gospels by 404, while in his ' Speculum '
and the ' De Civitate ' he follows the new Latin
text ?

We may indicate the answer which, in our narrow
limits, cannot be developed. St. Jerome, while creating
a literary masterpiece, wrought under conditions more
favourable than he believed. There was a Church-
Latin already in existence ; and although ' *sancta
quippe rusticitas sola sibi prodest,*' as he writes to Paulinus,
and he has often to insist on the privileges of sacred
learning, yet, like other creative minds, he took all that
suited him from the past. In an age when Ausonius,
a real decadent, was stringing together *florilegia* ;
when Claudian feebly echoed the hexameters of a dead
and gone antiquity, Jerome too might have droned
verses and indulged conceits as they did, were his subject not the Scriptures. There his natural taste for
rhetoric was curbed ; the matter he could not diver-
sify ; and inside a well-marked range even the words
had their prescription. As a Hebrew expert he was
bound by the text furnished to him ; in substance, not
altogether, it was the Massorah which is our actual
reading. As a Roman divine he recognised instinc-
tively, though sometimes chafed by the rule, that old
sacred terms were not to be cast away ; and in studying
the rustic Latin he caught more than he suspected of
its colour.

His style was hardy and expressive. Critics admire in the Vulgate ' the classic simplicity of its language,' and of this St. Jerome deserves all the praise. Large, nay continual, differences are observed between his translation and those which it superseded, especially as regards the Hebrew volume ; but he comes after the Old Latin and not in vain. Its influence may be for the most part unconscious, yet it is certainly real ; and he now and then incorporates in the text its very words. Thus, while Berger declares that he first made known the Old Testament to our Western peoples, which in a general sense is true, his own Vulgate in point of language has been described as ' at once artificial and archaic, and yet forcible, clear and majestic.' These diverse qualities lend it a richness that no other Latin work has ever equalled. Traces of the Septuagint mingle with Hebrew ; provincial idioms enhance the picturesque style. The laws of rhythm have not been overlooked, as St. Jerome himself points out, and Vallarsi notes in his edition. Energy and concentration are features of the ancient Bible ; they check the Latin eloquence which loves to flow abroad ; and this great version charms us most when its periods fall into brief musical phrases that are not verse but measured prose.

In principle its translator would have agreed, not with Francis Newman, who held to the letter (as the Old Latin did), but with his brother the Cardinal, to whom belongs a choice and well-known page on the subject at large. ' In a book intended for general reading,' says J. H. Newman, ' faithfulness may be considered simply to consist in expressing in English [or in any other language] the sense of the original ; the actual words of the latter being viewed mainly as

directions into its sense, and scholarship being necessary in order to gain the full insight into that sense
which they afford.' [1] This tells us pretty much what
St. Jerome was aiming at, ' *non verbum e verbo, sed
sensum exprimere de sensu.*' He justified his method by
the citations from Scripture in the New Testament,
which constantly exhibit verbal differences. Yet any
one who compares the Vulgate and the Hebrew will
perceive that even the order of the words is often
followed, so far as Latin syntax will permit. Repeti-
tions, indeed, which an Oriental for want of the indirect
narrative is compelled to use, do not find favour in
Jerome's eyes. Sometimes he interpolates a meaning ;
he amplifies or paraphrases ; but almost every portion
of his Old Testament has been singled out in turn and
highly extolled by good judges. Hagen praises the
Pentateuch, not without reason, as might be demonstrated, if space were allowed, from the numerous passages we have gone through for this article.[2] Kaulen,
whose treatment of Jerome's Latinity deserves careful
study, ranks the translation of the historical books
above the rest, and after that Job and the Prophets.
Our Saint was proud of his Samuel and Kings. But,
in fact, it is not easy to discriminate where all has merit.
Doubtless, we should have gained if the so-called
Gallican Psalter had given place to the direct version
from the Hebrew. Now that a critical edition of the
Vulgate is proceeding in Rome, this cannot fail to be
a matter for serious consideration.

Meanwhile, the power of St. Jerome will be appreciated only by going over his whole achievement. Let

[1] *Historical Sketches*, ii. 11.
[2] Look at Gen. xv., xl. ; Exod. ix.-xiv., xvi., xix. ; Lev. xxvi. ; Num.
xxii.-xxiv. ; Deut. xxviii. ; xxxi.-xxxiii.

us bear in mind also that no Latin Homer, Aeschylus or Pindar exists ; but here is a pen equal to every effort—history, the prose epic, lyrical and reflective poems, and the peculiar strain which we term prophecy. The liturgical year brings each kind before us, submitting it to a trial which would wear out Milton's iambics, and make intolerable the sound of most other verse. Yet our Latin Isaiah during Advent, the Lamentations in Holy Week, seem always new. Taken merely as literature, the Vulgate has been examined, in a volume now somewhat rare, by the late J. A. Symonds. He noted ' the austere and masculine virtues of Latin,' its ' naked strength,' and, in contrast, ' its studied oratorical magnificence.' The ' solemn march ' of Livy's historical narration fascinated him, as it charmed De Quincey. Virgil's tongue, he says once more, became ' the mother-speech of modern nations.' But how did this happen ? It was the task which the Latin Church undertook, and which she executed. St. Augustine, for example, whom Symonds thought an incomparable master, was ' steeped in the style of the Vulgate '—he means the Old Latin. That Bible was the ' chief monument ' of a transformation greater than we can parallel in any other thousand years. He adds with much force, ' This resurrection from the grave where Cicero, Tacitus and Livy lay embalmed is one of the most singular phenomena in history.' For it made Latin cosmopolitan during nine centuries, scattered and displaced the classics, yet gave a noble literature in their stead. St. Jerome has accomplished a million times more, he concludes warmly, than any other *vulgarisateur* by creating ' a new instrument of verbal utterance in the prose of the Vulgate.'

When we turn to details, we discover that Symonds

was particularly affected by the 'plangent music'
and 'deep reverberations,' as in Job, which express
'modern emotions.' He quotes the solemn chants,
Pereat dies, and their like, with some of which all are
acquainted in the Office for the Dead. A very different
chord is touched in *Veni de Libano*, from Solomon's
Song, a kind of prose 'artless in style, oppressive in
passionate suggestion,' as the dilettante calls it, remarking acutely that 'the language of Canticles aspires
towards music,' and he thinks of Palestrina. The
younger school of decadents—for there is something
a little morbid in Symonds' critique—would surely
substitute Wagner. Glancing at the Book of Wisdom
(which is Old Latin, not Jerome's) he draws attention
to the 'new structure' and the 'hitherto unappre-
hended colour-value,' destined to enhance 'the rich
sonority of ample Latin verbs and nouns.' Here was
'no laborious attempt to recapture the past,' but Latin
adapted to the Western races at the very moment,
marked by the death of Theodosius, when the Roman
Empire broke asunder, not to be united evermore.
The 'Confessions' of St. Augustine, it is admirably
observed, show us Latin Christianity in the making,
a worn-out language rejuvenated 'in the spirit and
manner of a modern artist.' St. Ambrose discards
quantity for accent, invents new rhythms and new
stanzas, adopts the ornament of rhyme. What St.
Jerome did, who shall measure? He gave to the
Middle Ages their Iliad and their Odyssey—laws,
histories, ritual, romance, devotion, cast into a universal mould, the dialect of Christendom. Or, to
apply the words which J. A. Symonds has used elsewhere concerning our religion, the Vulgate exhibits an
'ancient hereditary wisdom and sense of beauty woven

into the very stuff of simplest speech.'[1] Thus it became for the nations that developed Romance from Latin their literary primer, while it fixed the standard of ritual terms, gave to preachers a world of references and a vocabulary not to be exhausted ; overflowed into the Roman decretals, furnished the daily talk of the cloister, and was perpetuated in codices which are marvels of painting and caligraphy. No more brilliant chapter exists in the long story of the Catholic Church. And its central glory falls upon St. Jerome.

Most old manuscripts of the Bible, says Duchesne, served as lectionaries for the use of the clergy in their Offices. To accept the Vulgate or let it alone was no question for the learned, as it would be now, but instantly practical. This explains why it met with opposition of so decided a character at first, and how St. Augustine would not have it read in his diocese. The popular feeling was against it. By temper and training the Bishop of Hippo did not at all resemble the monk of Bethlehem. Their famous correspondence shows them in lights amusingly contrasted. St. Augustine, like many converts, desired to rest and be thankful. But he was too open-minded, as well as too sensible of literary excellence, not to perceive in the new version merits which outweighed its novelty. He praised and by degrees adopted it. As we have seen, the *Vetus Itala*, dear to him from its Milanese associations, possessed many things in common with our Vulgate. And much of the Old Testament, where St. Jerome was chiefly original, had no great hold upon the average Christians, who clung tenaciously to their accustomed hearing in Church The

---

[1] *Essays Suggestive and Speculative*, i. 282-297 ; *Autobiography*, i. 97, 256 ; ii. 183.

result, it would seem, was that in Augustine's last years (415–430) he gave the impulse by quotation and approval which carried the Hieronymian text over its initial stage. It is pleasant to believe that the two most eminent Latin Fathers may be joined, the one as originator, the other as patron, in this mighty work.

Others, indeed, as Rufinus, furiously incensed against Jerome, opposed it. The Donatists held to their ancient readings, as we learn from St. Augustine's dispute with Fulgentius, who quotes the Old Latin. Various Africans preserved this custom, while Italy, Gaul and Spain took up without reluctance a Bible distinguished for its clearness, accuracy, ease and elegance. Soon after 430 we find Vincentius of Lerins, Faustus Regiensis and Prosper of Aquitaine (the interesting school of Marseilles) citing their Scripture from the Vulgate. In the sixth century Isidore of Seville imagines that by the *Itala* was meant in St. Augustine this actual edition ; and so the mediaeval commentators with Walafrid Strabo generally understood. Some late critics would agree with Isidore. Still more important, in a world falling to confusion, was the practice of St. Gregory the Great. He tells his friend Leander, who had succeeded that prelate at Seville, in his preface to Job, that ' the Apostolic See uses both versions,' and himself preferred the later. It has been said by Kaulen that St. Columban, of Luxeuil, who died in 615, was the last to employ an exclusively Old Latin Bible. But scholars acquainted with MSS. all over Europe would perhaps not draw the line at this year. In any case, the mixture of readings, due to ignorance, caprice, quotations from memory and other accidents, went on increasing for well-nigh two hundred years afterwards. Ireland, it appears, had received the earlier text from St. Patrick, though he studied at Lerins. Irish missionaries, preaching in Britain, Gaul, Germany and Switzerland, writing their Gospels with unrivalled penmanship, mingled the lections in every conceivable measure. The Vulgate most widely adopted was, nevertheless, a good copy, represented by the Codex Amiatinus of 716 (*am* or A), which Ceolfrid the Northumbrian offered at St. Peter's shrine; it is now in Florence, and its true origin was found out by De Rossi. This magnificent volume is one among various tokens that the new Latin had made its way, slowly but surely, even in the British Isles, cut off though they had been from Roman influences at the moment when it first began its course.

But, as must be admitted, the Old Latin stood its ground in service-books, glosses and citations, nay, in the Bible itself, far down the Middle Ages, so that remnants of it survive till the thirteenth century (Codex Colbertinus (*f*) ; Perpignan MS.). Rome had no strictly official standard in times when learning had almost died out. The victory of St. Jerome was due to Charlemagne, yet not to the Emperor's direct ordinance. If Irish monks preserved the Gospel and other texts, it was an Englishman, Alcuin of York, Abbot of St. Martin's at Tours, who made the Vulgate their acknowledged representative. Over against him our attention is caught by Theodulf, Bishop of Orleans (787–821), a Wisigoth by descent and a native of Narbonne, whose labours, unhappily not completed, were based on the Spanish manuscripts, but included other materials from different sources. Theodulf's recension came before its time as a critical effort. It remains among the curiosities of literature. Alcuin succeeded where the Bishop of Orleans failed. Yet

in both cases the text wrought upon was Irish in its
pedigree, though one entered France from the north
and the other from the south.[1]

Charlemagne, by a capitulary of 789, had prescribed a revision of liturgical books,—*emendatos libros*
he desired to secure for the Church services. The
Bible he had not, we say, directly in view. However,
in 796, he ordered Alcuin, his Minister of Education,
as the French would now phrase it, to send for MSS.
from York, the home of the best readings, illustrated
by such works as the Amiatinus, the Book of Lin-
disfarne, and others. The Abbot lost no time. At
Christmas, 801, he was able to present the Emperor
with his newly edited Scriptures, sent by the hand of
Nathaniel or Fredegisius his disciple. Between 799
and 801 he had corrected the entire Bible. We no
longer possess an autograph of this memorable text.
It may, however, be followed in the Codex Vallicel-
lianus (V) preserved at the Chiesa Nuova in Rome ;
and the group of ornate MSS. which date from Tours
will afford us a second line upon which to recover it.
The consequence of Alcuin's publication was a certain
uniformity, troubled by variants in detail and the faults
inseparable from written copies, yet decisive as against
the Old Latin versions. These had forfeited their
authority. St. Jerome's Bible was not known, indeed,
as the Vulgate until the days of Roger Bacon. But
with Alcuin it acquired that supreme place among the
Latin nations which it is never likely to lose.

Englishmen may certainly be proud that their
country has taken a share so large in correcting and
editing the Latin Scriptures. After the great North-

[1] Berger has summed up the story in his preface, xii–xvii ; on Theodulf,
141–184 ; on Alcuin, 184–196.

G

umbrian we meet Lanfranc of Canterbury, who revised all the books of both Testaments, though his work is not extant. St. Stephen Harding made a recension preserved at Dijon. To Stephen Langton we are indebted for the present division of the Bible into chapters and much more ; while in Roger Bacon, a true disciple of St. Jerome, we may consider that scientific handling of the inspired text found a champion as well as a martyr. The current Bible in his day, the *Exemplar Parisiense*, was cheap, inaccurate and plentiful. Thus had the Old Latin overspread the West ; from Bethlehem the Vulgate which embodied or superseded it had been brought to the Northern nations. Corrected under Charlemagne, accessible to thousands of students from all sides in mediaeval Paris, not to be conquered even by the classic Renaissance, it deserved and won at the Council of Trent its place as the Latin Bible, the authorised text and standard of our teaching. The editors of King James's version acknowledge its merits. And the *Encyclopaedia Biblica* declares, ' It was the great good fortune of the Latin Church that so excellent a translator should have been raised up ; and it is his great glory that neither the sentimental associations of the old versions nor the increasing ignorance of the Dark Ages were allowed to interfere with the final acceptance of St. Jerome's labours.' [1]

[1] *Encyc. Bibl.* 5025.

IV

THE LITURGY OF TOLEDO [1]

'TOLEDO,' says a writer who shall be nameless, ' is after
Rome the sacred city of the West. What other can
compare with it ? Iona is a desolate isle and never was
a city ; Franciscan Assisi, though wearing the look of
Nazareth, is not crammed with the record of centuries
and crusades ; Oxford is the scholar's home ; Paris
was never sanctified ; Avignon remains the fair schis-
matic ; Seville and Cordova were Moorish brides and
have not put off their Paynim adornments. But
Toledo, girt by the golden Tagus, lifted high on its
seven hills, morose, burnt, empty in the scorching light,
has kept from the last days of the Roman Empire until
now its faith undefiled. It holds the primacy of all the
Spains ; it still recites the liturgy which St. Isidore and
St. Julian chanted ; its amazing Cathedral is the tomb
of kings and cardinals, preaching above them from 750
painted windows the Gospel of Christ ; and in spite of
Berber dynasties and Flemish-Burgundian Charles V,
as of that Philip II who discrowned it by choosing
Madrid for his royal presence-chamber, it reigns in
history, in romance, with a halo of religion surrounding
it, as Gothic, Spanish, Catholic, unconquerable and
unique. Such is Toledo, second only to Rome.'

[1] *Le Liber Ordinum en usage dans l'Église Wisigothique et Mozarabe
d'Espagne.* Par Dom Marius Férotin, O.S.B., Farnborough. Paris :
Firmin-Didot. 1904.

'The landscape of Toledo and the banks of the Tagus,' we read in M. Maurice Barrès, 'are among the saddest and most ardent things in this world. The city itself,' he continues, 'has all the colour, the ruggedness, the haughty poverty of the sierra on which it is built.' As though a mysterious living soul dwelt therein, it makes on the traveller an impression of energy and passion. Under the crude sky it appears 'secret and inflexible, in this harsh over-heated land.' It is hieratic, and cannot be modern ; 'magnificently faithful to its past,' it sleeps and dreams, but is austere amid its elegancies of architecture, which cannot dissemble the prevailing sternness ; and so it recalls the queenly widow (not the bride), who, when her husband dies, puts away crown and jewels to retire within a convent. Toledo is the royal dowager of Spain. She meditates on a prospect of 'ineffaceable desolation, incessantly exposed to devastating winds, swept by fierce rains and blinding dust and remorseless sun fire.' Her walls, dating from King Wamba, close round a 'mausoleum of petrified memories.' Her castellated bridges of Alcantara and San Martin lead you from the zone of the river into streets which are like desertravines, above which the Cathedral soars, a fortress, a shrine, a link between Christians, Moors, Jews, Romans, Carthaginians, all of whom have passed under the shadow of its hills. For the place was marked out as far back as the second Punic War. And its very name might be construed in Hebrew by the word 'Toledoth,' which means 'generations,' or 'the history of man.' [1]

'Hieratic' is the epithet befitting Toledo. Its

[1] Hannah Lynch, *Toledo*, 2–16, London, 1903 ; Gautier, *Voyage en Espagne*, 136–175, Paris, 1888 (originally 1843).

patron saint is Leocadia, virgin and martyr in 302,
under Dacian, the fierce lieutenant of Diocletian. On
December 9 her feast is kept, and three churches were
dedicated to her remembrance, in one of which outside
the walls, four of the Councils, well known to us by
name (the fourth, fifth, sixth and seventeenth), held their
meetings. The first Bishop was Melancius (283),
whom ten others followed, ruling without hindrance
over a people essentially Celtic, while the Roman
dominion endured. To the years 396 and 400 we
assign those Toletan gatherings which condemned
Priscillian, already executed in 386, and of late unex-
pectedly famous once more, thanks to the ' Comma
Johanneum ' and fresh studies on the Vulgate. But
the end was now near of Rome's western sovereignty.
Toledo barred its gates when the Vandals passed by ;
it yielded to the Visigoths under Euric (475), who was
an Arian, and who drew up a code of laws for his
barbarous people. Athanagild, his successor, pitched
on these gaunt rocks his capital or his camp ; but
neither he nor any of the heretical foreign rulers could
tear out of Spanish hearts their orthodox belief.
Hermengild the martyr conquered by dying (584) ;
and his brother Recared accepted the Nicene faith in
the Third Council of Toledo (586), as an inscription
on his statue, outside the Alcazar, bears witness. Goths
and Suevi followed their lord's example. The King
was a strong man ; but the hierarchy was stronger still,
as it ever has been in Catholic Spain.

Then Sisebuth overcame the Asturians and the
Vascons, drove out the Byzantines, gave his Jews in
Toledo the alternative of baptism within a year or expulsion from the kingdom, and erected the basilica
to St. Leocadia. In 653 the Eighth Council added

' Filioque ' to the creed of Constantinople. St. Ildephonsus, who was Archbishop in 659, wrote *De Vir-
ginitate perpetua Sanctae Mariae contra tres infideles*
—these ' infidels ' were natives of Narbonne, who came
long before the Albigensians—and his legend is highly
celebrated. He was buried in St. Leocadia's church.
Not long afterwards Wamba succeeded to the throne
(672). He built the walls, raised the great palaces,
and stamped on Toledo the gloomy Gothic character
which it still retains, and which not even the Moors
could efface, though softening it by their style of
ornamentation, called the *mudéjar*. We omit King
Ejica with his disedifying story ; glance at Rodrigo's
undoubted tournament, and just mention his legendary Cave of Hercules which the Toletans believe in
but have never found. Rodrigo, last of the Goths,
vanished during the fatal days of Guadelete, July 19–
26, 711. The Jews of Toledo flung open its gates,
and Tarik of Gibraltar came from Ecija to triumph in
the Christian capital. Here begins the chronicle of
the Mozarabites, whom, all along, we have kept in
view.[1]

' Mozarabes, or Mostarabes, *adscititii*, as it is interpreted in Latin,' says Gibbon. The word is a verbal
form, properly signifying those under Arab rule ; but
a certain degree of assimilation was charged upon them
by more fortunate Christians. They had 'submitted
to the practice of circumcision and the legal abstinence
from wine and pork ' in the middle of the tenth century,
as it appears ; they wrote and conversed in the Saracen
tongue ; but they would not pronounce the creed of
Islam. There is nothing fanciful in the resemblance

[1] Muir, *The Caliphate*, 371 ; Gibbon, iv. 287, 340 ; vi. 354–8—Smith's
edition, London, 1862.

which scholars have traced between the Mohammedan and the Arian formulas. That ancient quarrel which had troubled the Roman Spaniards was now to rage a second time during eight hundred years, until Granada should fall, Protestantism rise almost in the same hour, and the Socinian take up the doctrine of the Koran, *Deus neque gignit neque gignitur*. These names and dates fill us with astonishment. History, as we look at them, seems to be one immense drama, running into acts beyond counting. The Spaniard is always orthodox ; the Northern lapses into heresy ; the Arab is a Unitarian. Enough at present, let us turn to Toledo again.

The last great bishop, anterior to the Berber conquest, was St. Julian, who wrote much, including an apology for the Spanish faith which Rome accepted, and who died in 690. Though Tarik seized the sacred treasures and converted the churches into mosques, yet he left in Christian hands the seven which historians enumerate. No fresh ones might be set up ; processions and public ceremonies (including the ringing of bells) were forbidden ; but so long as the yearly tribute was paid, the city kept its arms and horses, observed its own laws, and pleaded before its own judges. The Moslem on both sides of the Strait came in no long while to prefer tribute above conversion, and a subject race to brethren in the faith. Hence his rule was often mild ; nor did he prosecute a holy war against those Christians who chose to be taxed rather than to feel the edge of his sword. Nevertheless, Toledo sulked and mutinied. In 763 Cassim, her Moorish ruler, threw off the yoke of Cordova. Abderrahman recovered the city in 766. The Christian renegade, Amrou of Huesca, contrived a mighty massacre of its nobles on the ' Day of the Fosse,' also termed for its sanguinary deeds *la noche Toledana.* Five thousand corpses filled a common ditch. Yet again, in 854, Toledo, says the Arabian poet, ' was desolate as a grave.' But twenty years later, in 873, she became a Republic under annual tribute and concluded an alliance with the Beni Casi of Aragon. Abderrahman III opened a siege round about her, in May 930, which lasted eight years and ended in capitulation. Last came Alfonso VI of Leon, who in exile had been made chief of the Mozarabes by King Almamun, and who treacherously or otherwise broke into the city, May 26, 1085, driving out Yahya Ibn Ismail. The fugitive went off to Valencia, which the Cid was to wrest from his grasp. So Toledo flung out the Moors three hundred and seventy years after the Jewish remnant had let them in.[1]

All this while, the noble Spanish-Latin rite had been practised in its seven churches. Now a tragic thing came to pass. Alfonso left his French wife Constance and the French Archbishop, Bernard of Cluny, to govern Toledo. They seized upon the Mezquita, formerly Christian, and in violation of treaty restored it to the ancient use. It was solemnly consecrated on December 18, 1086. But that was not the remarkable event which we mean. Bernard represented the widespread monastic movement which, beginning at Cluny in the former age, had seated Gregory VII in St. Peter's Chair, made war upon simony and a married clergy, and was now assimilating local rites to the Roman custom wherever it could be done. Previous attempts in Spain, of which we shall say something later, had not succeeded. Even now,

[1] Lynch, *Toledo,* 65-79.

though Aragon and Navarre yielded, Toledo called on St. Isidore and pleaded its five centuries of prescription, if not primitive usage. Legend declares that the holy volume was, in Gibbon's language, ' exposed to the doubtful trials of the sword and the fire' (vi. 370). In any case its doom was sealed. The Archbishop allowed it in six parishes ; but the Roman office reigned elsewhere in its stead. Only two parishes retain it now. As for the Cathedral, it was rebuilt in 1227, after the battle of Navas de Tolosa (1212), by the prelate Rodrigo Ximenes de Rada, who won that decisive victory, and who died in 1247. For 250 years the work went on.[1] Tradition says that the original church was founded by St. Eugenius and dedicated to our Lady under Recared, April 12, 587. We have only to add that a second Ximenes, Franciscan friar and Cardinal, Primate and Regent of Spain, munificent patron of the Alcalá Polyglot, established in this enormous pile a Mozarabic chapel, and in 1500 printed the *Missale Mixtum*, which is used by the canons. In 1502 he published the Breviary *secundum regulam S. Isidori*, which we now possess.

Let us go back to the period of St. Gregory VII or Hildebrand—for this wonderful man elected popes long before he mounted the Papal Chair. His policy was governed by one simple idea. Rome should be the centre, the pattern, the guide of Christendom. Local uses or privileges, however ancient, must not eclipse its religious dignity as *Mater et magistra omnium ecclesiarum*. Charges were brought against the Spanish Catholics of unsoundness in the faith ; and their liturgical offices fell under suspicion. The very name of Mozarabes lent itself to ambiguities, as we have seen.

---

[1] Description of the Cathedral in H. Lynch's *Toledo*, 150–190.

Learned men are disposed to think that Elipandus, the heterodox prelate of Toledo, forged certain texts in defence of his own errors, and thus drew down censure on the genuine ritual. If so, his inventions cannot be found. At any rate, towards 1065 the Roman authorities were decidedly hostile to the old liturgy and bent on suppressing it. What could the Spaniards do? Very wisely, their bishops appealed directly to the Pope, at that time Alexander II, a nominee of Hildebrand. They submitted to him four volumes—the 'Liber Ordinum,' the 'Liber Orationum,' the 'Liber Missalis,' the 'Liber Antiphonarum.' A fifth book, oddly entitled the 'Liber Comicus,' which contained the passages of Scripture read aloud during Mass, did not require presentation; it still exists in a copy of the eleventh century.[1] Alexander II examined, approved and returned the volumes in which his Council, after nineteen days' search, had discovered nothing heterodox. But this did not stay the suppression more than twenty years. Cluny and Rome in 1087 joined hands against Toledo. The ritual shrank into its half-dozen parishes; the books in which it was admirably penned and musically noted lay forgotten among the mouldered relics of old time. When Cardinal Ximenes would publish what was left of them, he knew only the Missal, and that overgrown with Roman additions; hence it was called *mixtum*, i.e. *plenum*. In 1755 Alexander Lesley, S.J., printed at Rome, with help from Acevedo, the edition which Migne reproduced *ad litteram* in 1862. Lorenzana, Archbishop of Mexico, brought out another, in 1770, at Puebla. The so-called 'Breviary' comprises portions of the Antiphonarum, the Psalter, the Canticles and a Hymnody. For these

[1] Edited by G. Morin, 1893.

we may consult Tommasi, Bianchini and Lorenzana. But no critical edition has yet been prepared.[1]

One volume was, it would seem, lost beyond recovery. Neither Ximenes nor the subsequent scholars had set eyes on the ' Liber Ordinum.' But we may say with Virgil, ' That which none dared to hope, behold the course of time has brought it unasked.' At Silos in Castile, renowned for its St. Dominic, who gave his name to another saint greatly more celebrated, there is a desolate abbey, with its *botica* or apothecary's shop and archives of unread manuscripts. And there, in 1886, Dom Marius Férotin was guided by the apothecary, Don Francisco Palomero, to a monument which, taken all in all, is perhaps the most important our age has recovered among treasures liturgical. For he had lighted upon the very copy, it would seem, of the ' Liber Ordinum ' which was presented to Pope Alexander II, and which contained a multitude of services never hitherto described by modern pens. An exceedingly beautiful volume it is, in 42 sheets or 344 folios of fine parchment, written in three colours, the style of caligraphy West Gothic, the scribe a priest named Bartholomew, and the patron, Dominic, Abbot of St. Prudentius, together with Santius Garceiz of Albelda and his wife Bizinnina, who were at the cost of it. Bartholomew finished his work on May 18, 1090 of the Julian era, which corresponds to A.D. 1052. The precious manuscript found its way to Silos, was probably used by St. Dominic, and about the year 1100 was laid aside. Hence it is in perfect preservation, except for a small number of folios. We may now, therefore, be certain that we possess the liturgical year as it was observed in the Spanish Church before 711.

[1] *Lib. Ord.* xi–xv.

'Which books,' says the Codex Æmilianus of the
Councils, 'our Lord Pope and all his advisers receiving,
diligently scrutinising and with sagacious study looking
through, found quite Catholic and clear of all heretical
depravity ; and by Apostolic authority forbade and
interdicted every man from vexing, condemning or
presuming to alter the office of the Church of Spain.'[1]

That office, meaning the Ritual which we are engaged upon, finds mention over thirty times in texts
ranging from the Fourth Council of Toledo in 633 to
the donation of Pelayo, Bishop of Leon, in 1073, when
he gave the 'Liber Comicus' to his cathedral, where it
still remains. As regards the 'Liber Ordinum,' our
editor has employed three MSS. besides the standard
one above—a Madrid parchment of 155 leaves, incom-
plete, from the Abbey of St. Millan de la Cogolla, and
of about the same epoch ; another at Silos of 1039 ;
and a fourth, also there, belonging to the eleventh century. We cannot linger among these details. Suffice
it that Dom Férotin has neglected none of the minutiae
dear to experts, in collating, printing, annotating, adding glossaries and indexes, which make of this great
volume a Benedictine and yet modern triumph in
scholarship. The editor has chosen a middle way
between strict palaeography and popular form. But
the text of the old Spanish Vulgate is carefully printed
as it is in the MSS. He subjoins six Mozarabic
Calendars hitherto unknown, but all in substance
dating from before A.D. 500.

Thus we are brought to a question as important as
it is difficult. What was the origin of this remarkable
liturgy ? Did it come to Spain by way of Rome, of
Gaul, of Africa ? Had we in our hands the earliest

[1] *Lib. Ord.* xix.

Roman books, we could perhaps reply ; but these are gone for ever. Did St. Paul visit the Peninsula ? Despite his known intention (Romans xv. 24) and the phrase of St. Clement which affirms that he travelled to ' the extreme bound of the West,' we cannot tell.[1] Nor does the legend of Santiago throw light on these investigations. Mgr. Duchesne is willing to ascribe with Pope Innocent I all the churches of the Occident, including Spain, their faith and their ritual, to St. Peter and his successors. The words are impressive : ' Aut legant,' exclaims the Pope, ' si in his provinciis alius apostolorum invenitur aut legitur docuisse. Quod si non legunt, quia nusquam inveniunt, oportet eos hoc sequi quod ecclesia Romana custodit, a qua eos principium accepisse non dubium est.'[2]

Remark how the language and policy of Hildebrand are here enunciated, previous to A.D. 420. But it is also manifest that Innocent I had never heard of St. Paul or St. James founding churches in the Iberian borders. Nevertheless, in 416, the date of this epistle to the Bishop of Eugubium, there did prevail a widespread ' use ' which was not Roman but Gallican, with its own peculiarities, whencesoever derived. It was followed, according to Mgr. Duchesne, in the ' diocese ' of Milan, as in Gaul, Spain, Britain and Ireland, but not in Africa. The ' Liber Ordinum ' should clear away some of this darkness. Meanwhile, we read, as if the common view, that ' the liturgy of the Spanish churches down to the eleventh century was identical with that observed in the Gallic churches before Charlemagne, and in the British Isles previous to the Roman

---

[1] See Lightfoot, *St. Clement*, ii. 30, on Ep. ad Corinth. v. ; and the Muratorian fragment in Westcott, *Hist. of Canon*, 517.

[2] Duchesne, *Origines du Culte Chrétien*, 87, Paris, 1903.

missions of the seventh century.' Duchesne concludes
that the Gallican rite, so far as it differs from the
Roman, is Oriental, not directly Ephesian or Apostolic
(a favourite English idea), but introduced at Milan
about 350, probably by the Cappadocian exile and
bishop, Auxentius (355–374), who played a great
part at the Council of Rimini, and was succeeded by
St. Ambrose.

To what extent this view will be modified on full
acquaintance with the ' Liber Ordinum ' it remains to
be seen. But, allowing it, we must register the learned
writer's inferences. He perceives in the Councils and
primacy of Toledo a solid foundation for the laws of
Spanish liturgy. There, in consequence, the Gallican
use maintained itself last of all ; everywhere else it was
fated to disappear. The Holy See, consulted by local
bishops sent them in reply its own volumes, as when
Pope Vigilius forwarded the Ordinary of the Mass to
Profuturus of Braga in 538. And so, by degrees, a
certain uniformity was established. Spain, however,
as being *in partibus infidelium,* escaped until the consecration of Toledo Cathedral by a French prelate, which
marked the passing of its native and yet glorious
liturgy.[1]

For us who are not experts the charm which
this ' Liber Ordinum ' holds in its pages will not be
lessened, whatever its origin. Like the other great
service-books of prayer and praise it is essentially
anonymous. The name of St. Isidore floats over it, as
that of St. Cyril over the liturgy of Jerusalem, and that
of St. Chrysostom over the Greek. But its real authors
are not known. It wears, indeed, a native air which is
unmistakable and, as the scholar would easily demon-

---

[1] Duchesne, *Origines du Culte Chrétien,* 91, 96–105

strate, even pre-Christian. 'The breath of Spanish genius,' we may observe with a most competent writer,

informs the Latinity of the Silver Age. Augustus himself had named his Spanish freedman, Gaius Julius Hyginus, the chief Keeper of the Palatine Library. Spanish literary aptitude, showing stronger in the prodigious learning of the Elder Seneca, matures in the altisonant rhetoric and violent colouring of the Younger, in Lucan's declamatory eloquence and metallic music, in Martial's unblushing humour and brutal cynicism, in Quintilian's luminous judgment and wise sententiousness.[1]

Then the Spanish Caesars, at least Hadrian and Marcus Aurelius, were men of letters—the one a dilettante, the other a saint according to his lights. Church Latin of the fourth century shines in the verse of the Christian poet Prudentius, in whom ' the savour of the terrible and agonising ' seems to anticipate Spagnoletto. These things are visible long before the Goths break in and establish their kingdom ; it is old Spanish rhetoric, Latinised under the Empire, to which we listen in the prayers, prefaces, exorcisms and hymns of the Mozarabite ritual. The Goth learned his florid style from the Iberian, who was mixed with Celts long ago ; it is doubtful if he bequeathed half a dozen Teutonic words to the Southern vocabulary.

Moreover, Licinianus, Bishop of Cartagena, corresponds with St. Gregory the Great ; and Leander of Seville is the Pope's intimate friend. Leander's disciple and successor acquires fame by his encyclopaedic writings, as ' beatus et lumen noster, Isidorus.' Braulius, Bishop of Zaragoza, edits that Saint's posthumous works ; St. Eugenius writes verses ; Claudius of Turin seems to revive Seneca ; Theodulf of Orleans

[1] T. Fitzmaurice Kelly, *A History of Spanish Literature*, 8 *seq.*, London, 1898.

attempts a critical issue of the New Testament, and composes for Palm Sunday the *Gloria, laus et honor*, which we chant every year. When Spain fell under the Saracens, its language did not perish. 'The rude Latin of the unconquered North remained well-nigh intact'; and at Cordova Livy and Quintilian were studied in the schools. If many Christians took on the Saracen tinge, we read likewise of the *Moro latinado*, the Castilian-speaking Arab, who 'multiplied prodigiously.' Thus, from the Silver Age to the troubadours we follow in its changes one strongly marked form of speech, rhetorical, epigrammatic, forcible, tender, abundant, in which the verse borders on declamation and the prose rings out high and swelling. Here is the very medium for liturgical achievement. Prayer has always demanded rhythm, which is the token of deep feeling; but for exhortation a certain check must be laid upon verse. Gothic Latin resolves this problem with a majesty, eloquence and warmth of colour not easily matched, if at all, in any other Western dialect. St. Ildephonsus describes it well. 'The word of exorcism should not be with artifice, nor hard to understand, neither wrought in strange terms, but simple, decorous, ardent, so illuminated by virtuous intention that the prince of this world may flee before its rebuke.'[1]

With exorcisms, piquant in detail, but comparatively modern, the book opens. It falls naturally into two parts, divided by Holy Week—a ritual which comprises the sacraments, the great days, various blessings, and funeral services; followed by a collection of votive Masses, answering to some of these high functions. St. Eugenius of Toledo had remarked on the splendour

[1] *Lib. Ord.* 25, note.

of the Spanish votive Masses in the seventh century. ' Ideo non scripsi,' the Saint replies to a petition from the Bishop of Tarragona, ' quia in hac patria tam accurati sermonis habentur atque sententiae, ut simile non possim excudere.'[1] There is nothing like them in the Roman Missal. They are, in fact, surprisingly rich, devout and touching. But in the first part, or Sacramentary, as we may call it, the Annus Sanctus with its round of observances pictures the church of Toledo as though in a series of stained glass windows lighted by the southern sun.

For, though we are in presence of the general Spanish liturgy, we view it as observed in the Basilica Praetoriensis, or royal chapel, which King Wamba raised to a bishopric, the primate opposing him and finally getting it reduced again. This was the Church of the Holy Apostles, in which the Councils were held from 653 to 702, and Wamba received the crown (672). Its name recalls the Praetorian camp at Rome ; from it the army set out on every war against the infidel ; and the special service for that day is given here at length. Other indications prove that we are at Toledo on Palm Sunday, Good Friday and Easter Eve. Allowing some of the formulas to be rather late, very few pass beyond the seventh century, according to Dom Férotin. The whole rite of baptism, most of the ordinations and benedictions, the public penance, the anointing of the sick, a large part of the long and magnificent sepulchral ceremony, all the offices of Holy Week, the Mass *Omnimoda*, and many other Masses, should be dated, says our editor, previous to the invasion of the Barbarians.[2] Little was added after 711. We know from different sources that during

---

[1] *Lib. Ord.* xxiii.　　　　　　[2] *Ibid.* xxi.

H

the terrible eighth century Spanish literature was all but silent. The Abbot Salvus of Albelda in the tenth century is perhaps the only writer who added new formulas, themselves now lost, to the sacred liturgy.

Our ' Liber Ordinum ' takes us back, then, fifteen hundred years, to the period of the Latin Fathers. It falls far within those six centuries, appeal to which has recently been made as if decisive for Christian tradition. Pope Alexander II certified that it was entirely ortho-dox in its teaching ; and of this we may convince ourselves at leisure as we scan its copious pages. By assertion, by repetition, by creed and preface and rubric, it declares the faith of Christendom. With no doctrinal change it might be followed in Westminster Cathedral, at St. Paul, Minnesota, at Sydney, Calcutta, Jerusalem or Rome—wherever, in short, the Catholic Church flourishes to-day. For us its language has not grown obsolete, nor its ceremonies unmeaning. A resurrection so unexpected brings home to the reader such an argument as, in lines of colour and symbol, the Catacombs offer to Roman pilgrims. It is concrete fact, solid and tangible ; so much better than a course of theology as it exhibits clergy and people united in the divine action which lay at the heart of their belief.

Two characteristics in general we cannot overlook —the note of Holy Scripture and the note of the Sacraments. Quoted or suggested by implication, the Written Word is always present in these varied rites ; they do not evaporate in preaching, but wield and express a supernatural power. Citations, as we might expect, were most numerous from the Psalms ; then from the Gospels, especially St. Luke and St. John ; Genesis, Exodus and Job furnish many allusions ; the Epistle to the Romans and First to Corinthians add their own ; the Apocalypse is not forgotten. We remember also that the ' Liber Comicus ' was made up of Biblical passages for reading to the faithful at Mass. But, in truth, all our liturgy is set in the key of Scripture, and its prayers do but enlarge upon the sacred text. Patriarchs and prophets, apostles and evangelists, form that cloud of witnesses who encompass the Communion of Saints. Were Holy Writ called in question, the lofty building would fall to the ground. Spain had its own treasure of the Latin Testaments. ' No group of readings,' we learn from M. Berger, ' except the Irish, present so exclusive an originality ; but Spain had the advantage over Ireland of preserving the entire Bible.' We cannot turn aside to dwell upon the palimpsest of Leon, the Ashburnham Pentateuch with its illustrations betraying a Spanish origin, the Codex Toletanus or the Codex Cavensis, the Bible of San Millan, the Codex Gothicus, the Bibles of Alcalá and Avila. But these wonderful relics of a world laid in ruins exhibit the Vulgate Latin as it was known under the Visigoth Kings and back even to Priscillian. The erudite Vercellone had already shown that this composite text was found in the Mozarabic Missal and Breviary. Scripture, then, could not be wanting to the ' Liber Ordinum ' in the same recension.[1]

Three great mediaeval ceremonies which we should look for in this Pontifical are absent from it : the consecration of a bishop, the dedication of a church, and the King's coronation. It is certain that all three belonged to the ancient rite. Of churches built under the Visigoths few are yet standing. Pope Vigilius in the document previously cited to the Bishop of Braga has a note, ' De ecclesiarum restauratione in fabricis

[1] Berger, *Histoire de la Vulgate*, 8–28, Paris, 1893.

vel dedicatione quid sit observandum,' which declares
that the consecration of any church ' in qua sanctuaria
non ponuntur' is effected by saying Mass within it.
Various Councils between 561 and 691 legislate in
these matters and name the episcopal unction used,
which it was not allowable for a priest to bless. Lapi-
dary inscriptions give dates of the ceremony all over
Spain from about the year 600 or earlier to 730, which
is late enough for our purpose. They constantly mention the relics of saints as though appertaining to the
ritual, and among them we note ' de cruore Domini,'
and ' sancte crucis,' as also ' de pane Domini.' At
Guadix, near Granada, which held these memorials in
652, were others connected with ' the seven sleepers in
Ephesus,' celebrated at large by Mohammed in his
Koran (xviii. ' Chapter of the Cave '). We may read
in the *Comes* manuscript of Leon (eleventh century)
and in that of Silos the portions of Scripture which
were recited on the feast of dedications. And the
Mozarabic Breviary furnishes three hymns for the
same day.[1]

St. Isidore describes in several passages how the
bishop received staff and ring, and was anointed with
laying on of hands ; the Councils speak of his ' consecration' or his ' ordination' ; the Antiphonary of
Leon (1066) records the chant, *Sono*, at this function ;
and the Codex of Compostella gives one arranged from
St. Paul's first Epistle to Timothy.[2] In our book
the ordinations written out deal with clerks, deacons,
archdeacons, archpriests, the primi-clericus—a rare
description—the priest, to whom a *Manuale* or Sacramentary is delivered ; the abbot, who receives the
pastoral staff ; and the abbess. There were no regular

---

[1] *Lib. Ord.* 505–515.   [2] *Ibid.* 60, note.

monks in Spain until about 546. Then they spread
very fast ; Recared is known from the year 586 to have
built and endowed monasteries, while he speaks himself
of the abbots whom he had sent on business to Gregory
the Great. Abbots sat and voted in the famous
national Council of 653. Their monks followed the
Eastern rule (which St. Isidore takes for granted), not
the Benedictine. In 580 the Council of Zaragoza
forbids women under forty to take the veil ; in 506
we read of a *monasterium puellarum* ; and St. Leander
about 584 addresses to his sister Florentina rules for
nuns living in community.[1] The superior was entitled *virginum mater*, not *abbatissa* ; she received at
consecration the blessing of Deborah and Judith ; was
saluted by the bishop ; had the staff and the book of
rules given her ; and, as we learn from a MS. of 976,
which appears to have copied an older rite, this admirable benediction was included, ' Sit enim mulier sancta,
discreta, gravis, casta, dilecta, humilis, mansueta,
amabilis et docta, etiamque divinis experta documentis.'
Such was the conception of woman's rights among
Spaniards in the darkest ages. From other historians
we know that religious sisters copied out the Bible,
and could not fail to be intimately acquainted with its
contents. Let us remark, finally, that in and round
about Cordova there existed during the ninth century
houses of Mozarabic nuns, some of whom underwent
martyrdom.

Those ' Councils of Toledo ' were national Parliaments, at which nobles and bishops together laid down
laws for the King as well as the people. In 633 the
Fourth Council prescribes how a king shall be chosen ;

---

[1] Dom Férotin's identification of Etheria as the author of the *Peregrinatio
Silviae* proves the existence of Spanish nuns in the fifth century.

it was presided over by St. Isidore, the six metropolitans attended, and sixty-two other prelates. There is no mention of anointing the elected prince until Wamba in 672 was crowned by Quiricus in the Palatine or Praetorian chapel. St. Julian tells the story at length: ' He would not suffer himself to be anointed before entering the royal city, the home of his father's race, in which it was fitting that he should take the standard (*vexilla*) of the sacred unction and quietly await the consent of those at a distance to his election.' The Gothic king of ancient days was by no means *el Rey neto*, absolute like Philip II or Ferdinand VII. Before all things he was a crusader. When he set out on an expedition, he first came to the Praetorian, was met by the clergy, and prostrate before the altar prayed in secret. The bishop chanted a supplication for victory, and presented to the king a cross of gold, which was to be carried in front of him during the whole campaign and brought back in peace on its conclusion. St. Dominic, as the record tells, bore such a cross aloft at the battle of Muret, where Pedro of Aragon and the Albigensian cause went down. Then the king embraces the bishop, mounts on horseback, and rides off to the war, his cavaliers and footmen following him, while the clergy sing ' Domine Deus, virtus salutis meae, obumbra caput meum in die belli.' [1]

Not always did the king come home again. But for a thousand years it may be said that he took the cross when elected to the crown. Recared in 586 swore to be a Catholic prince ; in 1588 the world gazes after Philip's invincible Armada, sent on a crusading errand to the English Channel. Moreover, these open conflicts were exasperated by plots, real or imaginary,

[1] *Lib. Ord.* 478 and 149–153.

of Arians, Jews and Moriscos against the faith, which
many of them had been compelled to adopt, although
they could not believe in it.   The execution of Priscillian and his comrades, the decrees of Sisebuth, who
persecuted Israel, prepare us for gloomy episodes in
the days to come.   Our 'Liber Ordinum' has no
ritual which implies an *auto de fé*.   But it contemplates
the reconciliation of Jews and heretics.   The Fathers
of Toledo forbade, in 633, that Israelites should be
made Christians in their own despite ; Sisebuth's procedure was condemned by St. Isidore as ' non secundum scientiam.'   The Council of Agde in 506 desired
genuine catechumens to be under instruction for at
least eight months.   To the Arian a series of renun-
ciations was prescribed.   The Donatist was not rebap-
tised but prayed over with laying on of hands, ' ut haec
ovicula . . . non Donatiste vel cujuslibet, sed tui sit
nominis Christiana.'   No form of reconciling a Jew
is found in the West outside our volume.   It contains
the peculiar word *cespitare*, to slip on the grass ; and
prays that the neophyte ' tetrum fetorem horreat syna-
goge, quem ydolorum spurcitiis inquinata lupanari
prostitutione collegit.'   This very strong language,
amusingly inapplicable to the children of Israel who
were contemporary with its authors, would be more in
place at an exorcism.   However, we cannot pretend
that our Spanish brethren were at any time fortunate
in their handling of the Jews, whom they called
Marranos and were continually vexing, until the day of
the great exile arrived under Ferdinand and Isabella
(August 2, 1492).[1]

Far more pleasant it is to consider with what happy
turns of speech and instinctive accuracy these prayers

[1] *Lib. Ord*, 100, 103, 105.

can set forth religion. Sometimes we light upon a discourse which in its sharp antitheses reminds us of St. Augustine ; for example, the sermon dated by Dom Férotin as early as the fifth century, which was given out 'in die Apparitionis Domini,' when the Church celebrated our Lord's birthday, the adoration of the Wise Men, the baptism in Jordan, the marriage feast at Cana, and the multiplication of the loaves. We hear in it the terms of Chalcedon, ' Et tamen non duo sed unus Christus ; nec dividitur locis nec confusus est in naturis. Unus ergo in utraque substantia, naturarum proprietatem in una persona conservat.' But an older and less abstract style, that of Augustine or Leo, has been sounded first : ' Vide ergo parvulum in gremio matris, sed crede perfectum ineffabili manentem in sinu Patris ; ad non procedentem, sed numquam exinde recedentem,' and the rest. Devotion expresses itself here in a glowing theology, which is neither sentimental nor sensuous, but coherent, luminous, persuasive. *O si sic omnia !* we are tempted to exclaim, when we contrast certain modern prayer-books with a language and spirit so elevated.[1]

The very notices of high days are thus made edifying. For Easter, at the close of the above sermon, ' Therefore, dearly beloved brethren, after the mystery of our Lord Jesus Christ born in the flesh ; after the showing forth of so many great marvels ; we announce to your devout minds the Paschal solemnities. . . . I exhort you, most dear brethren, let us endeavour so to live justly and piously, in chastity and soberness, that we may arrive at this sacred feast without crime and with abundance of good works.'[2] It would surprise controversial writers who deem our belief in the sacraments

---

[1] *Lib. Ord.* 527.   [2] *Ibid.* Append. iv. 526.

incompatible with a true ethical system, to find faith
and morality blended so firmly together by the Spanish
Church, when proclaiming Lent and Eastertide.   This
insistence on good works, however, meets us in every
service, baptismal, eucharistic or funeral.   Equally
prominent is the doctrine of grace.   But no one has
charged on Spanish Christians the heresy called after
Pelagius.   Quite as little should the falsehood be
tolerated which would degrade their feasts and sacraments into an indulgence for vices unrepented of, or
scandalous living.   The heart of this 'Liber Ordinum'
is sternly and emphatically clean.   Note, for instance,
in the blessing of the Baptistery those touching words,
' Nec confiteri possumus, nisi confessionis affectum tuo
munere sumserimus.'   The contrite spirit is God's gift.

Certainly, the term *Indulgentia* plays its part here.
It has more than one meaning.   In particular it enters
into the supplication for the dead.   But its origin takes
us back to primitive rules of penance ; and with such
it is associated in the remarkable ceremonies which
occupy Good Friday.   This was the end of the Lenten
rigours, when the people cried aloud to the bishop for
pardon and reconciliation with Christ whose minister
to them he was.   On that day all Christians acknowledged themselves to be ' penitents,' and broke forth
into the petition, *Indulgentia !* which they repeated
seventy, or one hundred, or even three hundred times.
The Fourth Council of Toledo (638) ordained that in
this function the ' mystery of the Cross ' should be announced—as is done in a most admirable sermon—
' atque indulgentiam criminum clara voce omnem
populum postulare ' ; so that the faithful, cleansed by
repentance, might take the Sacrament of Christ's body
and blood.   The Bishop does not give absolution

according to our modern form, but impetrates it in three prayers of singular beauty, and says over the penitents, ' Exaudi, Domine, supplicum preces, et tibi confitentium parce peccatis, ut quos conscientiae reatus accusat, indulgentia tue miserationis absolvat.' When the Arian was reconciled we find this formula, ' Et ego te chrismo in nomine, etc. . . . in remissione omnium peccatorum ' ; and for a lapsed Catholic, ' Tu eum ad sacramentum reconciliationis admitte.' The direct imperative absolution does not seem to occur ; but the priest's deprecatory petitions, both for the living and the dead, exhibit a strength as well as a tenderness of appeal which it would be difficult to match elsewhere.[1]

We have somewhat neglected the order of things in our book while pursuing these observations. That no sacred rite can be performed, except by a duly ordained cleric, is manifest in all it lays down. The priest's office, to bless and consecrate, touches the common life at every stage. A pretty complete picture might be drawn, as on the shield of Achilles in Homer, from the prayers adapted to all occasions in the career of a mediaeval Spaniard. We see him brought to the baptismal font which has been dedicated with impressive ceremonies and opened on Easter Eve. He is anointed, plunged into the water a single time, confirmed with chrism blest by the Bishop ; his head is veiled in white, and he receives Holy Communion. As a child he is offered by his parents *ad doctrinam* in the Christian school. Like a Greek youth he consecrates the first cuttings of his hair at the altar, even though not destined for the priesthood. But many children were made clerics. The warrior, as we saw,

---

[1] *Lib. Ord.* 200–202 ; Absolution of Arian, 100.

took his cross and banner in church, setting out for a campaign. Travellers by land or sea had their appropriate collects.[1] The seed in the furrow, the springing blades of corn, the sheaves and the threshing-floor, were blest in due season. There were benedictions for the vines, for the house, the well, the boat, the fishing-net. Oil with perfumes was set apart for the sick in a peculiarly beautiful Mass on the feast of SS. Cosmas and Damian. Crosses and crowns to be hung above the altar were frequently dedicated. The oldest crown, now in Madrid, bears its donor's inscription, ' ✠ Suintilanus Rex offeret ' (621–633). But the finest is that of Receswinth (649–672), which with seven others was hidden at Guarrazar, west of Toledo, when the Moors entered, and lay there until its discovery in 1858. All this treasure-trove is now at the Museum of Cluny in Paris ; but we hope it may one day return to the cathedral which it formerly adorned.[2] Such crowns were offered to Christ, our Lady and the Saints as defending the kingdom against its enemies— a form of mediaeval homage to God not obscurely connected with what has been called the Papal monarchy over Christendom.

Among additions not much later than 1052, and by the same hand, to the manuscript of Silos are the blessing of the bridal-chamber, of the wedding rings and pledges given by the bridegroom, and of the veil (*sipa, jugale*). The ceremony of marriage follows after Mass, and is concluded in a short preface, with prayers and a double benediction. As the newly wedded pass out the choir sings, ' Vos quos ad conjugale gaudium

---

[1] One of these, ' Ploramus et gemimus,' p. 345, goes back to the invasion of Spain by the Goths.

[2] Description in H. Lynch's *Toledo*, 44.

perduxit Dominus,' a fine antiphon. They had, of course, communicated at the priest's hands during Mass.[1]

The last anointing and the funeral rites take up one of the most remarkable chapters, much too long for quotation—' Ordo in finem hominis diei,'—but abounding, as Dom Férotin rightly observes, ' in magnificent formulas and curious rubrics.' If time allowed, Communion was to be administered ; the priest anointed with oil the dying man's head, pronouncing a series of invocations ; all gave the kiss of peace and said farewell (*valefactio = ave atque vale*) ; many psalms were recited, and after death came the ' Suscipe,' in a form greatly superior—though in substance not unlike—to our modern ' Proficiscere.' It is found in the Sacramentary of Gelasius. A litany follows ; the cross is fixed above the head of the bed, and the mourners lift up their lament (*clamor*) ; after which the body is incensed and lauds are chanted. In the long procession churchwards an acrostic hymn is sung, with its refrain, ' Deus miserere, O Ihesu bone, tu illi parce.' And the people cry, ' Indulgentia ! dicamus omnes.' The tomb is consecrated, the body laid in it ' in sinistra ' ; four more prayers are uttered, ' pro anima famuli tui ' ; and as the earth receives its own, a pathetic supplication arises, ' Si ascendero in celum, Domine, tu ibi es ; et si descendero in infernum, ades. Mitte manum tuam, Domine, libera me ex inferno inferiori.' Seven anthems follow, broken by the verse, ' Ubi mors non est, ubi dulce gaudium perseverat.' The command is given, ' Terra, terra, audi verbum Domini ; suscipiant te angeli Dei.' So the grave is covered in, with a lugubrious voice as of

---

[1] *Lib. Ord.* 433.

the dead himself, ' Hec requies mea in seculum seculi.'
But still the Church prays for her child and bids him
hope.   She will not cease to remember him, for her
faith is sure ; ' Mutatur vita, non tollitur.'   The whole
of this wonderful ceremony is bound up with Christ's
death and resurrection, as we are taught in the Requiem
Mass that accompanies it.   And we must never forget
that no mere creature comes at this supreme of moments
between the soul and its Redeemer.   Nothing is
more impressive in the long supplication than that
solitude round which the prayers of priest and people
echo, as it were, but which they cannot violate.[1]

Such were the rites of every day, adding to human
life a grace and significance, disclosing at the hour of
death a light in darkness, and turning to poetry the
fierce prose of an age otherwise rude even to barbarism.
The stately Latin of our classics had never moulded
popular speech outside Rome.   Here it is the *sermo
plebeius* which has taken a lofty flight, quickened by
the deeds and personalities that together make up
the Christian message.   All centres round the daily
Sacrifice.   It fills the *Missale Mixtum* of Ximenes ; it
constitutes in detail one half of this *Liber Ordinum* ;
it explains the Calendar of festivals and saints ; it is
the treasure bestowed at ordination, the votive offering
which the priest celebrates on his own account, for the
sick, for captives and for the departed.   Let us call to
mind with Dom Férotin that the Mozarabes inherited
their chief ritual, unbroken by heresy or schism, not
only from St. Isidore, but from a period anterior to the
Gothic invasion.   Its affinities with Eastern forms
have been acknowledged.   It was always orthodox.
It represents, therefore, the primitive or Apostolic

[1] *Lib. Ord.* 108-125 ; Masses of Requiem, 391-447.

tradition, both in what it enacts and in the doctrine
which it proclaims so eloquently. But, except for a
variation in the place occupied by some of the prayers,
or slight and immaterial adjuncts, it is the Mass which
every priest in the Catholic Church is bound to say.
These are grave considerations. Historically, the
Mass is one as the Church is one ; and it carries with
it priesthood, hierarchy, jurisdiction, creed, sacraments
and Scriptures. That was our meaning when we said
of the ' Liber Ordinum,' laid up at Silos for eight centuries and witnessing to almost as many more, that it
contained an argument not less indubitable than the
testimony of the Catacombs to primitive usage.

We should now pursue the changes of this sacred
action as the year moves round. But space is failing
us ; we can only invite those who seek the best of
prayers to study the ordinal for themselves. They will
find in it ancient relics. Here is a blessing of the
palms older than the fragment of Bobbio—not later
than 700. The ' sermon ' includes a peculiar version
of the Creed, which is said by the catechumens three
times, the Bishop guiding them, for it is not to be
written down ; ' Sit vobis codex vestra memoria,' the
prelate charges them. The palms are consecrated
with six admirable prayers in one church ; and then
the procession moves to another in which, as above, the
symbolum fidei was delivered to all who should be
christened on Easter Eve. Large variations from the
Roman ritual may be noted on Holy Thursday ; but
the Maundy is performed after stripping the altars
and quenching the lights. Until evening the fast was
rigorously kept. On Good Friday came the great
office of Indulgence, which comprised the veneration
of the cross during a long alphabetical rhythm hitherto

unknown, *Ab ore Verbum prolatum*, and the public
absolution, but no Mass of the Presanctified.   There
might be a private Mass on Holy Saturday in the titular
churches at a distance from the Cathedral, if need were.
But the solemn service was held there by the Bishop,
beginning with the new fire, going on to the Paschal
lights and the deacon's chant (attributed by Elipandus
to St. Isidore) which corresponded to our ' Exultet ' ;
then baptism with water from the Tagus in the *agnile*
or fold, i.e. the Baptistery ; and bidding prayers such
as we recite on Good Friday, but each following its
own lection from Scripture.   The ' Liber Ordinum '
is here mutilated, and the Easter Mass cannot be found.
It is implied, however, in the blessing of the Paschal
lamb, which was performed at its conclusion—a custom
observed among Greeks on their Holy Saturday, as the
present writer was told not many years ago at Delphi
on that day.   In the printed Mozarabic Missal it is
assigned to Easter Eve.[1]

Thus we have completed what we had to say
touching the Spanish liturgy and the Christian use of
Latin—a subject as inexhaustible as it is instructive.
Whether our Latin Bible was translated first in Antioch
or in Asia Minor is of small importance compared with
its diffusion throughout the West, its place in our
religious ceremonies, and its influence on mediaeval
and modern devotion.   It remains to us the greatest
of literary possessions.   And the ' Liber Ordinum ' ?
We cannot be grateful enough to the Benedictine community, now in exile, which has produced it, or the
editor who gave to its worthy setting forth the labour
of fifteen years, or those royal persons who have taken
so strong an interest in its publications.   From Toledo,

[1] *Lib. Ord.* 178–244.

from Silos, to Solesmes and Farnborough, the liturgy
has travelled along a path strewn with tragic memories.
It is one great Book of the Dead. It seems to chant
a Requiem over the Iberian Christians who were vanquished by the Goths ; over the Goths themselves,
broken on the days of Wady Becca ; over the Mozarabic Church, whose prayers were silenced by Bernard of
Cluny in the hour of its triumph ; over Toledo, proud
and defiant, which could not save its freedom, though
it had the hero Padilla to champion it against absolute
rule ; and over the Imperial dynasty whose tattered
flags are laid upon the granite monuments in the crypt
at Farnborough. Better so, perhaps, than to have
taken a common tinge by use and wont, to be soiled by
the mixture of modern vulgarities, familiar yet unknown to a generation which is fast losing the sense of
reverence, and which cannot pray, for it does not
believe. The past, revealed by such a long-hidden
treasure, is yet heroic and beautiful, though laden with
its own sins. It is our past. Had we the virtue of it
still abiding in us, we might make it our future, and
renew the face of that Christendom which our fathers
created.

V

POPE AND EMPEROR [1]

THREE great powers divide the modern world (which includes America), and are struggling for supremacy— the Roman, the Teuton and the Jew. Rome has tradition on its side ; the German has force ; the Israelite money. But there is a deeper account of the antagonism which sets them in array one against the other, and it must be sought in the region of ideas. History, from the fall of the Roman Empire, is nothing else than the conflict on a large scale between instincts which have grown into philosophies, with Church, State and civilisation as their direct outcome. Now, when we appear to have reached a turning-point in the drama, its precise character is thrown into relief by contrast with a new situation arising suddenly where least expected. The yellow race, incarnate in its Japanese hero, springs on the stage ; and at once we perceive that Roman, Teuton, Jew belong to the same group or species, have more in common than they ever dreamt of, and together constitute the European type. Unless they acknowledge these facts in time to be reconciled before the invasion breaks upon them, it is an even chance that all will go down as world-powers—

[1] *Catholic Church and Christian State*. By Dr. (afterwards Cardinal) Joseph Hergenröther. English Translation by C. S. Devas. London : 1876.

I

we know that the Church cannot fail—in presence of a movement which the sternest logic governs at every step it takes.

Europe is at odds with itself. The Latin nations waver between an omnipotent state and their Catholic hierarchy. In the wide spaces and vast populations which are controlled from Berlin, London and Washington the confusion of thought is amazing, but English freedom holds its own. Everywhere the Jew meets us, in our Bible, our Church, our market-place, our newspaper. He wanders from Russia to Oregon ; he inspires the Socialist propaganda ; he puts on the colours of the Primrose League ; he is flexible, obstinate, modern-ancient, always reminding us that the Apocalypse has not yet been fulfilled. He is a prophetic figure, pointing to the consummation of the age.

This it is which lends to Roman history a charm and an importance justifying antiquarian research. We study its documents with pleasure, for they are written to delight us ; but they also furnish the origins from which all our present problems have taken their rise. In such a light we cannot but echo the Shakespearean words and own that we are ' made and moulded of things past.' Impatient America would scorn history ; but it is not to be done. The Roman himself looks at it chiefly in one aspect ; he finds a change of bearings difficult and still judges English or Teutonic literature as the work of Barbarians. Yet he might consider how significant it is that the most profound of Latin historians, Tacitus, begins the modern era precisely by sweeping into his survey the Christian, the Jew and the German. Livy's exuberant style adorns what was even in his time the dead past, beautiful in remembrance. Tacitus, at the French Academy or in Oxford, would not be deemed an antique ; he is modern because the elements of strife and progress which he describes are with us still. We have added nothing to them. The Roman majesty, the fierce freedom of Germania, the religious fanaticism of Judaea, the Christian martyr's hope,—these have played their part during well-nigh two thousand years ; and religions, laws, languages, literatures, merely exhibit them in endless combination. The Catholic Church and the Roman Empire, coalescing into a civilised polity, have subdued the peoples of the North and spread with their conquests, but have never won a permanent footing outside these bounds. Christendom is the universe which Tacitus had before him, enlarged by geographical discoveries, but otherwise unchanged. The black and the yellow races lie outside it. When it numbered its churches by the thousand in Africa and Asia Minor, it did but touch the fringe of those vast Continents. Beyond the Atlas or the Euphrates Christians have never felt at home.

Now, perhaps, we may understand how the Roman circle was broken, yet only to be enlarged and closed in again, by the Hebrew with his revelation from on high and the Barbarian who lived a free man of the woods about Elbe and Danube. If anything in history is clear, we must grant that a new synthesis had been swiftly growing up since Alexander took Greek ideas into Western Asia and the Romans absorbed his dominions. From Alexander to Constantine is six hundred years. When the first Christian Emperor founded New Rome on the Bosporus, that intermingling of Jewish religion, Greek philosophy, old Republican and Imperial jurisprudence, was become so com-

plete that we may term it the Christian idea in practice.
Henceforth education was to be cast in this mould.
Now one element might get the upper hand, and now
another ; but the Middle Ages, the Renaissance, the
Revolution itself, all bear witness to an identity in the
spirit which marks them off from the world of Islam,
not to speak of systems reigning in the Farther East.
Every Christian talks Hebrew when he prays, Greek
when he philosophises, Latin when he goes to law.
There is no help for it.   The Teuton in all his varieties
cannot escape this great tradition.   He brings to its
handling one instinct, due to his overmastering energy,
—individual freedom, 'veterem Germaniae liberta-
tem,' says Tacitus.'[1]   This, too, becomes an idea in
time, and with it our problem is fully stated.

In the Apocalypse Rome is a persecutor of the
Saints, drunk with their blood, and Jerusalem is the
Holy City.   This point of view remains fixed for
several generations in Christian apologetics ; it dominates the invectives of Tertullian ; it affords a principle
to St. Augustine on which he has wrought out his
monumental 'De Civitate Dei.'   Yet there was
another, quite distinct and not less primitive, as we
read in the Acts of the Apostles, where Roman Law is
invoked by way of defending the Christian from his
Jewish assailant.   In course of time the first yielded
to the second ; Rome was actually transformed to a
Catholic Jerusalem ; and down to the twelfth century
we may say, the Apocalypse faded out of Western
imaginations.   Then a remarkable change took place.
The reforming sects, Waldensians, Albigenses, and
finally Protestants, identified Papal with Pagan Rome,
called the Pope Antichrist and his theocracy the reign

[1] *Annals*, xi. 16.

of Satan. This was a triumph for the Jew, with whose Old Testament ideas the Reformers had so many things in common. And if we discount mere language, we shall find the same intense fanatical hatred at the heart of those associations, whether terming themselves Christian or free-thinking, which under the name of Templars, Illuminati, Masons, Carbonari, Saint-Simonians, Socialists, and the like, have waged war upon the Holy See during the whole modern period. They are sects inspired by some Utopian scheme, enthusiastic for the propagation of an Eternal Gospel, enraged against the Pope as ' him that letteth,' —in plain English, as the great European bulwark which anarchy assaults in vain.

Here is the connecting link between all phases of Roman history, the kinship in spirit whereby Republic, Empire, and Popedom are united as instruments to carry out one vast plan, embracing nations and centuries. It is the spirit of Law, divine by origin, human as regards matter and scope, theocratic because appealing for its sanction to heavenly powers, hierarchical and selective in the persons by whom it rules, rather than feudal or hereditary, when fully developed. Early Rome grew upon a basis of family worship ; but the Imperial legislation, while conferring on Caesar a *patria potestas* without limits, has attained to the idea of man as man, the subject of rights and duties springing from his very nature. So there is a *Lex Naturalis* into which we are all born, bound up with what Burke might call the frame and constitution of the world itself, or divine Reason and Justice, prior to any social compact, and needing none for its establishment. To the Roman Peace we may apply those magnificent words of St. Augustine, ' Nullo modo aliquid legibus summi

Creatoris ordinationique subtrahitur, a quo pax universitatis administratur.'[1] The sovereign conception of a divine order upon earth, as it is in heaven, governs Catholic theology from its beginning and comes to its perfect type in St. Thomas among the schoolmen, in Dante among the poets. Nevertheless, we say, there was a parallel development of which the *Digest* is a record among heathen legislators, so curiously identical in many points that one set of terms will express the Christian or the Roman principles. So Justinian writes, ' The laws of Nature which all peoples alike observe, being established by divine Providence, remain fixed and immutable.' The Emperor has in mind Ulpian as well as the other famous jurists when he lays down this axiom. But long before their date Cicero, in his ' De Legibus,' had recapitulated the sayings of Greek and Italian wisdom to this effect, ' Lex vera atque princeps, apta ad jubendum et ad vetandum, ratio est recta summi Jovis.'[2]

Nowhere, then, was the reign of law more splendidly exemplified than in the Roman Empire, which made its conquests permanent by superseding the laws of the conquered. On this very ground of a rival theocracy at death-grips with Rome do we account for the ' obstinate faith ' in themselves which Tacitus ascribes to the Jews, who alone of all Easterns would not suffer their Deity to migrate with a crowd of vassal gods to the Pantheon, and whose ' pervicaciam superstitionis ' the historian connects with their hatred of mankind.[3] It was temple against temple, law against law ; so was brought to pass the destruction of Jerusalem. But neither Tacitus nor Trajan could have dreamt that in fulfilling Christ's prophecies they were yielding

[1] *De Civ. Dei,* xix. 12.   [2] *De Legibus,* ii. 4.   [3] *History,* v. 5 ; ii. 4.

up Rome to a dynasty, the heir at once of both laws
and able to reconcile them. 'If there be wise men,
judges in equity,' says Lactantius, 'who have composed the Institutions of Civil Law, how much more
shall we set down in writing the Divine Institutions,
wherein we speak of life, immortality, and God, to the
ruin of superstition?'[1] Hence it has been boldly
asserted that Canon Law grew up in the shadow of the
Civil and, as the Decretum of Gratian proves, borrowed
from it the form and procedure by which ecclesiastical
courts are regulated.[2]

Taking a more general view, we cannot but observe
how soon and how steadfastly the Roman genius makes
itself felt in Papal documents. It gives to St. Clement's
Letter a judicial strength which has been acknowledged
by every modern critic. In the decrees of Victor concerning Easter, of Callistus regarding public penitents,
of Stephen on rebaptism, it provokes opposition but
wins to Rome the assent of Catholics at large. When
the Western Empire shrinks behind the marshes of
Ravenna, it comes forth in the classic majesty of St. Leo
confronting Attila and protecting the city from the
Huns like a new Camillus. With Leo the fusion of
Law and Gospel is triumphantly accomplished. He
prevails in East and West. He fixes the style of the
Curia. He puts down the Manichees by aid of the
secular arm. He is recognised at Chalcedon as 'the
holy Archbishop of the world.' He persuades Valen-
tinian III to issue the 'Perpetual Edict,' by which a
supreme court of appeal was recognised in the Lateran.
The immunity of clerics had been, it appears, a rule of
long standing and is insisted upon by St. Ambrose in
380. What were afterwards known in England as

[1] *Instit.* i. 1. [2] Dodd, *Hist. of Canon Law,* 135-149; Sohm, *Institutes.*

' Courts Christian ' had already begun to take over a
certain proportion of cases dealing with secular matters,
but submitted to the Bishop as an equitable ' daysman '
between litigants. The Emperors not only allowed
but encouraged a jurisdiction which in the rapidly dis-
integrating West supplied for their own impotence,
while at Constantinople or Alexandria it respected,
often beyond what was decent, the high theocratic
privileges claimed by the orthodox Caesars. With
Byzantium, however, we are little concerned. It was
in Italy and the Western half of Christendom that
civilised society started on the lines which it is still pursuing ; there, and not among the Lower Greeks or the
decadent Christians of Egypt and Syria, we may watch
the world's debate, turning ever on the opposed yet
necessary points of authority and freedom. From that
arena we have not yet emerged. Our future lies at
stake in the midst of it ; and if history can teach us
how the quarrel ought to be decided, we may well be
grateful to historians.[1]

First, then, let us remark that Judaism had won,
so far as it had established in the Empire a Church
no longer dependent on the State. Caesar was henceforth not to be a priest, much less the Pontifex Maximus. He had no jurisdiction in the holy place. The
Bishop was inviolable at the altar, in his court, when he
attended a Council, nay, even though he fell into crime.
He could be judged only by his peers. And the
meanest clerk shared in this immunity. There was
a true ' Imperium in imperio,' consequent on the jurisdiction which no crown lawyer could supersede or
invade without sacrilege. And while the Civil Law

[1] See in *Histoire Littéraire de Fénelon* the valuable dissertation, ' Droit
public du Moyen Age.'

was losing its power, the Canon Law waxed mighty
and overshadowed it until, after the fall of the Western
Empire, a confusion of tribal customs set in which left
the Church courts manifestly supreme during six
hundred years and more.

The Pope, as Johannes von Müller expressed it,
became ' tutor of the Barbarians.'   But he held supremacy over them by Divine Right, not by concession
from kings who themselves were subject to him in
virtue of their baptism.   A new Pater Romanus dwelt
in the Lateran.   The Emperor had gone away to
Byzantium ; the Pontifex Maximus stayed behind.
Rome, which had always been a theocracy, its ruling
principle worship of the Invisible Powers, did not
change its character, but was exalted to a loftier place
and wielded a larger jurisdiction by absorbing the
tribes and abolishing the gods of the North, as it had
incorporated with its worship the Asiatic, Egyptian,
Hellenic rites.   The Roman road was to be the road
of history, Hebrew prophets leading the nations forward, serving as pioneers of progress towards a distant
but definite ideal which may be summed up in the
single word Righteousness.   What could the Vandal,
Frank, or Saxon contribute to this great Messianic
movement ?   They needs must have been taught as
children before they could enter into its purpose.
And we ask even now whether one solitary thought has
come to us by their lips which is not derived from
Greek, or Roman, or Hebrew sources.

' The isthmus of Rome,' says De Quincey with
daring felicity.   Or we may symbolise what happened
by the Pontiff sacrificing on the Sublician bridge that
carries civilisation across the stream of time.   As for
the Barbarians, who well deserved their title, we

inherit from them chiefly the Feudal System (now strangely transformed as Toryism), or service by oath and tenure between a man and his lord. This romantic attachment is founded not on law but on compact ; it implies a freely chosen loyalty, answering to the other notable creations of enthusiasm in the Middle Ages, —Knight-errantry, troubadour worship in the Cour d'Amour, the Crusades, and the chivalrous Orders in which soldier-'monks followed their Captain Christ. But no feudal hierarchy would have been possible in the shape which is familiar to us, had not Pope Leo III, obeying an instinct deeply rooted in Italian minds through all vicissitudes of fortune, created the Holy Roman Empire.

In that magnificent conception as Dante saw it,—nay, justice compels us to declare, as it appeared to Pope Gregory VII and his champion St. Peter Damiani, the two powers, spiritual and temporal, were to be ever distinct yet ever united, wielded by diverse persons, directed to the same end, their meeting-place Rome, their sphere of action the world. The Empire and the Church were to make up one grand Federation, of all peoples, tribes, and tongues, like a vision in the Apocalypse. Two swords, but one Christ, and the sword of flesh subject to the spirit. Augustus had combined both powers in himself. Charlemagne and Leo were to share them. On this principle Europe has founded what is now known as liberty of conscience ; it was then termed the independence of the spiritual order, its immunity from State-control.

If we rehearse these well-known commonplaces of our story-books, it is not for their own sake. The object which we keep in view is modern and practical. As the world now moves, it would seem that European

society is going one way and the Catholic Church
another. What explanation are we to give of such
a divorce between powers in their nature so akin as
civilised government and the old religion ? Many
illustrious thinkers, especially among ecclesiastics,
attribute the dissidence which is weakening Europe in
face of the Eastern Renaissance to matters of creeds
and dogmas. But we cannot overlook the question of
Law ; and it is plain from a multitude of facts to be
found in all our histories that kings and Parliaments,
rather than divines or Councils, have guided the revolution thanks to which the Papacy now stands for an
influence exercised mostly on individuals or through
minorities, whereas during a thousand years it controlled the public order.

From St. Gregory to Leo X Catholic Rome represented not only a conservative tradition but a force of
advance. There was no element in the West which it
did not make its own. It exhibited the most vigorous
life, the highest sum of intelligence possible to the
races governed by its rod of empire. Rome and civilisation were tending, as years went on, to become
synonymous. Take the eighth century with its
Charlemagne ; the twelfth with its University of
Paris ; the thirteenth with its St. Thomas Aquinas ;
the fifteenth with its revival of learning ; at each of
these periods the Catholic, that is to say the Roman,
supremacy in things human no less than divine was
unmistakable. Abelard and Aristotle, the philosophy
of the Saracens drawn from Greece, the printing-press,
the classic literature, the Bible, and all the arts, were
serving the central idea of a Christian Theocracy.
One antagonist, more formidable than speculative
tenets however zealously propagated, held out against

the Pope. It was the secular spirit, the lay or anti-
clerical ethos, which under many names had begun to
stir in the Feudal System itself long ago. That spirit
wakened in rude, unkempt Germans like Henry IV a
resistance to churchmen the significance of which they
could not measure, and which seemed liable to everlasting defeat until, by the discovery of the Pandects
and their application to the Western Emperors, it contrived to get law on its side. When Frederick Barba-
rossa proclaimed his Divine Right as Caesar, dependent
neither on Pope nor people, in the plain of Roncaglia
(1158), the modern state was born. Roman Law had
turned against the Roman Pontiff.

How difficult it is to beat this view of history into
men's heads those know best who have tried. It was
not the Albigensian or the Lollard that struck out a new
line of development in the heart of the Middle Ages ;
it was the lawyer, dazzled and inspired by Justinian's
Imperial Code, most favourable, as Michelet says, to
despotism—yes, certainly, to a despotism of the crown,
with its axiom from the Lex Regia, ' Quod principi
placuit legis vigorem habet.' This mighty word, as
lawyers construed it, broke the Feudal System in pieces
and took from the Pope his temporal jurisdiction over
the world's rulers at a single blow. It substituted the
Royal Supremacy for the Papal Monarchy. It justified Philip the Fair and Henry VIII by anticipation.
When the Hohenstaufen, after a hundred years of
fighting and chicanery, lost the battle and Conradin
was executed at Naples, the Pope looking on, first
France and then England seized the glove which that
unhappy boy had thrown down as a challenge to the
Guelfs. Thirty years had not elapsed before King
Philip was sounding in the ears of Boniface VIII his

haughty claim to absolute dominion over all French subjects, not excluding the clerical order. Philip meant to exercise his prerogatives without let or hindrance from the Holy See, giving a rehearsal in the thirteenth century of that great anti-papal drama which Henry of England was to enact more fully and carry on to its *dénouement* in the sixteenth. For, as Hergenröther observes, a conflict on principles had broken out between Pope and King. Whoever had been the persons engaged, the issue would have been the same. That France alone was not concerned ; that the behaviour of Philip or Boniface towards one another is of little moment compared with those hidden forces which were urging them both onward in their public policy ; and that we ourselves have a stake yet depending on the solution of their quarrel, is beyond a doubt.

By way of clinching this point, let us read the Statute of Appeals, passed in 1533 by the English Parliament, declaratory as it professes of the law already existing, as laid down in acts of Edward I, Edward III, Richard II, Henry IV, and ' other noble kings of this realm.' It will be found, we say, that this bold language affirms explicitly the conception of a supreme civil society, competent to manage its own affairs in every instance, which the German Emperors and the Kings of France had been feeling after as the basis of their authority, but had never so clearly formulated. Caesar was now the crowned and sceptred layman, whose power the priest could neither limit nor revoke, under any pretence whatsoever.

Whereas [says the Statute] by divers sundry old authentic histories and chronicles, it is manifestly declared and expressed that this realm of England is an Empire, and so hath been accepted in the world ; governed by one supreme head and

King, having the dignity and royal estate of the imperial crown of the same ; unto whom a body politic compact of all sorts and degrees of people, divided in terms by names of spirituality and temporality, be bound and ought to bear, next to God, a natural and humble obedience : he being also instituted and furnished by the goodness and sufferance of Almighty God with plenary, whole and entire power, pre-eminence and authority, prerogative and jurisdiction, to render and yield justice and final determination to all manner of folk resident or subject within his realm, without restraint or provocation to any foreign prince or potentate of the world . . . in consideration hereof, all testamentary and matrimonial causes, and all suits for tithes, oblations, and obventions, shall henceforth be adjudged in the spiritual and temporal courts within the realm, without regard to any process of foreign jurisdiction, or any inhibition, excommunication or interdict.[1]

Such was the English reply,—we are speaking historically and not now judging the right or the wrong of it,—delivered in 1533, to the Bull ' Unam Sanctam ' of 1302. Boniface had reiterated the famous doctrine of the ' two swords,'—one spiritual to be wielded directly by the clergy, i.e. by the Holy See in ultimate appeal, the other temporal, to be in the hands of kings and warriors, but ' ad nutum et ad patientiam sacerdotis.' Henry VIII answers by denying the system of appeal, terming the Pope a foreign prince, and asserting for the Crown supreme jurisdiction in both courts. The mediaeval Christian State, accurately delineated in the words of Boniface, which echoed Innocent III and may be followed back to St. Bernard, St. Anselm, St. Gregory VII,—had ceased to exist. The idea lingered still in the Roman Chancery ; the conditions under which it had been realised were a dream of the past.[2]

---

[1] *Acts of the Realm*, 24 Henry VIII., cap. xii.
[2] Hergenröther, ii. 97–145, ' Boniface VIII and Philip the Fair.'

That dream took its most glorious shape in the Holy Roman Empire. It supposed Western Christendom to be a single society, all the members of which were bound in feudal submission to one temporal chief, anointed at Rome as the Church's Protector. As such he swore an oath in the Pope's hands before receiving the insignia of royalty ; and Charlemagne, lying prostrate in St. Peter's on Christmas Day, 800, while Leo stood up to bless and consecrate him, presented a symbolic illustration which after-ages dwelt upon with rapture. The innumerable volumes where these incidents are discussed by Gallicans, Ultramontanes, and modern critics, allow us to conclude that all Popes asserted a spiritual right in crowning the Emperor, not a concession from any earthly potentate ; and if they acted as Christ's Vicars in bestowing their sanction on what the electors and the people had done, it seemed by parity of reasoning that for good cause they might withdraw their benediction, unmaking the prince they had made. In the language of Councils, they might declare the Emperor a heretic, excommunicate him by name, shut the churches throughout his dominions, interdict all but the necessary offices of religion, and if he persisted in his contumacy, depose him outright. He then fell under the ban, which according to feudal usages put him beyond the law. Every baptised Christian was member of a system which dealt with his body and soul for salvation and correction. To lose spiritual caste was to become an exile from civil society. The excommunicate forfeited all claim on his fellowmen ; he was dead in law, to be shunned as a leper, and punished for his treason to Christ by imprisonment, by stripes, and, under the growing severity of legislation, such as Frederick II put forth in his

Sicilian Code, by death. In a theocracy exclusion from religious rites had its own logic, and these were its consequences.[1]

We may quote St. Thomas on this head, who brings out the whole mediaeval view with his accustomed clearness:

> Infidelity as such [he observes] does not conflict with sovereignty ; for sovereignty came in by the law of nations, which is human law, but the distinction between faithful and infidel is by divine law ; and this takes not away the human. . . . It does not belong to the Church to punish infidelity in those who have never received the faith. . . . But in those who have done so, it can punish their lapse from faith, and in this they are reasonably chastised, viz. that they be not suffered to rule over the faithful. . . . Therefore, as soon as the man is judicially declared excommunicate because of apostasy, by that fact his subjects are released from his rule and from the oath of fealty by which they were bound to him.[2]

In these words the Dominican jurist lays down a principle already affirmed by the Fourth Council of Lateran in 1215, when it was dealing with Raymond of Toulouse and the Albigenses.[3] We have no space to recite its Canons, which, however, is the less required inasmuch as mediaeval practice, in what may be termed the pattern instance of Henry IV and Gregory VII, had made it manifest that an Emperor judged contumacious by the Pope lost his crown and all other civil prerogatives, distinctly on the ground which St. Thomas enunciates. The Hebrew and the Saracen were exempt from Papal jurisdiction, according to the dictum of St. Paul, ' Quid mihi de his qui foris sunt judicare ? ' But the apostate Catholic must be

---

[1] See, especially, the Suabian Code in Senckenberg, *Juris Alamannici*, c. 127.

[2] *Summa Theol.* 2a, 2æ, ix. 12, art. 2.   [3] Hergenröther, ii. 319.

sharply handled, lest he should corrupt others and, if
not checked in time, break up the fair fabric of Christendom.   Society was a closed State.   Once more,
speaking historically, it cannot be denied that in proportion as the mediaeval law grew weak or was evaded,
a certain dissolution set in.   And the services of the
Papal Monarchy in building up civilisation are acknowledged on all hands.

At this point so many considerations demand our
interest that we must select from them one or two lines
of argument which the reader can follow up for himself.   First, let us grant a principle of progress at work
in the Middle Ages, and identified with spiritual supremacy (in however rudimental a form) striving always to
transcend brute force, now by subduing it to the old
Roman Law (as much of it as survived), and again by
the dedication to religious ends of the Feudal System
in all its details.   But remark that, although antiquity
gave the rule and men lived by tradition, the outlook
was ever towards a world beyond sense.   History had
become a pilgrimage from time to eternity.   Thus the
Middle Ages recognised in their very nature a symbolic meaning, compared with which the present was
dwarfed and merely a shadow.

Dante is the immortal singer of this Christian
Odyssey, which sacrifices all that man has in the search
after ideals.   So deeply is the feeling ingrained in us,
that we take it as a matter of course and expect every
saint to be a reformer.   St. Bernard innovates on
St. Benedict ; St. Francis throws open the cloister ;
St. Ignatius forms his disciples into a military battalion.
The Popes, almost in their own despite, become kings,
are clad with imperial garments, give away crowns,
act as suzerains over Europe, call out Crusade after

K

Crusade, and from being simply the Bishops of Rome
are compelled to take measures against Islam in the
field, as veritable Commanders of the Faithful. St. Leo
was the subject of an empire dying at the heart ;
Innocent III or Gregory IX decides who shall be the
Western Caesar. And, undoubtedly, this meant progress in the general conscience, a higher grade of civilisation, achieved as human conquests are, not without
evil deeds, yet a permanent addition to law and order.
' Not force, but justice in the name of Christ,' said those
Papal investitures and depositions that have given such
offence. They were not infallible,—far from it, but
their appeal rings like an Old Testament prophecy
through the endless confusion which, left to itself, had
literally been ' bellum omnium contra omnes.' The
true social compact between rulers and subjects,
admirably expressed in the rite of a King's coronation,
dates from the time when bishops began to dedicate
the royal sword in the Church's defence.

Progress, again, not only by development of spiritual institutions, but in the arts of life, in learning,
manners, commerce, architecture, poetry, philosophic
meditation, and above all in respect for humanity. If
Christ was king, the Madonna was queen ; perhaps no
more decisive step has been taken towards the realising
of ideals than this which exalted Mary, and all women
in her name, as the embodiment of virtues now seen to
be essential in a perfect society. The everlasting types
whereby mankind is drawn onward and upward were
thus complete. But, as being heavenly, they could not
be exhausted. Moreover, in themselves they were
neither lay nor clerical but transcendent above these
differences. The saint occupied a throne, a cell, a
palace, or a hermitage. He refused the Papacy or he

accepted it. The bishop was a prince ; the monk a builder of cities ; the friar a philosopher. Women ruled monastic orders, studied the classics, read and transcribed the Scriptures, preached in the public squares, went on embassies for the Holy See. Greater freedom within the bounds of faith has never been known. The creative imagination, as soon as Barbarian raids from the north could be checked, wrought wonders in the twelfth century and reached in the thirteenth an eminence equal after its own style to the Greek or the modern. And of all these achievements Rome was the centre as it had been originally the source. It is impossible to conceive them without religion, or religion triumphant if the Popes had not claimed and exercised a supremacy which no temporal ruler could gainsay.

Hence, no sooner did a Clovis, a Recared, or a Pepin Heristal, aim at establishing a kingdom on the site of a military camp, than he threw himself into the arms of the clergy. To make his crown independent, the sovereign of Toledo, chosen by bishops and nobles, offered it to Christ. He became the Pope's vassal and put his royal estate into sanctuary. This was all one with declaring it to be inviolable. Hungary, Bohemia, Denmark, England, Portugal, Castile, Aragon, and in a special way Naples and Sicily, were feudatories of St. Peter. When Innocent III revoked Magna Charta, and his successors confirmed it by their legates, we see how the Law of Nations was embodied in the Papacy as arbiter between the king whose allegiance it had received and his subjects, who had also their right of appeal in Rome. Such were the beginnings of our modern Constitutions, at once a protection to the sovereign and a check on his encroachments, for he

could not even lay fresh taxes on his people without
licence from the Holy See, as the Bull ' In Coena
Domini ' declared. No mediaeval kings were absolute ;
all were members of a great Catholic federation which,
as Urban II proved at Clermont in 1095, any Pope
could summon to a Crusade involving the most heroic
self-denial and an infinite expense of blood and treasure.
When Frederick II took the cross but evaded his
engagement, Pope Gregory IX warned, excommuni-
cated, and deposed him. Nor did any of his fellow-
sovereigns, among whom was St. Louis, question the
right which in a manner so peremptory had been exercised against their Imperial colleague. Twice before,
at Canossa in 1076, at Venice in 1177, Emperors had
made atonement on their knees to St. Peter for high
crimes which they had perpetrated to the injury of
the Christian Commonwealth. Now Frederick II
also submitted ; but he was deposed a second time
at Lyons in 1245, and the Hohenstaufen dynasty
became extinct.

These tremendous object-lessons were copied with
violence in a later age, when deposition was followed by
execution on the scaffold at Whitehall or in the Place
Louis XV. But here we light upon a distinction,
always admitted in terms, yet in history tending to be
forgotten, between the temporal power lodged in Papal
hands, direct or indirect, and that which secular princes
may claim. Every one has quoted the Gospel text,
' Regnum meum non est de hoc mundo,' as determining the nature of Roman jurisdiction ; all, except
a few extreme apologists, grant that the Pope is not
Caesar in his own right over the Christian world.
Leaving aside the States of the Church and their origin,
we must hold the Petrine privilege to be simply spiri-

tual in its essence, and the weapons of Papal warfare unearthly. Religion is a moral influence ; the Gospel wins by persuasion ; it is a voluntary law which we take on ourselves, and conscience, not mere brute force, gives it a sanction. St. Peter had no soldiers ; St. Paul bowed his neck to the jurisdiction of Nero, concerning whom he had written in energetic terms, ' He beareth not the sword in vain.' For seven centuries the Popes were subjects of the Empire and made not the slightest attempt to cast off their allegiance. When Councils like the Second, Third and Fourth Lateran decreed temporal penalties against heretics, Bossuet and the Gallican writers justly observe that by the presence of lay lords, or of bishops who were feudal chieftains, they became Parliaments and legislated in the double capacity. So far as forms availed no spiritual person could take part in a judgment of blood. Facts, indeed, are stubborn, but principles will hold their own ; and in the growing secularisation which disfigured the mediaeval Church as it absorbed property and privileges during its later career, this axiom was never denied. Even Boniface VIII did not call in question—he distinctly asserted—the divine origin of the State, and the difference between the two swords. In quoting St. Paul he was admitting that kingly power comes from on high ; there is a divine right which the Papacy has not created but has always acknowledged in the social order, be its form royal or republican, democratic or mixed.[1]

Thus, in whatever degree civilisation is equal to its own ends, strictly human and temporal, the Church is set free from tasks which it had undertaken only because ' caritas Christi urget nos,'—there was no

[1] Hergenröther, ii. 235-274, ' Origin of the Civil Power.'

other way of getting them executed. Missionaries have taught savage tribes agriculture, invented grammars, acted as pioneers of trade ; but their calling was to preach the Gospel, and these things they attended upon as preliminaries, not as a part of it, however compatible with its lessons. In like manner the Papacy fostered art and science, interposed in secular government, decreed war against the infidel. But there is no revealed system of politics, no science in the Bible, no style of architecture, no economic pattern, to which we are bound in detail as Christians. Creed and Sacraments, not learning, taxation, commerce, hygiene, the fine or the useful arts, come within the Papal jurisdiction and furnish its matter. The rest, however sublime, is a serving of tables ; when society is able and willing to serve itself, the Apostle gladly turns to his own work, the propagation of religion pure and undefiled.

It is instructive to compare, from this point of view, the attitude of the Holy See towards East and West. Never once did a Pope act as though suzerain of the Byzantine Empire. Those Lower Greeks inherited the crown of Caesar, and their legislation renewed the juridical omnipotence which old heathen Rome had exercised over the nations ; yet the Pontiff looked on in silence. Hellenic culture owed nothing to Hebrew or Christian ; it was flourishing when the Apostles began their travels ; under its influence their converts were born ; and the Rome of the Popes was its debtor, not its creator. Had the Iconoclast Emperors not lost their hold on Italy, the peculiar features which distinguish mediaeval Christendom could never have been observed—a sure token that they belonged to the accidents rather than the substance of religion, and

might pass away, leaving it intact.   No Eastern bishop
comes forward as a temporal prince ; the Churches of
Thrace, Asia Minor, Syria, and Egypt, recognise in
Constantine a right of protection founded on no compact but on his supreme and God-given power, which
the hierarchy did not dream of challenging, though the
best among them withstood Imperial heresy again and
again.   The Papal Monarchy took its rise only when
Islam had overrun the fairest provinces of Asia and
Africa ; when the free Barbarians put an end to the
Western Empire ; when Constantinople faded into
a legendary distance as the Golden City guarded by
fires of magic against Moslem hordes, but otherwise
unknown to Frank or Saxon.   Whatever privileges the
Gregories and Innocents affirmed to be theirs in the
West, towards the genuine heirs of Antoninus, Theodosius, and the last ecumenical Caesar,—that never
to be forgotten Justinian whose law is the foundation
of the modern State,—they did not exhibit the fierce
procedure which in dealing with later kingdoms was
dictated by the stylus Curiae.   Rome had originated
or set its seal upon the feudal dynasties ; therefore
regarded them as its creation.   Hence the difference,
marked at every stage, between its tone of command in
the West and its more primitive or spiritual language
when addressing the Greeks.

On the subject of civilisation at large, Cardinal
Newman has left us words very much to the present
purpose:

First [he says] we must grant—and it is difficult to determine
how far we must go in granting—that both the Mosaic and the
Christian dispensations took the existing state of thought as it
was, and only partially innovated on or corrected it. . . . On
a far larger scale is the absence of meddling with the social and

secular world. God speaks 'for the elects' sake.' He leaves
the popular astronomy as it was. Heaven is still above, and the
powers of evil below. The sun rises and sets, and at His word
stops or goes back, and the firmament opens. And so with
social and political science ; nothing is told us of economic laws,
etc. So from the first there has been a progress with laws of
progress, to which theology has contributed little, and which
has now a form and substance, powerful in itself, and independent of and far surpassing Christianity in its social aspect ;
for Christianity (socially considered) has a previous and more
elementary office, being the binding principle of society.[1]

Progress, then, as a human instinct, came to a
knowledge of itself in Greek thought and found expression in literature, law, civil polity, and the Pax
Romana, without help from Christian theology, to
whose course it moved antecedently or in parallel lines.
We need only glance over the pages of Thucydides,
Plato, Aristotle, and Cicero, to be persuaded that men
who lived before the Gospel knew in theory and practice a social order which greatly excelled any that the
uncultivated Christian could have devised. The reign
of the Saints need not imply proficiency in secular arts,
or deep scholarship, or inventive science, or the most
perfect methods of jurisprudence, or direct interfer-
ence in politics. Revelation has never drawn out a
Republic, such as Plato dreamed of, complete in all
its parts. Neither does it guarantee the Canon Law
against defects arising from national prejudice, ignorance, rudeness of manners, or a backward civilisation.
Temporal prosperity is a dubious note of the Church.
In any case, it is one thing to serve the altar, another
and a different to build up the State. As we travel
down the chronicles bequeathed by mediaeval historians, we cannot but feel sensible that a change for

[1] See letter in W. S. Lilly's *Essays and Speeches*, p. 95.

the worse comes over the scene with accession of power
to clerics, whose office of preaching was too frequently
absorbed in their great public charges, and who ruled
with a rod of iron, by penalties of which the spiritual
nature almost disappeared under secular fines, im-
prisonments, and executions. Interdict was made a
weapon of diplomacy. After the Crusaders took
Constantinople the Holy War, which had hitherto
been directed against Saracens, was not seldom used
as an expedient to harass anointed Kings ; it was proclaimed by Gregory IX in his conflict with Frederick II,
against the Roman Emperor himself. The Church,
as heretics maintained, now became more oppressive
than the State, and Constantine's donation (in which
all men believed) had been the greatest of calamities.

There is no call on us, at this time of day, to take
sides with Guelf or Ghibelline. It is enough to bear
in mind the repeated protests of which our English
Parliaments keep the record that testify to melancholy disputes between Crown and Curia ; while
the hundred ' Grievances of the German Nation ' at
Constance and Basle were a distinct overture to the
Reformation. These and the like symptoms of widespread disaffection showed, as we know now, but as
authority could not realise till too late, that the Middle
Ages were passing. The momentum of power, so
long in favour of Papal Rome, had swung towards
Caesar. And lawyers, aided by rebellious or designing ecclesiastics, in the long and confused struggle of
Louis the Bavarian with many Popes, found in their
national codes an Edictum Perpetuum which made
the King more than a match for ' Ultramontane '
canonists.[1]

---

[1] Hergenröther, ii. 52–61.

The Great Schism now broke Europe into rival
' Obediences ' ; it all but anticipated the Reformation-
principle, ' Cujus regio ejus religio,' for it was the
monarch who decided which Pope should be acknowledged. At Constance the Emperor Sigismund was
arbiter between claimants to whom the Council declared
itself superior. No King has been effectively deposed
by a Papal judgment since that day. Then came the
Renaissance, of which, if we seek a definition, one com-
prehensive word may suffice to describe it,—in every
phase and vicissitude, high or low, sublime or degraded,
the Renaissance is equivalent to Humanism. It is
precisely the antithesis, but need not lapse into the
negation of Christianity. It is Reason acting under
its own lights, moving in response to an inward law,
calling up man's faculties to their proper exercise along
every line. It is eternally Greek, for such was the conception of human training which Athens upheld and
the classics display. But it keeps as its aim progress
in the world that now is, not the Christian life or the
virtues which we term supernatural. Here is the
beginning of our strictly modern age ; here, too, the
danger looms upon us of a contest more formidable
than the brute strength of Barbarians from the North
could have carried to an issue between the saints and
the sages. Here, finally, we note a curious likeness
to the mediaeval story in its two periods of triumph
and decline. For the Popes welcomed the Revival of
Letters with open arms. They blessed the Renaissance altogether ; they have anathematised the Revolution which claims to be its offspring. So had they
consecrated the Holy Roman Empire, as the rod and
staff of their spiritual dominion. But when the
Christian Caesar made his law independent, his

parliaments anti-clerical, his courts supreme, the power which had created disowned him.

The long series of protests uttered by the Holy See, from Gregory VII to Pius X, covers a period of eight centuries and a half.   It turns always on one subject under many names—the Church's freedom.   But that freedom has been embodied in a multitude of forms and privileges corresponding to the general movement of things.   Church and Empire, for instance, were both divinely ordained, as the Middle Ages held.   Each had universal jurisdiction ; but in last resort the temporal ruler must yield to the judgment of the spiritual. Such was the Papal theory, founded on a deep truth, viz. that all human activities must be subject to God's law, which is the immutable standard of right and wrong.   But in applying this great principle we see the free spirit of the Gospel itself crystallising by degrees into enactments and procedures that call forth resistance on all sides, ending in the catastrophe by which the mediaeval system was broken up.   The rule of religion had become a rule of law, enforced by civil penalties.   As we are all aware, the Reformers did not deny that governing axiom of the earlier time.   They accepted and acted upon it.   The change was not in principles but in conditions.   A divided Christendom after the furious combats in which neither party could annihilate its adversary, brought in the long run toleration, as at least an armed truce.   It implied, however, infinitely more.   The battlefield was henceforth to be society, the weapons knowledge, enterprise, scientific research, criticism, metaphysics, literature, and political enfranchisement.   Compared with mediaeval struggles, the modern is on a higher plane, involving forces of which no one in the thirteenth century could imagine the existence. Forces of intellect, subtle, far-reaching, self-protected, at work in a social order complex and diverse in the elements which make it up, obedient to no single impetus, and in every progressive stage cosmopolitan, if not by the influx of peoples yet always by contagion of ideas. Thought is international ; the press cannot be tuned even by syndicates, much less by governments, for any length of time. Civilisation, as a whole, is its own sovereign, autonomous and free.

These are the circumstances under which the Catholic Church must deliver her message while the modern period lasts. We will endeavour, in a concluding article, to answer the question with which we started—how is it possible for Rome to fulfil its divine mission while recognising the ' ancient German freedom ' now making the round of the world as English or American law, and not putting to the ban that democratic equality which is the last and best outcome of Imperial Legislation ? For ourselves we deem such reconcilement an ideal greatly to be desired and in its nature compatible with all Catholic dogma. The Papal deposing power is gone, perhaps never to return ; but the Pontifex Maximus abides and Christ reigns still in the hearts of His people. Liberty, equality, fraternity are inspiring words. If the Renaissance brought intellectual freedom, the Teuton had never lost the conception of individual rights. And what is the Communion of Saints but human brotherhood according to the pattern shown in the Mount ? To unite these divided ideals is, let us say with Goethe, ' Im Ganzen, Guten, Schönen fest zu leben.'

VI

THE ANGELIC DOCTOR [1]

The Dominicans are once more in Oxford. With splendour of procession and a Roman Cardinal laying their foundation-stone, these Black Friars renewed, on August 15, 1921, the Feast of our Lady's Assumption, that solemn entry which they made just seven hundred years ago, Stephen Langton blessing them, within the University precincts. This time they brought in their hands the 'Summa Theologica,' written by St. Thomas Aquinas, now translated into English for modern students. It is true that mediaeval Oxonians had always favoured Duns Scotus, whom J. A. Froude calls, rather undiscerningly, 'the greatest of the Schoolmen,' and mocks as 'the constructor of the *memoria technica* of ignorance, the ancient textbook of *a priori* knowledge, established for centuries the supreme despot in the Oxford lecture rooms.' When Leigh and Leighton, royal commissioners, put down the 'old learning' with rapidity and violence in September 1535, on arriving at New College, they 'found the great quadrant full of the leaves of Duns, the wind blowing them

---

[1] (1) *The Summa Theologia of St. Thomas Aquinas.* Literally translated by Fathers of the English Dominican Province ; 1906–1922. London : Burns, Oates and Washbourne.

(2) The same : Latin text with French translation. By F. Lachat ; 1854–1861. Montréjean and Paris. See also the present writer's article on 'St. Thomas's Theory of Human Knowledge,' in *Dublin Review*, 1875.

into every corner.' Reasons why the Franciscan
genius would appeal to that of Oxford are not difficult
to comprehend ; nevertheless, who now reads Duns
Scotus beyond a small company of experts ? He is
a memory ; while St. Thomas, the Angelic Doctor,
has taken to himself his great power and reigns. He
reigns without a rival among Catholics ; and the vast
world outside, where little more than his name is
familiar, does him homage by the voices of Huxley,
Harnack and Eucken. Of all our books to be chosen
by way of letters introductory to Oxford, which are
the three we might best name ? Surely they are the
' Imitation of Christ,' the ' Divine Comedy,' and the
' Summa.' Each is a work of high and unique achievement, perfect in beauty, and, humanly speaking,
inspired. Our religion, poetry, philosophy, meet in
them, form and spirit, lucidly rendered in pure mental
equivalents, poised, self-centred, complete. And of
the Angelic Doctor it must be said briefly that his
writings convey to every age the mind of the Church.

But why does he come back to learned Oxford
in translation ? The answer implies a far-reaching
story. When St. Thomas lectured or preached, as he
did in Paris, Cologne, Bologna, Rome, and Naples,
the common language understood by all who had any
culture was Latin ; moreover, a certain recognised
philosophy prevailed, with its terms fixed almost as
in mathematics, though disputes about their contents
went fiercely on, and would grow apace. There was,
in Western Christendom, a unity of mind to which
corresponded the one sacred speech, ruling alike over
Liturgy, Canon Law, Scripture, and History. Now,
all that is changed. Latin has lost hold of the civilised
nations, rich in their several languages and literatures ;

while the double movements we sum up as Renaissance
and Reformation have between them broken the
mediaeval mould, brought strife into religion and controversy touching first principles into men's minds.
One immediate consequence is that St. Thomas returns
a perfect stranger to Oxford, his thought forgotten, his
dialect unknown in comparison with many later, such
especially as the Kantian, Hegelian, and Spencerian,
not to speak of Schopenhauer and Bergson.   He seems
to candidates for academic laurels far more antiquated
than Aristotle, who keeps a certain rank in the schools
and ever will, so long as Greek is not sacrificed to the
inner Barbarians.   This condition of things would
probably have ensued, although Tudor England had
not cast away the Roman yoke ; for that wider and
more permanent influence which the ' poets ' glorified
in the neo-classic age of Leo X was decidedly scornful
of Thomas, Scotus, and their commentators ; but the
break with Pope and Curia made it inevitable wherever
Protestants got the upper hand.   Thus intellectual
barriers conterminous with religious differences arose
in the West, and the republic of letters went fatally
asunder.   By the year 1600 this unhappy schism of
reason as well as of faith was completed.   To-day sees
it still in force.   There is a Roman Index of forbidden
books, as all the world knows ; but one equally severe,
while not so explicit, decrees that Catholic writers in
any department shall be passed by without mention
in the leading modern journals, reviews, and biblio-
graphies, or handled only (with rare exceptions) by
strangers to their creed.

A striking illustration occurs in the case of St.
Thomas himself. Like his great fellow-Catholic,
Dante, during century after century he was deliberately

overlooked, or named with contempt by the heralds of
revolt from Christian Rome. In our critical inquiring
time, however, not even the Scholastics might be left
out of a general survey ; and we shall find an article
on Aquinas in the 'Encyclopaedia Britannica' devoted
to his memory. But who were appointed to give an
account of him ? Two writers, one a Principal of the
Scottish Free Kirk, Dr. J. M. Lindsay ; the other,
Mr. J. M. Mitchell, Lecturer in University College,
London—certainly not a member belonging to his
Church. That scores of Catholic students profoundly
versed in St. Thomas were available is beyond per-
adventure ; and Cardinal Mercier's fame as a modern
Thomist could not have been unknown to the British
editor. I am far from disparaging the article in question, which admits that the 'writings of Thomas,'
whom Dr. Lindsay is careful not to style Saint, ' are of
great importance for philosophy as well as theology ' ;
and that ' by nature and education he is the spirit of
scholasticism incarnate.' Why not, then, invite one
among his best qualified disciples to interpret him ?
No, the custom of the country demanded otherwise ;
and so a Scots Presbyterian draws for us a portrait, not
indeed untrue, but without animation or sympathetic
power, of the typical Catholic thinker and Angel of the
Schools. To the 'Encyclopaedia' such philosophy
seems dead and buried ; it informs us—and we hardly
know whether to smile or sigh—that ' the last of the
Scholastics ' was Father Suarez, S.J., who died in 1620.
We have ourselves met a few since that date who were
sufficiently alive to quarrel with Father Suarez.

Clearly, from all this it follows that St. Thomas
needs translation into modern vernaculars and will gain
by it, as Dante gained when his Tuscan was made

English or High German.   Even among Catholic students, especially in our seminaries, the advantages to
be reckoned are exceedingly great.   For we none of
us live now in the Middle Ages ; neither do we talk
Latin in familiar dialogues or write in it our correspondence, as Erasmus did.   Our manuals of science
appear in the language of their respective countries,
and only by translations could they circulate round the
globe.   Newton published his ' Principia ' in Latin ;
what mathematician would now dream of inditing a
Ciceronian treatise to defend or attack the formulae of
Einstein ?   My copy of Mendeléef's ' Chemistry ' is
translated from the Russian.   In short, we have ceased
to think in Latin habitually ; and its correlations with
our minds are difficult as they never were to the universities of the thirteenth century.   With so many
schemes of thought crossing one another in the air,
words take on confused shades of meaning, and these
we can scarcely keep apart from the Latin of our text-
books, while a good translation would lessen the danger
by its idiomatic precision.   My argument, as will be
seen, favours reverent study of St. Thomas in his own
Latin, with lecture or comment on it in the mother-
tongue, thus doing for the ' Summa ' what has been
long since done for the Bible, and on grounds as
weighty.   ' Understandest thou what thou readest ? '
That is ever the question, leading on to a second of
incalculable moment to priests and preachers.   ' Canst
thou explain it when read ? '   Many a consummate
scholar who knows the Angelic from beginning to end
will be dumb or unintelligible on such topics for want
of the English equivalents, which he has never thought
upon.   And here is one most serious reason why St.
Thomas remains a hidden treasure, when his wealth of

wisdom should be scattered abroad. Speaking from my own experience, it cost me nearly two years of continuous reading to master the vocabulary and assimilate the logical procedures which are indispensable, if we would be at home in the School where Catholic philosophy holds its court. We think, I repeat, in English ; and our clerical training requires us to be quite familiar with another tongue, with recondite terms derived from ancient Greek metaphysics, and with Christian adaptations of the same to revealed doctrine. It is a triple knot which we are set to loosen, perhaps the hardest we shall ever take into our grasp.

' There is a book,' says the French translator of the ' Summa,' ' which contains the true system of philosophy, the substance of Christian tradition, the mind of Holy Scripture, and the brilliant expression of divine lore.' On the other hand, let us take into account with what imperfect control of classical Latin our average students are equipped when they have passed out of their ' Humanities,' and how simply unknown to them is the technical diction now first presented for use and comprehension while they are diving into metaphysics, a deep sea, the very existence of which few among our own lads have ever so much as suspected. Leave them to grapple at once with language, thought, and argument, we not only may, but hitherto mostly have done ; as I call the consequences to mind they would admit of improvement. At any rate, since a Latin version of every Greek author used to be printed in earlier editions of the classics (and, *me judice*, with good effect), so might a rendering into well-chosen modern terms give to St. Thomas a quite unrivalled influence on the priesthood of to-day, which would before long shape their teaching and preaching to finer issues. The

Bible and the ' Summa ' furnish by far the best of sermon-books.

Such as these were the motives that prompted M. Lachat, in 1854, to begin the French translation of the ' Summa ' which lies before me in sixteen volumes, not completed until 1860. It is truly a monumental work—the Latin text done into admirable French, with notes and the most reputable commentaries, a full index and quintessence of the whole by way of conclusion. The author points out how marvellously well adapted to this great undertaking is the language of Catholic France. It has been steeped from the earliest days in Christian tradition ; it is analytic by nature, clear, rapid, direct, impatient of roundabout involved phrases ; and we may subjoin that its genuine affinities have always been close to the Latin, never Teutonic or Eastern. These qualities of brevity, precision, order, and common sense make French the fit instrument for teachers in all the sciences, but especially in mediaeval scholasticism, and St. Thomas might have written in the language of Descartes or Pascal had it been developed during the thirteenth century, as it was three hundred years afterwards. M. Lachat contends that his version has cleared up doubts and escaped ambiguities incident to the Latin style, in which I am disposed to agree with him. ' The perfection of strength,' says Newman, writing on Cicero's diction, ' is clearness united to brevity ; but to this combination Latin is utterly unequal. From the vagueness and uncertainty of meaning which characterise its separate words, to be perspicuous it must be full.' Who, we may ask, could be more unlike Cicero than St. Thomas Aquinas ? Rhetoric was entirely forbidden him ; pure intellect was the faculty which he addressed, logic the method of persuasion ; and yet again, as Newman goes on to remark, ' Latin is not a philosophical language, not one in which a deep thinker is likely to express himself with purity or neatness.' The Angelic Doctor did, indeed, triumph over these difficulties ; without being diffuse he contrived to be in a very high degree perspicuous ; and he added to his Latin style not a little of the Attic ' clearness, energy and harmony,' to which by native grace it could not lay claim. Nevertheless, French, were it only by possession of the definite and indefinite articles, and by a precision that the Schools themselves had greatly assisted in development, holds advantages of its own, peculiarly felt in a good translation like that by which M. Lachat has enriched Catholic literature.

On turning to the English, now presented in a handsome and convenient form by the brethren and heirs of St. Thomas, we have to congratulate them on so grand an enterprise happily ended after sixteen years of labour upon it (1906–22). It is surely another of the cheerful signs we may observe that our second spring is hastening unto the harvest. Of late a shining constellation of genius native to the Church, moving round about her as a central sun, has been telling her glory—I mean the centenaries of Columbus, Cervantes, Shakespeare, Dante, Napoleon, Dominic, and Francis. What a magnificent roll of honour this recital unfolds! The range is immense, the height beyond any modern achievement. All these except Shakespeare were Catholics born and bred, while *his* pictured world is not Protestant but mediaeval. What is my conclusion ? I foresee that in the happier time to come our Faith will be adorned by men of science, explorers, poets, actors and chroniclers of romance, mighty organisers, prophets, philosophers, and saints, as in the days of old. For the Church breeds men ; her ideals inspire them ; her discipline forms them ; and she is never weary of making fresh beginnings. ' *Quare fremuerunt gentes, et populi meditati sunt inania ?* ' The taunt of the Psalmist smites that century from which we have just escaped, with its blind rage against our creed, its empty Nihilism in philosophy. Bankrupt it died, having with infinite toil dug its own grave. As for the Church, ' incessu patuit Dea ' ; the glory of going on reveals her strength and majesty. At such a time we are glad of these newborn volumes. They bring the credentials of our religious teaching before philosophers, men of letters, educated readers in every class, who may well be at the pains of learning what Catholics hold and why it is held by them. I have spoken and written much concerning the ' heralds of revolt.' St. Thomas Aquinas comes forth now with splendour and authority as the herald of our Faith.

' My copy of the " Summa " of Aquinas,' I read in Dean Milman's ' Latin Christianity ' (vol. ix. 132), ' has above twelve hundred of the very closest printed folio pages in double columns, without the indexes. I pretend not to have read it ; but whoever is curious to know, as it were, the ultimate decisions of the Latin Church on most theological or ethical points, will consult it ; and will see the range and scope of that theology, and the groundwork of all the later casuistry.'

More fortunate than the versatile Dean of St. Paul's, there have always been numbers of Catholics who knew their St. Thomas well. It is long since Possevin reckoned seven hundred commentators on his works which, by law and custom, never lost pre-eminence in the Catholic universities or the schools of religious Orders, although certain vicissitudes may be noted to which I shall return by and by. Thanks to the digest of the ' Summa ' that lies at the foundation of all theological treatises inside the Catholic borders since the Council of Trent, we must needs be all alike disciples and St. Thomas our Master. This it is which qualifies me to review any translation, not without much direct reading of the original. But I shall not claim to have turned over all the pages contained in the Blackfriars version. Every distinct portion has had my intent study, with hardly an exception ; and I find each faithful to the text, precise in giving an equivalent which appears to me sound English without pedantry, and everywhere readable. Difficulties, of course, remain, such as the necessary but never quite unambiguous employment of the word ' form,' which refuses to signify in our language either ' essence,' or ' energy,' or ' constituent principle.' And I much prefer ' transitive ' to ' transient,' when applied to the effect of a cause outside itself. These are points of debate or adjustment ; but I rise from my voyage of discovery with an admiration all the greater that I used to wonder if the thing could be tolerably done, and here it excels both in correctness of rendering and in use of the vernacular. No doubt we read St. Thomas for knowledge or insight, that is to say, for science, not for style ; and he must be taken seriously and tested as we go along ; in short, he is akin to mathematics, not to literature.

And since, in mathematics, it is not the teacher's name that signifies, but the demonstration, so when we have glanced at the briefest of prologues ever set

in front of an *opus magnum* like the ' Summa,' no more
is heard of St. Thomas himself ; he becomes an impersonal voice except on the very rare occasions when
to register dissent from prevailing opinion seems called
for by the argument.   Not a line, not an epithet, so far
as I remember, tells us anything by which we might
infer that he suffered or was sad, like other pilgrims in
this vale of tears.   He might be the Great Anonymous
of the Schools.   Contrast a silence so unbroken with
Montaigne's delightful garrulity and draw the conclusion.   If the French essayist did not babble concerning his life and opinions, always with a personal
touch, the ' Essays ' would lose not only their charm
but their secret, which is persuasion.   Much turns on
this difference and will turn.   After studying the chief
systems of philosophy, Tennyson, who was nothing if
not a poet as Montaigne was an observer, felt ' a certain
terror of minute scientific analysis in matters of religion.'
His was at no time ' the faith that cannot be content
without parcelling out its information into scientific
sections ' ;   and herein he may well stand for the
average man of his race, who prefers action, with
mystery left in the impenetrable background, to theory
and dogma.   That is an additional reason why St.
Thomas holds no rank among the great men of
times past whom Britons revere although not knowing
much more than their names.   Who was Aquinas ?
The ' Prince of Schoolmen '—and who were they ?
' Pedants,' it was replied, ' writing bad Latin, who six
hundred years ago divided their " dreary intellectual
world " into furious factions, quarrelling over questions
unanswerable or not worth answering.'

St. Thomas, however, was a great man who still
awaits and will reward a modern biographer, although

Digby calls the story of his life, as related by Touron, one of the most delightful of books. He rises conspicuous among an imperishable company of 'heroes,' in Carlyle's altogether human sense, on what has been termed the ridge or watershed of mediaeval history. By this we ought to understand the crisis prepared and fixed in its chief consequences, while the thirteenth century was in mid-course, that broke up Western Christendom, brought the system of Empire and Papacy governing Europe to an end, set France on her ascending path until she became *la grande nation* ; with Avignon and Constance, Wittenberg and Trent, hidden in the gloom afar off, but as their day came to be revealed. So completely has the thirteenth century been thus dissolved into its elements that modern imaginations know it only under aspects which fail to create a single united impression. Hence it has grown to be a field for experts ; but not even Frederick II, once called ' *Stupor Mundi*,' will compare in fame with later crowned men of genius, although probably their equal. Now St. Thomas, by birth and condition, was at the very centre of all the movements which entered into this judgment-scene of the Middle Ages, and a leading actor in them. His pedigree, Norman-Sicilian, connects him with Frederick of Hohenstaufen, but likewise with the royal houses of France, Aragon and Castile. He met Popes and Kings on familiar terms. That his family, after keeping him two years a prisoner in their castle of Rocca Secca, gave him leave to join the Dominicans in 1243, was owing both to the Emperor and the newly elected Pontiff, who were to be most resolute enemies ; so that Frederick and Innocent IV may be considered his sponsors in religion. The Saint's kindred fought under the

Ghibelline flag ; but he was always an ' ultramontane,' as journalism now speaks, devoted to the Holy See. Personal griefs were not wanting to him ; a sister was killed by lightning, a brother starved to death in captivity, the castle of Aquino destroyed. His own death is attributed by Dante and Villani to poison, who lay this sacrilege at the door of Charles of Anjou, let us hope untruly. But when he died, in 1274, Thomas had perhaps not reached his fiftieth year. Of a stately presence and silent meditative habit, he took his own way through life ; yet was ever obedient to the authority which commanded him not only to lecture but to travel on diplomatic errands, to preach where the Pope resided, and to labour towards the extinction of the Greek schism. On the tragic events which filled his time he has left not a syllable. How tragic they could be the piercing lines of Dante, when he meets Manfredi in the realm of purification, tells us. What, I wonder, did the Angelic feel and judge on hearing of the execution at Naples of his kinsman, the bright-faced lad Conradin, whose dying cry still moves all hearts ? And the tragedy of Frederick himself, with whom an empire and a dynasty found their sepulchre ? These were Sicilian dramas in which Thomas had his place, were it only as related to the victims ; but his feelings we shall never learn. And yet he knew the philosophy of love and friendship by more than his readings in Aristotle. The rest is silence.

He writes then impersonally, with an Angel's aloofness from our human agitations, and as one wedded to the ' passionless bride, divine Tranquillity.' None that I know of among Catholic commentators has drawn his character in this respect so vividly as Milman, who remarks : ' He approaches more nearly than most

philosophers, certainly than most divines, to pure embodied intellect.   He is perfectly passionless ; he has
no polemic indignation, nothing of the churchman's
jealousy and suspicion ; he has no fear of the result of
any investigation ; he hates nothing, hardly heresy ;
loves nothing, unless perhaps naked abstract truth.
In his serene confidence that all must end in good, he
moves the most startling and even perilous questions
as if they were the most indifferent, the very Being of
God.   God must be revealed by syllogistic process.
Himself inwardly conscious of the absolute harmony
of his own intellectual being, he places sin not so much
in the will as in the understanding.'   And thus he
' examines with the same perfect self-command, it
might almost be said apathy, the converse as well as
the proof of the most vital religious truths.'   While,
therefore, he ' has assigned its unassailable province
to Church authority, to tradition or the Fathers, to
faith or works ; yet beyond, within the proper sphere
of philosophy, he asserts full freedom.'

All this we hear with satisfaction, recognising how
precisely it corresponds to the original, and what an
answer it affords to those who charge Rome with
fostering ignorance.   But something must be added.
St. Thomas indeed ' gives every advantage to his
adversary,' and states the case for him better than
most disputants could state it for themselves.   He is
a judge who not only sums up but passes sentence.
And in so doing he acts the part of the great Reconciler
between Reason and Revelation.   In such a blending
of the divine with the human sources of certitude
Scholasticism finds its task, wins its guerdon, which is
peace—peace intellectual and permanent.   To quote
St. Augustine's magisterial sentence, ' *Beatitudo est*

gaudium de veritate,' happiness means rejoicing in the truth. The Angelic Doctor can throw himself into the attitude of sceptic, atheist, or heretic, when opening the debate by which he constantly proceeds. When, however, he takes up the reply, St. Thomas brings to bear on it all the resources of his inexhaustible learning, which not even Dante could surpass. Legend affirms that the memory of the wonderful Sicilian retained all he had ever read. His quotations appear to be waiting always at command ; they cover the writings of classic and Christian authorities so far as the West was in possession of them ; and a work such as the ' Catena Aurea ' cannot but fill us with amazement, when we take into account its mastery of the Gospel text and the Fathers' comments upon that portion of Scripture.

Critics have remarked that Albert the Great was even more encyclopaedic in his pursuit of knowledge ; Scotus and Roger Bacon were apparently daring beyond their Dominican predecessor. But we must not overlook the great sovereign idea which St. Thomas obeyed, and which determined the contents no less than the design of his colossal undertaking. He was, if we may so describe that function, reporter of the Catholic Church to every succeeding generation ; not a speculator but an editor-in-chief of her doctrine, the actual concrete inheritance of which Providence had given her the charge, ' *Depositum custodi.*' And what was that deposit ? She was heir, by default if you will, of Greek wisdom, not less than of the Hebrew and Christian treasures admittedly her own. There had come down to the Middle Ages not simply the rumour of lost knowledge, but, as Novalis calls it much to the point, a ' mysterious tradition of philosophy,' bound up with mighty names, the divine Plato and the most

judicial of Hellenic minds, Aristotle.　These unrivalled
teachers were scions of the ' House of Socrates ' ;　and
his method of cross-examination could never fall into
disuse without injury to sound reasoning.　If Plato
was a supremely gifted theologian, Aristotle had come
to be honoured in the lifetime of St. Thomas, by
Catholics no less than by Greeks, Jews, and Arabians,
as *par excellence* ' the Philosopher.'　Now, was the rich
estate of human intellect thus acquired to be cast away
in deference to sheer doubt or self-devouring scepti-
cism ?　If not—and everything of value, private or
universal, was at stake—it followed that the system of
teaching must keep in view demonstration rather than
acquisition.　Not such dreams as a David Hume might
indulge, shut up in his library, but wisdom for life here
and hereafter, should be the copious matter of university
training.　Or shall we insist—we ought surely—that
the first and last of sciences never can be brought down
to a bare method without contents ?　The Lucretian
' void ' in which atoms fleet aimlessly for ever but ideas
have no real existence, leaves mankind helpless and
hopeless.　But our Scholastics moved ' in the serene
light of eternal truth,' and their reflective thought con-
templated reality, instead of making it an insoluble
problem, at best a ' riddle of the universe.'　No
method, however, can work without premises which
are more than logical forms.　If the central tradition,
which carries forward the experience of the race to
their descendants, be flung into the abyss, dreams
will usurp its empty seat ;　and, as we now feel with
growing apprehension, society will run the risk of destruction at the hands of intellectual Nihilists.　Our
wise mediaeval masters combined a fearless method of
reasoning with a regard for the past which no doubt

fell into credulity or even superstition where moderns would not be led astray.   But we owe to them a tradition by which we can live as moral agents and baptised Christians.   Where is the constructive philosophy of to-day that denies their fundamental principles ?   To the Scholastics, therefore, Reason was in presence not merely of its own notions but of a real universe antecedent to analysis, given by experience, and always at hand as the touchstone of assertions, true and false. Emphatically, I repeat, something was given before and after the mind's reflections termed by us philosophy ; experience, past and present, was a reality which we never might put by.   Thus did Reason and Reality meet in a living embrace.

Socrates sought true definitions ; Plato dwelt in a heaven of exemplary ideas ; Aristotle perfected the process of syllogism and built up a system where each individual was found under its proper genus and species.   This Organon of thought St. Thomas applied all through the ' Summa ' with an effect at once conclusive in detail and of striking symmetry in the general view.   Now the question arises whether, as Hume said and Arthur Clough sang, ' all is juxtaposition ' ; or do real causes produce distinct effects ? Aristotle maintained that the supreme cause which set all others in motion was the end, or intelligent purpose of them, each and all, a doctrine calculated to throw the modern man of science into a paroxysm compounded of rage and fear.   He rages lest it be verified ; and he fears lest it should show him the face of God.   ' Juxtaposition,' with a formula, is the idol he adores.   But in upholding the philosophy of ' motives ' acting on otherwise inert Nature, the Greek and the Christian give to all things a meaning and thereby a value. There is, indeed, a 'stream of tendency'; not an aimless round of dead electrons chasing one another, but an upward going—whither, except to the First, who is also the Final Cause?

In such a system philosophy delineates a Pilgrim's Progress, or man's journey from the seen to the unseen. The stages, means, vicissitudes, fall into a drama, with its crowning success or self-determined failure. All the Middle Ages were intent on this Quest, which sought through wild woods and by perilous waters for the way to Paradise. In gleaming prose it becomes the 'High History of the Holy Graal'; in poetry, the 'Romaunt of the Rose,' and far above all other achievements the mystic song of Dante. Twin stars in the Catholic skies at their loftiest height, St. Thomas and Alighieri shine for ever, alike and yet unlike, the tranquil Sicilian over against the fiery Florentine, Guelf and Ghibelline holding one creed, both disciples of Aristotle, curiously docile to the master of those that know, yet each independent and unique. Thomas begins where Dante ends, with God as term of the creature and the divine Exemplar, thence coming down to the Human Image and Likeness, finally showing the means of attainment through Christ, who is both God and Man. Dante, on the contrary, loses himself in the dark forest, goes down through all the gulfs of misery, ascends by painful stages, and by flights from sphere to sphere until he reaches the blessed Vision of Peace. And for the guide of his ascent to the Empyrean Thomas appears in glory, though not yet canonised on earth. Such a regal assumption of authority as by right divine is, in the Angelic, not surprising. Pope Leo XIII quotes Cajetan, who wrote of him : ' So great was his veneration for the ancient and sacred Doctors that he may be

said to have gained a perfect understanding of them all.'
He, indeed, made the humble confession to a brother
Dominican that by God's gift he comprehended whatever his reading brought him for study ; earnest prayer
was the spiritual Organon of all his discernment.   We
may take our view from a slightly different angle, by
contrasting the deference of most mediaeval writers (and
I include Arabian as well as Latin) for the wisdom
of the ancients with a proud or calm self-sufficiency,
visible in Luther, Descartes, or Kant, which bows to
none other than its own thought, and assimilates only
what it seems to create.   St. Thomas delights in
agreeing as a disciple with his Augustine in truths
revealed ; but quite as willingly with Aristotle in
reasonings he could have made out alone.   So Dante
worships low before Virgil, his master and guide, from
whom he has learnt the lovely style that does himself
honour—Dante, chosen to a grander sublime than
sweet Virgil ever attained.   There is a simplicity in
such avowals of genius, very winning.   And so the
Tuscan goes to school in the ' Summa ' ; borrows from
it the scheme of virtues and vices on which to frame a
world where justice retributive or vindictive reigns ;
throws into the most enchanting verse its ordered scale
of being ; and, as Pico della Mirandola well observed,
rises on the wings of Thomas and Augustine to
heavenly heights.   ' After Thomas,' it has been said
by one who found in the ' mystic unfathomable song '
of Dante deep joy, ' what is left but the light of glory ? '
That radiance which glows brighter and brighter, as
we move on from the ' gentle hue of eastern sapphire '
through many-zoned splendours, even to the Eternal
Rose about God's throne—whence falls it on the
Tuscan's meditative, sorrow-darkened brow, except

from the tranquil mind of St. Thomas ? Concerning these two Catholic luminaries we may thankfully write :

> Voice answering voice, so musical and clear,
> That can be known but where day endless shines.

St. Thomas, therefore, has brought to fulfilment the design promised but left a forlorn ruin by Lucretius, to erect above all confusion and distress of mortals the ' *templa serena* ' where wisdom might dwell sure, the human spirit find rest. The ' Summa,' like a garden enclosed, is complete within itself, and deserves to have inscribed on its title-page the name long since given it, ' *perennis quaedam philosophia* ' ; or the doctrine of the centre, real in affirmation, ideal in scope, spiritual in essence, derived historically from the House of Socrates, but purged and crowned by the Christian revelation. In structure it bears a suggestive resemblance to other great works of the later Middle Ages, not only to the ' Divine Comedy ' but to the intricate and refined Church architecture prevalent when Aquinas taught. Not, indeed, that the word ' decorated ' ever could be applied to a style which in its Greek sobriety is austere, appealing strictly to the judgment without bias ; yet a true analogy runs between the infinite rich detail of Gothic shrines controlled by a master-builder, and the countless arguments serving one immense plan where nothing is overlooked in the philosopher's idea. His object was the very same which inspired Dantean stanzas, lifted high sanctuaries towards Heaven, led holy men to write meditations, as in the volume attri-buted to the Franciscan Saint Bonaventure, ' Itinera-rium Mentis in Deum,' how to reach the goal of Humanity, or the union of man with his Creator by thought, love, obedience, self-sacrifice. Pure intellect, yet not unaided by sense and imagination, thus views time and eternity from the heart of the universe where, according to Aristotle and St. Thomas, God the Prime Mover dwells, desired of all that He has made. Here is the splendour of light without a cloud. The language is therefore cleansed of earthly dross, lucid, concise, adequate, simple, that is to say, free from double meanings in the measure allowed by Latin which, we have already granted, was not designed for abstract reasoning. The Latin of St. Thomas will repay special comparative study, with reference not merely to classic authors whom he was not copying, but to St. Augustine, St. Gregory, and Boethius ; it is a subject on which one had better keep silence than offer a few desultory observations ; and so I hasten to the concluding stage of my present venture.

Great, undoubtedly, St. Thomas is ; but unknown as well as known, and to latter-day thought and thinkers, *magni nominis umbra*. Leibnitz, whose apologetic treatise, called ' Theodicy,' was drawn up under his influence, remarked on this fact more than two centuries ago ; and a fact it remains. Towards recent systems of philosophy the Angelic Doctor seems to hold a position resembling that which the Catholic Church holds towards heresies dating after the first period of the Reformation. Both are worlds apart, and a great gulf separates them. St. Thomas, intellectually a Greek, rejects once and for all time every system which subordinates Reason to Unreason. With all his might he opposed the ' Impersonal Mind ' which Averroes would have substituted for the living, personal Trinity of our creed. Nevertheless, how large an undertaking would it not be to disengage from the

M

'Summa' those arguments by which he has refuted in anticipation the sceptical assault of Kantism on our intellect, and the dangerous deceits of Hegelian sophistry? 'His conclusions,' we are instructed by Leo XIII, 'have the very widest reach, and contain in their bosom the seeds of truths well-nigh infinite in number. These have to be unfolded with most abundant fruit in their own time by the teachers who come after him.' Something, then, still requires to be done, building on the sure foundations laid. Moreover, the argument is to move by process of thought, not simply by fiat of authority. And again, we must discover a meeting-place where we can argue, for if we and our adversaries have nothing in common, how shall we join issue? Reflections in this key, long and carefully taken into account, have led to various movements, which are celebrated as forms of neo-Scholasticism. They fully recognise the Angelic and do him honour.

That St. Thomas always had praise without end from the Holy See requires no demonstration. In life he was constantly employed by the Pope of the day; with John XXII, who called each of his articles a miracle, begins the series of documents bearing the Roman seal which in their language declare his teaching not only safe but to be followed, almost as if it were infallible. The supreme distinction shown to him at the Council of Trent, where the 'Summa' was laid on the altar side by side with the Holy Scriptures, canonised the book itself, and remains without imitation as it had no precedent. His theology could not become obsolete, for it was the marrow of all school books in Catholic universities and seminaries down to the French Revolution. But undoubtedly, as physical science advanced, as the literary taste of the Renaissance would not endure mediaeval Latin, as Descartes invented an extreme form of private judgment in his ' *Cogito, ergo sum*,' or atomic intellectual method, and as Locke reduced thought to reflection upon sensible experience, the continent, so to call it, of Scholasticism underwent submersion like Atlantis, and men sailed over it unawares. German philosophism, deriving from Descartes and Spinoza, wanted neither its matter nor its form from Aquinas. Our own schools during the eighteenth century were languid, if not decaying ; and the French armies, overrunning Europe, did not encourage the idea of their resurrection. A hundred years ago, the ' Summa ' was little studied, even in the Eternal City. A rather shallow kind of eclecticism, more or less inclining towards Locke, but still protected by religion from the legitimate consequences of his principles, held sway. Neither did a revival of the School-philosophy seem at all likely for many years to come. In 1846, Newman, at Propaganda, ' found, to his surprise, that both St. Thomas and Aristotle were now out of favour in Rome.' We can see from Wiseman's observations, in passing, on the ' crabbed ' philosophy of the mediaeval schools, how neglected they were by his friends, the learned on both sides of the Alps. My own master, Dr. Charles Meynell, who was by temperament a thinker and a man of unquestioned mental ability, bears much the same witness to a later date (about 1857), for he did not study the ' Summa ' till putting it into my hands at Oscott, yet he had taken a Roman degree. However, by that time a reaction had begun to set in. The writings and disputes of Italian leaders—especially to be named are Gioberti and Rosmini—could not leave St. Thomas without mention. Among writers known to me was Liberatore, who quoted the ' Summa ' to refute these new systems of Ontologism and the Ideal Light. At a distance from Rome, on the tower-crowned hill of Perugia, Cardinal Pecci was absorbing the wisdom of the Angelic during an exile that lasted thirty-two years. In 1878 his opportunity came ; and on the Feast of St. Dominic, August 4, 1879, Leo XIII announced by his magnificent Encyclical, *Aeterni Patris*, that the Angelic Doctor had been recalled from a still more protracted exile to his rightful place among the scholastic divines, as ' their master and prince.' ' The glorious teaching of St. Thomas Aquinas should be restored and win its former renown,' said Pope Leo. He kept his word.

But, as Lord Morley reflects in a passage worth noting for its unexpected conclusion, ' the mediaeval spirit wears something of a ghostly air in the light of our new day. This attempt, which has been made many a time before, " to unify two ages," did not carry men far in the second half of the nineteenth century. Nevertheless, it were an idle dream to think that the dead hand of Dante's century, and all that it represented, is no longer to be taken into account by those who would be rulers of men.' Saul here finds himself among the prophets. Lord Morley had in view the failure of Romanticism, Guelfism, and even the Tractarian Movement, when compared with such counter-influences as did achieve triumph and empire down to the Leonine era. Since then, what a discomfiture of unbelief by hard facts has not the world witnessed ! ' Back to positive spiritual convictions, and to a constructive scheme of life ! ' is the cry. Yet the past never returns. And when Pope Leo described the writings of St. Thomas under the figure of a seed-bed,

he put upon Catholic philosophy the duty of development, vital and not simply formal, which must enlarge
the synthesis already established between Faith and
Reason.   There was much dead wood in mediaeval
physics ; new powers of criticism, sources of knowledge, acquaintance with vast world-religions, demanded attention.   It was for special research to
indicate where and to what extent St. Thomas had
borrowed from non-Catholic authors—such as Mai-
monides and Ibn-Gebirol.   But far more important
was direct dealing on methods universally accepted
with systems, agnostic, monistic, or materialist, which
had sprung up since Occam's revolt from the central
philosophy left Christendom a prey to the forces of
negation.   The things that remain unshaken are such
as Plato's doctrine that Eternal Mind has called into
being an intelligible universe ; Aristotle's appeal to
first principles which are self-evidently true ; the
sanctities and sanction of the Moral Law ; the immortal destiny of man.   As regards Christian apologetics, knowledge has been widened, fresh problems
appear and will multiply, for in this region East and
West are drawing closer with every decade.   We can
no more expect to discover in St. Thomas a critique of
the Upanishads or the Buddhist Scriptures than a
prophetic refutation of Fichte or Schopenhauer.   The
Angelic wrote for his own age.   But in the ' Summa '
we have a standard of truth, and consequently a touchstone of falsehood, to which every system must conform.

Truth is the watchword of St. Dominic, ' Veritas,'
a challenge no less defiant than austere.   It is a challenge because an affirmation ; and by the method
of St. Thomas a reconcilement after combat.   The
word that returns in his pages, made current in our

scholastic tournaments, is *Distinguo*, which implies
criticism but holds out a prospect of qualified acceptance, seeing that every possible error distorts some
real truth. Question and perpetual analysis look
onward to the unity of all partial views in a light where
Reason transfigures experience, and Revelation is no
longer Faith, but sight. A most consoling foregleam
of that dawn meets our gaze in the beauty and pathos
which St. Thomas sheds over his treatises on the incarnate Christ and the Blessed Sacrament, not to speak
of the Corpus Christi office and hymns. Truth and
unity embrace when the Word becomes Man, just as
the Communion of Saints is made perfect in the
Eucharist of which all partake. No false philosophy
creates anything by its falsehood. Hence the modern
chaos, out of whose devouring jaws civilisation is
trying, however feebly, to escape. The truth alone
will make us free. And St. Dominic holds it forth to
Oxford in the ' Summa '—to the Oxford of late years so
devoutly read in Dantean lore, best of all novitiates for
a lifelong dedication to Catholic truth. Our supreme
poet might have written the verses with which I end in
the volume of St. Thomas, where he learnt so much of
his wisdom ; they fit the great translation I have been
praising ; and should be quoted for their music in the
original Tuscan :

> I see full well the mind can ne'er exist
> Content, unless illumed by that True Light,
> From whom dissevered may no truth consist ;
> Therein it rests, like wild thing in its lair,
> Delighted, when 'tis reached, for otherwise
> All human efforts unavailing were.[1]

[1] *Paradise*, iv. 124–129.

VII

THE GOLD OF DANTE [1]

FLORENCE and Rome, Verona with Ravenna—these are
the cardinal points in Dante's life and pilgrimage, the
places of his birth, vision, exile, death. Florence, a
cruel stepmother to her most wonderful son, thanks to
whose inspiration the crown of Christian poetry en-
circles her brows ; Rome, the City of God, centre of
Empire and Papacy, the gate of Heaven where all
nations, kindreds and people came together for worship
at St. Peter's shrine ; Verona, the home of a race from
which he received shelter, one of whose sons he trusted
might set Italy free ; and Ravenna where he lies
dead, an exile to this day, six hundred full years since
the tomb closed over him, on September 14, 1321.
Dante was born in May 1265, on a day which is
uncertain, perhaps the thirtieth—in any case, three
centuries all but a year before Shakespeare, whose birth
was on April 23, 1564. We associate the citizen and
Prior of Florence for ever with its beautiful, yet gloomy
and tragic, Duomo, with its Baptistery, ' mio bel San
Giovanni,' and Giotto's marble tower, the flowerlike

---

[1] From the immeasurable literature I select Edward Moore's original
text of all Dante's works, with his three volumes of *Studies* ; Hettinger, on
the *Scope and Value of the Divina Commedia*, translated by Bowden ;
Gardner, *Dante and the Mystics*, etc. ; and as a rare curiosity, Lyell, *The
Canzoniere*, Italian and English (Bohn, 1840). Versions are mentioned in
the text.

campanile known to all the world. On the bridge of
Sant' Angelo we imagine him at Easter, 1300, among
pilgrims moving towards the Vatican to earn the indulgence of Jubilee granted by Pope Boniface VIII, his
deadly foe at that very time, soon to shut him out from
his native city, afterwards to be assigned by the indig-
nant poet a dreadful doom among the lost, nevertheless
not without pity for the day of September 1303, when
Nogaret and Sciarra should pull him out of the Papal
Chair, smiting him on the face, and renewing in His
Vicar the passion of Christ. Again, we are at Verona,
in the Piazza dei Signori with monuments of the
Scaligers all around, the shadowed presence of Dante
haunting us even in sunshine, his bitter cry still audible,
' How steep the stair of exile to a homeless man, how
salt the bread of aliens !' And then Ravenna, the
forsaken, amid its marshes, the enchanted wood
covering what was once the harbour of the Roman fleet,
Sant' Apollinare in Classe bidding him seek rest and
oblivion as he returns from his foiled embassy at
Venice, along the Adriatic, which is not his own sea,
through a pestilence-laden air, so unlike that of the
Tuscan hills, of Fiesole and San Miniato. There he
dies and there he is buried. Penitent Florence would
fain bring him home now with honour ; but she must
leave his dust untroubled ; he will not return.

It is a world far away from England that we gaze
upon, the landscape wholly different, whether we view
it as a scene, a background to history, or a place of
conflict between ideas. Which of the Italians belonging to it survive in men's thoughts to-day ?

Among divines and philosophers St. Thomas
Aquinas, after ages of neglect, is winning recognition
n ce more ; Giotto has entered into his glory with the

Primitives and their genuine successors ; but the name
of names is Alighieri.   We may safely predict that he
will not pass under eclipse again so long as our civilisation endures.   Homer, Dante, Shakespeare, each
himself and without a fellow, live apart, beyond change
or decay, as the epic, the mystic, the romantic singers
of Humanity, ' in a kind of royal solitude, none equal,
none second to them.'   A few years ago, Shakespeare
had his centenary in the midst of war.   Now we transport ourselves from Stratford and Blackfriars to Italy
as it was when the Middle Ages, having reached their
height, were falling into chaos, and upon Dante the
burden was laid of chanting their Apocalypse.   To
such a task he dedicated his life—youth in the ' Vita
Nuova,' which corresponds after a way of its own to
St. Augustine's ' Confessions ' ;   and manhood until
verging on old age in the ' Divine Comedy,' where the
strange title conceals a resemblance of design and at
last of treatment to the ' City of God.'   Let us keep to
the thought and figure of a mediaeval Apocalypse, with
Dante fulfilling St. John's prophetic office, the unseen
kingdoms made visible, the judgment set, the saints
executing it, and the heavenly Jerusalem revealed.   In
that sky Dante is supreme, *Sopra gli altri come aquila
vola.*   He abides, I say it for remembrance, as the
St. John of Christian epic and tragic poetry ; he is the
Catholic seer, miraculously fitted by temperament,
training, trial of good and evil, by the time when he
appeared, and by his very wanderings of twenty years
about the land that denied him any haven of rest, ' to
embody musically the religion of the Middle Ages, the
religion of our modern Europe, its inner life.'

I borrow these memorable words from Carlyle,
who was a Puritan contrary in grain to the Papal

Church, and who, by professing to have found salvation in Goethe, might seem the last of men to allow
that the inner life of Europe and the Catholic Creed
were in any sense identical. Yet he does grant so
much ; ' Dante has given us the Faith, or soul,' he
says ; ' Shakespeare, in a not less noble way, has given
us the Practice, or body.' It is not, however, in
reliance on Carlyle or any other that I register this
momentous conviction, but after the study of a lifetime. Fifty-six years have fallen into the gulf of the
past since I began to read Italian for the sake chiefly of
its divine poet ; and no year has gone by without fresh
travels through his realms of sorrow, light, and joy.
Every season that brings us along the great Catholic
liturgy to Easter Eve I find myself with him in the
Earthly Paradise ; and still I am sensible of the deep
impression it wrought, as I went over those tender and
exquisite lines after listening to the Mass of Pope
Marcellus in the Sistine, and retired apart in a vale
a little beyond St. Peter's, while the bells of Rome were
ringing Easter in. Memories of Dante, studied where
he went sadly to and fro, lend a poignant charm to the
' mystic unfathomable song,' with which I have been
occupied during as many years as he lived altogether.
For though he reckons with the Psalmist that his thirty-
fifth brought him to ' the midway of this our mortal
life,' the end came long before he was seventy. His
unjust exile and bitter meditation upon it, upon the
woes of Italy, the failure of his own hopes in Henry of
Luxemburg, the corruption which was dimming the
fine gold of the sanctuary, the translation of the Holy
See from Rome to Avignon—all this had proved to
be more than his high and loving spirit could bear.

As Frederick II the Hohenstaufen was last of the

mediaeval Roman Emperors, and as Boniface VIII
closed the dynasty of Pontiffs who consecrated and
gave away crowns, so Dante sums up the elements of
strife which had driven Guelf and Ghibelline, each
appealing to the same authorities, into a storm of
antagonism where the Kingdom of God on earth,
which they both undertook to perpetuate, was smitten
with disaster.   Frederick and his house perished ; we
stand before his magnificent tomb in Palermo Cathedral, at once melancholy and admiring, awed by so
tremendous a fall from such a height of dominion.
Boniface VIII lost Rome to the Popes for seventy years,
and opened thus the way for that Great Schism of the
West which made some sort of reformation, or attempt
to build up National Churches instead of the one
Catholic Church, inevitable.   To our Florentine, as to
the inspired seer of Israel, the vision came of things
accomplished and of things yet to be, retrospect and
prospect, line upon line ; and to him was the message
delivered, ' Go, set a watchman, let him declare what
he seeth.'   None other could be found ; Dante is the
watchman steadfastly regarding, swiftly and pregnantly
declaring, the whole pageant of that time—call it a
hundred years complete—as it passes over the stage
and makes an exit, to come back no more for ever.

When the splendid structure of the Middle Ages
fell, and the proud Renaissance, the latest birth of time,
discovered or created new worlds, in and out of Europe,
Catholic Christendom seemed to shrink into an episode,
even a ' barbarous intermezzo,' cumbering the centuries by which a classic antiquity was divided from
modern scientific and progressive days.   According to
the Reformers, who were men of the ' new learning,'
the world had been sunk in idolatry for eight hundred

years. But the men of the Renaissance condemned its culture during the same period no less vehemently. And under·this sweeping anathema Dante was hurled with all his contemporaries into the abyss. A literary exile now overtook him, the scorn of modern minds being forcibly illustrated by a succession of mockers that extends from Voltaîre to Savage Landor, and by a neglect as unbroken as that in which the Ossian of Macpherson now sleeps. With Aristotle and Aquinas he was sent far into the outer darkness, to dwell among the horrors of his own Inferno. We can scarcely give credit to the story ; but the classical spirit, becoming exclusive in its triumph, grew deaf to the Dantean harmonies even as it was blind to the beauty and grace of an architecture which it called insultingly Gothic. To us now Voltaire has become himself an episode, Landor is only a pastiche, and the interpretation of Greek and Roman classics on Renaissance methods appears as pedantic as it was unreal. The Romantic movement which once crowded the *Via Sacra* of literature, bore along with it the *spolia opima* wrested from a pseudo-classic enlightenment, always justly open to the sarcasms of Erasmus and Montaigne.

Undoubtedly, the disdain, and even hatred, of Dante which prevailed among learned men, poets no less than critics, for more than two hundred years, were prompted by motives not hard to decipher. Dante was, first and last, the prophet of the Supernatural. He came as though sent by God out of the Holy of Holies to tell living men that which he had seen. All his teaching—and it is impossible that a poet of supreme power should not teach—was Catholic and sacramental. Indeed, as I shall be pointing out later, this word ' sacramental,' and not merely the word

' symbolic,' renders precisely the form and pressure of all Dantean writing, as by inward necessity it must have been. His dream or vision was not mere reminiscence of things done or seen during waking hours ; it was communion with eternal truth, fashioned into fit imaginations which body it forth in speech and song. The whole is rather premonition of the world to come, than memory of what unbelievers deem a creed outworn ; and, in every case, the core is one thing, the outward show another. That vital change, however, in the orientation of Europe (forgive this technical, yet apposite word) consisted in moving away from the supernatural, now held to be either a delusion or beyond our knowledge, and in a deliberate return to nature, cultivated by science, worshipped under all its forms by all the arts, and taken as the ultimate, the veil of Isis which no mortal could lift. Instead of Supernature, then, the ' eternal things,' as Pierre Loti calls them with a rare apprehension of the creed at this day paramount, are just those appearances of earth and sky and sea in the presence of which man is consumed. And the practice resulting is Paganism ; the religion of instinct, energy and passion ; of the Great Mother, of Demeter, Cybele, Aphrodite. Given this mood which, after the ecstasy of the early Renaissance, by degrees made itself felt in the poets and thinkers, the men and women of genius, who taught Christians to cast aside their inherited beliefs as Philistine, can we be surprised if the more essentially Catholic or supernatural a work of art was so much the less did it win either attention or praise from Neo-Pagans ?

Such considerations will teach us why the ' great Pagan,' Goethe, called ' The " Inferno " abominable, the " Purgatorio " dubious, the " Paradiso " fatiguing.'

His own ' Faust,' in conception a mystery-play, might have pleaded a little on Dante's behalf ; but when we contrast Gretchen with Beatrice—to compare them would be sacrilege—it will become clear that the sage of Weimar, ending with his lifelong Feminism—his apotheosis of Woman as mere attraction—falls into a region *dove il sol tace*, where the Sun of Revelation is eclipsed. Under such an eclipse, not partial but total, the greatest single poem that ever came from the hands of man lay hidden and despised till the last century was well on its way. Then a reaction set in to which, so far as my reading and observation extend, nothing similar, and assuredly nothing equal, has taken place in the vicissitudes of literary fame. For two miserable centuries the descent of Italy from its pride of place to servitude under Spaniards and Austrians had brought in its train what I venture to call the dissolution of Dante. With the Florence of Michael Angelo he seemed to die ; and when the Risorgimento dawned, he, too, rose from the grave. He rose, let me not be deemed over-daring if I say it, by some divine power always persisting within his works, defeated, but unconquerable. First, however, he seemed utterly to perish.

After the sack of Rome in 1527 by a Lutheran army, and the last siege of Florence by the Medici mercenaries in 1530, Italy became ' humble ' indeed, a low-lying, subdued ' geographical expression,' a museum of antiquities and *virtù* which usurped the name of valour, and the Mother of Western civilisation suffered indignity as at once a mistress and a slave. Her noble arts, dedicated to religion, freedom, liberal commerce, were now grown secular and profane, the amusement of dilettantism enjoying the grand tour.

The Tuscan idiom went out of fashion before the
French of Louis XIV ; it fell silent while German
literature set forth on its expedition of conquest, to be
checked only yesterday by a world-war.   Dante might
have written in a dead language, so far as polite readers
even within the bounds of Italy, and naturally still more
beyond the Alps, were troubling to comprehend his
terza rima, though couched in a virile and majestic style.
He had chosen for his models of composition the
learned—nay, frequently too learned—Roman poets ;
Virgil, his master and guide on the unearthly pilgrimage, who had taught him in the Sixth Book of the
' Aeneid ' what the supernatural world was like ; but
also Lucan, the singular patriot who preferred Cato's
judgment to the verdict of the Gods ; and the Lucretian love of didactic science could not be foreign to a
mind which had taken all knowledge for its province.
But mediaeval science was rendered obsolete by Coper-
nicus and Galileo ; the philosophy of Aquinas went
down before Descartes, Locke, and Sensism ; if any
one dogma more than another was flouted by all the
Reformers, it was that of Purgatory, or a Middle State
after death ; and who could waste the golden hours
in ascertaining how those obscure Italian adventurers
celebrated by him won or lost the Hundred Cities of
the Peninsula ?   The Book of Tyrants was crowded,
disgusting and obscure.   What did it signify to the
world's historic sense whether once upon a time
Aldobrandeschi lay in wait for Siena, whether Baglioni
disgraced Perugia, Malatesta lorded it over Rimini, or
Bevilacqua held Bologna ?   Many among our English
or French Catholics, otherwise well-disposed towards
the ' Divine Comedy ' by reason of its transcendent
and unique religious value, have turned away from the

intricate scandals of mediaeval Italian condottieri in which it abounds. This, I believe, was the feeling expressed by Cardinal Newman, whose taste and reading drew him to the Church of the Fathers in preference to the later Middle Ages. Of Dante, we must allow that he is nothing if not local, personal, and yet enigmatic, as he leads us along a gallery of portraits, doubtless vivid in every feature to himself, and to his friends or foes from Sicily to the Alps of Friuli, but long since forgotten. We look at them, being compellingly invited, but we know them not, and soon look away. Generations will weep with Dante as he tells the tale of Francesca, so passionately sad, so inexorably severe ; but is there anyone except an archaeologist who minds whether she was Francesca of Rimini ? No one, I think. We do incline to believe that the poet, who took refuge with her people, may have set eyes on this pitiable victim of fortune and misguided love ; but the scene lies in our hearts ; it needs not a local habitation or a name.

Thus, then, physics and metaphysics, astronomy and geography, science, history, religion, and his very language, combined to dissolve the influence of this exalted singer, until both Reformation and Renaissance had their day out. Each, be it observed, was a movement of ideas or doctrines, general and cosmopolitan by nature, appealing to abstract principles. The resurrection of the nations was yet to come. It followed hard on the French Revolution, partly by imitation, partly by reaction, but very swiftly spread over Europe. The changes to which we owe the Third Italy began in France, when Avignon was annexed to the Crown ; not long afterwards a great captain, by pedigree Florentine, in character a soldier of fortune, led his French troops into Lombardy, shattered the political system that had prevailed since the time of Clement VII, and as Napoleon, King of Italy, inaugurated the Risorgimento.   I possess a very fine edition (four volumes in folio) of the 'Divina Commedia,' published at Rome in 1815, and reproducing the critical text of 1791 ; between these two dates the new Italy had come to the birth.   And although Napoleon, the centenary of whose death, May 5, 1821, falls near to the natal day of his Tuscan kinsman, died like him in exile, the enterprise to which poet and emperor set their hands may well demand the honours of a Roman triumph.   Italy is now safe ; Dante is immortal.

Reaction or revival, whichever you please, marks the last century, little as it may have been adequately measured by observers intent on a more ambitious programme, bearing the name of Liberalism.   Not only did the nations resist an all-devouring French Republic and Empire ; the Roman Church ascended out of her catacombs where she had long been immured ; the Tractarians gave to the almost expiring Anglican institutions a new lease of life ; the Romanticists, a motley host, found leaders everywhere in the West, and made of the despised Middle Ages a motive in art, letters, politics, which fascinated even their opponents.   This curiously simultaneous attack put to flight a host quite as motley on the other side, of Lutherans and Calvinists, French defenders of the stage unities, commentators on the classics who ground the heroes of antiquity into powder and who had never dreamt of Greek or Roman in the flesh—I need not pursue the catalogue.   We talk, and rightly talk, of the ' Revolution,' implying an advance along the whole

N

line of Humanity, in however many detachments. The point of view had, after this fashion, been altered, the horizon grew larger, fresh heights and depths came in sight.   If the classic genius relied on reason as a law which is justified in itself ; and if the romantic glories in its gift of invention, its passion, strangeness, and mystery ; we may laud and magnify the time out of which our own generation has sprung, in that by a consummate spirit of criticism it was capable of thinking really back to the past, and by a philosophic impartiality of desiring to overlook none of its phases. To such criticism, as to impersonal science, all the phenomena that ever had genuine existence were welcome.   But the claim of Dante to recognition was instant and great, beyond all else in literature.

For his were ' the first words Italy had said,' and still he cried aloud against the Barbarians that held her down ; he was the voice of the Catholic Church, seen to be the main outstanding bulwark on whose deep and strong foundations anarchy made assault in vain ; while Rome appeared no longer as a Babylon hated by true Christians or a pleasure-city for tourists, but as the historic centre of religion never to be removed.   The voice, too, of a culture that, echoing Virgil, preluded to the free romantic dramas of Shakespeare, and in the faculty of seizing the soul through features and action equalled them.   So soon as comparison by this new critical method was attempted, it became evident to all scholars that the Florentine must be given rank with Homer, who chanted the heroic world of Hellas in ' Iliad ' and ' Odyssey ' ; with our English bard who held the mirror up to nature in such wise that he promised to be the universal poet of mankind.   These were not fashions or fancies, but the judgments of

Reason raised to its highest function, dealing with the
works of Dante as it deals with Sophocles or Aeschylus
or Plato, not regarding national prejudice, or religious
bias, but only the quality and achievement of thought,
its correspondence to reality by portraiture, significance, expression, and its magic charm.   A picked
' Company of the Rose,' by knowledge kindled to enthusiasm of Christian art, the Pre-Raphaelite Brotherhood, broke down the barriers set up when pseudo-
classicism reigned, recovering for our delight large
periods of painting, sculpture, and architecture, of
which the spirit was profoundly in agreement with
Dantean ideas and the technique adopted in prose and
rhyme by the Master, who was a Tuscan or local poet
no less than a prophet to his own and future ages.
When the passion for liberty spread after Napoleon's
defeat to every oppressed people, with it came a revival of languages, folk songs, national epics ; and the
' Lay of the Nibelungs,' the Finnish ' Kalevala,' the
' Chanson de Roland,' called for the ' Divine Comedy '
to consecrate their second spring.

On turning to the Catholic landscape, as we may
describe it, which came fold after fold into view during
the last hundred and twenty years, we are struck by its
curiously blended, often opposed colours, nor have
we yet arrived at ' the calm sunset of a various day.'
There were still Guelfs and Ghibellines, both laying
claim to the unique Italian who had passed from one
camp to another, but was never at home with partisans,
however much he strove to discern something of the
ideal in their contrivances.   The resurrection of Italy,
promoted by Carbonari, Papalini, and the astute
Piedmontese ; by Manzoni and Gioberti, by Leopardi,
Mazzini and the circle of Rossetti, by D'Azeglio and

Cavour, found its herald at every stage in the patriot,
Catholic, and exile, who was, according to Carlyle and
in truth, a 'Saint of poetry.' The nation that had
a Dante could not perish. In his musical accents
Italy was ever pleading her cause at the bar of Europe,
subduing men's hearts until her captives should be
set free and by sword and pen Italia Irredenta had
been transformed to an Alpine shield, an Istrian bulwark. To this *opus magnum* of justice, of a civilisation
reinstated where its throne had been originally set up,
all the writings of Dante were gifts, precious like the
achievements of Michael Angelo, sacred as the
sufferings and death of Savonarola, testifying also to
a martyrdom long drawn out, a shame and a glory to
Florence, which once solemnly decreed to burn him
alive, as it hanged Savonarola on a cross.

In vain had it mocked 'Dante Alighieri,' when
some fifteen years of banishment were expired, with
hope of recall, if he would submit to fine and censure.
On such terms he, the innocent, would never set foot
in the guilty city. Could he not 'everywhere look
up to sun and stars, contemplate most delightsome
truths, yes, and even find bread not wanting '? So he
answered, proudly enough. And at length has been
wrought by many heroes and a whole nation the Via
Gloriosa which he demanded, high above political
reactions and military triumphs—the way of peace.
I would symbolise the events thus conspiring to a great
act of reparation under the figure of a meeting in
Paradise between Dante, St. Thomas the Angelic
Doctor, and St. Francis, the seraph of Assisi. All
three were cast aside in scorn by a period of 'enlightenment' which rejected the 'Divine Comedy' as
a barbarous allegory, left the 'Summa Theologica' to

moulder unread on monastic shelves, and thought the
Franciscan poverty sheer madness ; and lo, all three
have been restored with honour to their seats on high !
Nor yet by Catholics only, as neither by much advo-
cacy of ours ; the secret influences of time and what
may reverently be taken for the counsels of Providence
have guided men through and beyond the desert stages
of Luther, Voltaire, and materialist science, to the edge
of the Promised Land. We are returning towards
Dante, having ourselves been led on a pilgrimage
through the dread Inferno, whence with infinite
endeavour we must climb into a more lightsome world.
In the prologue to a late Oxford translation of the
' Paradiso ' we read, ' Custom, the social fabric, civilisation itself, are hung precariously over an abyss of
blackness, like a thin crust that may give way. . . .
In something beneath and above them is the only solid
base of life, the reality of which life is the moving
shadow. Dante is one of the great masters to whom
at such a time we can turn, not to seek distractions or
to drug our senses in dreams, but to be enabled to see
the things about us in their true proportions, to realise
how slight and transitory they are.'

Higher praise than this no man need desire. Yet,
fully to reckon its value, we shall bear in mind always
that our poet is not a mere Ecclesiastes, the preacher
of ' All is vanity,' but has learnt like St. John to behold
with open eyes the City of God which is the Tabernacle
of Adam's race redeemed. This it is, the belief in true
human progress and its goal of divine perfection—the
Vita Beata—which divides him eternally from the poets
of disillusion and despair; from the ' Satanic School,'
though he paints in lurid burning colours vice with its
fierce disdains and moods rebellious against Heaven ;

as from the delicate or decadent votaries of art for art, who care only to render an impression as it is experienced, whatever be its ethical or religious quality, and know nothing more. Of the absolute Catholic poet we are delighted to affirm that, while he had not listened to Diotima teaching Socrates how man might ascend from earthly to ideal beauty, and thus attain the vision of God, he was instructed by a teacher still more august to seek in things visible the image, vehicle, analogy, and presentiment of things invisible, the mystery which is at once the secret of art, the knight's quest through mediaeval forests, the Holy Graal to be conquered in the far-off city of Sarras, the Wood beyond the World, the Isle of Hy-Brasil, the Land of the Hyperboreans, the vision splendid vouchsafed to heroes and saints, the white radiance that overhung those Middle Ages, so turbulent, chaotic, and yet creative, to which we feel ourselves so much more strongly drawn than we could ever be to the chill academic, or unrestrained sensual heathenism of the Renaissance. Was, then, the ' so-called nineteenth century,' at once unbelieving, critical, agnostic, swayed by scientific materialism, yet attracted to the fierce, tender, adventurous paladins of mediaeval Christendom? Even so, I reply with Victor Hugo ; it was a time of light and dark ; *les rayons et les ombres* were mingled in a strange twilight, lingering still in the mental atmosphere of elders like myself, who have grown into the years, and possibly the platitudes, of Gerenian Nestor. But now to the man and his work, with whom I have lived so long.

Shakespeare is a name ; not even by the dream-fugues of the Sonnets can we be sure that we hold him. Dante is real and singular, as well known to me as

Swift or Montaigne. I see him, doubtless, in the portrait of the Bargello, attributed to Giotto ; but, in
comparison with his living self revealed by the ' Vita
Nuova,' by the ' Comedy,' that picture is a faded photo-
graph, telling me little I want to ascertain. He is one
of the men who must needs create on their peculiar
pattern, while they appear, like Jonathan Swift, dis-
dainful of the crowd and its opinion. As in a dream,
he makes all the personages, their attitudes, actions,
speeches, out of his own fancy ; he is the stage, the
play, the dialogue, the orchestra. Whatever he sees
he shows you ; and you are compelled to see it as he
does. There is no science of the individual ; there is
only vision ; and the Etruscan Dante had that power
which we note in all Tuscan artists, in the saints of
Florence and Siena, whereby they become disciples
in the school of the Hebrew prophets, so that all
their wisdom, of earth or heaven, takes on the form
of imagery. Remark, however, what a contrast lies
between the modern poet and the mediaeval. To a
modern imagination the figurative language denotes
only moods ; it has rather a musical than a symbolic
meaning, and its value is evanescent. To the imagination which Dante ruled with an astonishing delibera-
tion, the task assigned was not at all to delineate the
poet's attitude towards life or conduct ; its function
was like that of the Catholic ritual with which it had
such intimate connection, to body forth supernatural
realities, otherwise beyond the reaches of our souls.
In the ' Convito ' we find this method of teaching is
termed allegory and symbolism. But we must not
suppose that Dante uses mere artifice of which the
significance is exhausted in time ; for it conveys a
message from eternity. ' Great would be his shame,'

said the poet-critic, ' who, rhyming under the garb of
figure and rhetorician's colours, knew not how to strip
his words bare that so they should win true understanding.'   Of this explanation Dante made a beginning, and even a sort of Latin prose-version, but it was
left a mere torso, not only when he sketched his fancy
of a ' Symposium ' resembling (however little it did so
in fact) the mystic and incomparable dialogue of Plato,
but likewise when addressing to Can Grande the epistle
which expert scholars now grant to be authentic.   The
sum of my argument, then, is that Dante, inspired and
shown things hid from mortal sight, was a seer, not
merely a singer of love-songs, or a weaver of dreams,
at midnight terror-striking, then lit up by radiant dawn
and tranquil sunset.   I come back to my definition ;
he is the poet of the Catholic Apocalypse.   But he is
always himself and not another, by which note he
remains the antagonist of all Persian Sufis yearning to
be absorbed in the One Essence, and of all adepts in
Buddhism enamoured of Nirvana.

From the Vulgate Bible, that most fortunate
rendering of the Scriptures which he knew by heart,
and from its fourfold sense, literal, spiritual, moral,
anagogic, Dante derived his idea—strictly Platonic
also—of a perfect composition.   To the author, as he
judged, fell this duty of wrapping up deep meanings in
significant speech, to the reader a corresponding task,
the unravelling of that which had been concealed.
Modern science proceeds on a contrary method ; it
aims at the utmost clearness and is a secret only to the
untrained intelligence.   So, too, modern literature
demands from the crowd no second glance ; allegory
is more than out of fashion, it has become an extinct
language, shut in its tomb for ever.   Dante, says

Dr. Moore, ' firmly believed that he lived in a world of mystery ' ; its hidden meaning was divine ; the allegory was real and true ; but the outward-seeming only a painted veil, an instrument of good or evil controlled by spirit, and that more than human. What marvel if a student who is not a Catholic or in any other sense mystically given, should confess with Dr. Moore that between the age of Dante and ours an ever-widening gulf is fixed, and that the poet's supreme point of view is irrecoverable ?

For us, however, who keep the doctrine of the Incarnation and the Sacraments, and hold to the ' prophetic soul of this wide world,' it remains indubitable that things have a significance no less than a reality ; and, ' through every star, through every grass-blade, and most through every living soul, the glory of a present God still beams.' I grant even to the ' soul within the soul ' of Alighieri some cloud of inconsistency, to his artist's hand moments of trembling. To me it does not seem unlikely that he tangled various threads in his enchanted web—seizing hints from all he came across, plucking out secrets from a deeply wounded heart, playing with Love's mediaeval ' Romaunt of the Rose,' yet serious during such pastime ; and thanks to the solely-singular being he was, we must give up the ambition which would enable us to sound him to the top of his compass—how vain in such as we, the average, the mediocrities ! But our Catholic training helps us not a little to feel at one with Dante while he pilgrims along the way that we ourselves must travel. He deemed, for instance, Boethius, the scholar and lover of Italy, who died in exile on his country's behalf, to be a model and light upon his own suffering career. In the pages of Boethius he saw Philosophy personified, a gracious lady, Wisdom herself, beautiful in all her ways.   But was Dante ignorant of the association long consecrated by Church and Liturgy between Mary the Mother of Our Lord to whom he cherished so ardent a devotion and the Wisdom whose praise we hear in the Proverbs of Solomon and the Book of Job ? Reverence forbade him to claim as his guide the Virgin-Mother ; a bitter-sweet experience of young affection, untouched by passion less worthy, and sealed by death, may well have determined him to celebrate Beatrice dei Portinari as none other lady had been glorified, and why not ?   Such a heavenly grace springing from mortal mould appears to the Catholic imagination altogether credible, and it would not stand alone.   The principle to bear in mind is that our Faith deals in realities, not in generalised abstractions, and that our wisdom is never simply of the head but takes to its heart the will, the fancy, the conduct of life—all which Dante knew and had made his own while bent in thought over the pages of Aquinas.   Therefore, to sum up, the supreme point of view being on this wise sacramental, we Catholics are not simply in the dark as regards it ; on the contrary, to us it appears calm, distinct, luminous, positive ; and such the poet describes it, in words unmistakable.   The height and light combine for him as for us in the Beatific Vision, where all things are beheld according to their true proportions.   Dante's spiritual message is indeed Love, but tested and sanctified by the grace of Christ the Redeemer.   We admire the miracles of construction which make his ' Vita Nuova,' his ' Divine Comedy,' each a design of infinite detail, complex and opulent as the Gothic cathedral, simple as the unity of creed and worship to which they owe their existence.

Alighieri will be always the greatest of didactic poets by his blending into a single work of the charm of Nature, the power of the Supernatural, and the pathos of human joy and sorrow, with Justice over all.

Such I take to be the gold of Dante, purged from mediaeval Italian and other dross, tried in the fire, proved everlasting by vicissitudes of honour and dishonour moving through centuries. After being, as it were, canonised in Chaucer's delightful verse, then cast into oblivion by the neglect of almost all Tuscan literature among English readers down to some hundred and twenty years ago, he has had a noble revenge ; Shelley, Byron, Tennyson, leading him back with glorious chants of recognition ; Carlyle and Ruskin setting his praises forth in impassioned prose ; Cary, Longfellow, Wright, Wicksteed, Okey, Caley, Norton, Shadwell, the Greek Musurus, and not a few of lesser note, translating him ; and Oxford, by the hands especially of Edward Moore, determining his text from Bodleian manuscripts even to the enhancement of Karl Witte's labours, though Witte was the father of Dantean studies in the century past. Among Catholics the place of distinction belongs to Edmund Gardner, whose elucidation of the *Ten Heavens,* an astronomical problem, led up to what is the decisive question, far more momentous than that of Ptolemaic cycles or Italian parochial pedigrees—I mean how Dante was related to the Catholic spiritual writers, and from which of them he drew most. That his foundations may be discovered in St. Augustine, Dionysius the Areopagite, St. Bernard, the Victorines, as well as in St. Thomas and St. Bonaventura, we may convince ourselves from his admirable pages ; and he keeps within due bounds, neither giving all the glory of Dantean

theology (which is so entrancing) to Aquinas, nor
making of the poet a spiritual Franciscan beyond the
warrant of history.   But I must break off ; and what
shall be my brief concluding word ?

Dante, according to Ruskin, was ' the central man '
of all this world ; to Carlyle his book was ' the sincerest
of all poems,' he was the ' spokesman of the Middle
Ages ; the thought they lived by stands here, in everlasting music ' ; his ' Divine Comedy ' is ' the most
remarkable of all modern books ' ; and ' one need not
wonder if it were predicted that his poem might be the
most enduring thing our Europe has yet made ' ; it
remains, and he by virtue of it, ' the possession of all
the chosen of the world for uncounted time.'   Dante
and Shakespeare are the two voices of Catholic Christendom.   Stratford-on-Avon stretches out a brotherly
hand to Florence-on-Arno—Florence, the ' most
famous and beautiful offspring of Rome,' but towards
this unique citizen ' all too inexorable.'   He dies in
a strange city, on the feast of the Exaltation of the
Holy Cross, which is a signal date in the life of St.
Francis, not without symbolic value.   In twenty years
of suffering how much had this lonely wanderer not
accomplished while his age was going down head-
long to ruin ?   He had written a Bible for Italy,
become the herald's voice of the Catholic religion while
the world lasts, and proclaimed to every succeeding
generation that in God love and righteousness are one.
The triumph of Christian art in its highest and most
enduring form we owe to Dante Alighieri.

. . . . . .

A great surprise was waiting for the Sixth Centenary of our poet's passing away.   In 1919 Don

Miguel Asin, Professor of Arabic at the University of Madrid, published a volume in which he traced the 'Divine Comedy,' its narrative and structure, to Moslem sources.   But he tempered the significance of his argument by insisting that Islam itself was a sort of Christian heresy (which is undeniable) and that Dante would be justified in reclaiming heirlooms from the folklore of the East which were by rights our own. To Christendom, in fact, none of this Arabic literature was within reach save to a few experts.   The unique value of Dante's life and writings remains as transcendent as ever.

VIII

FRANCIS THOMPSON'S LIFE OF ST. IGNATIUS [1]

OUR latest Catholic poet, who died in 1907, is now secure among the shining choirs to which, by grace of predestination, he belonged. Francis Thompson was, however, not less a martyr than a poet ; and he adds another tragic name to the *Newgate Calendar* of authors, unknown and yet known while they lived, upon whose grave the laurels that were flung made small atonement for the neglect and misery inflicted on them by a blind world. The law that men of genius are doomed to suffer, and the more exquisitely the rarer their gifts, has been exemplified in this new instance with a perfection that mocks our age of light. But the martyr is gone to his high place ; the poet remains. And his legacy, rich in spiritual treasures, holds one pearl of price, dropped from his dying hand, the ' Life of Saint Ignatius Loyola,' which will stand alone as the biography of a Catholic hero, written in choicest English, by a master of prose, by a seer and son of the Renaissance, born out of due time.

It is an Elizabethan work, this new Life, in its unflagging energy of presentment, its wealth and colour

---

[1] *St. Ignatius Loyola.* By Francis Thompson. Edited by John Hungerford Pollen, S.J. With one hundred illustrations by H. W. Brewer and others. London : Burns & Oates.

of speech, its solid concrete handling, its freedom from conventions reckoned sacrosanct in the literature to which its subject invites us. No writing ought to be more profound in the knowledge of the spirit, more delicate and heartfelt, than the Book of the Saints ; but surely none has proved less equal to demand, so far as it is not the composition of saints themselves. It requires, let us boldly say, an inspired pen ; and the mystics who are at home in this secret realm would probably declare that something of inspiration is needed likewise in the reader. Sympathy, at all events, a mind intent on the story, power to transport the imagination into distant unfamiliar scenes ; these cannot be lacking if the true effect is to be obtained. Passive delight, which in our Ovidian time appears the one thing sought by skimmers of novels and lookers on at spectacular drama, betokens, I think, that literature is ending from sheer intellectual fatigue. How precious, then, a work which on every page witnesses to the alert fancy, the straight glance, the grip and judgment of a whole-hearted man, who dares to lift his eyes even to a saint, and who sketches what he sees ! If we term this volume the portrait of Ignatius of Loyola drawn by Francis Thompson, we shall have described it in a phrase. It is a portrait from life, not a copy ; the intuition gained as poets and historians seize the past through means not accessible to the average, but in the result justified. For we feel sure, while we read these lines, that the founder of the Great Company stands before us in his habit as he lived.

Two ways of putting together that ' Second Nocturn,' which in our Breviaries attempts to portray the Saints, are conceivable. We may deal with our materials for edification—and such is the common aim

—or we may test every incident on its merits, suffer the correspondence left (when there happens to be any) to tell its own tale, insist on rigorous proof, and where it cannot be had qualify the statement accordingly. In idea, these two methods should yield the same outcome ; but in fact they often diverge, somewhat as science differs from tradition. They are also characteristic of unlike ages and tempers. When uncritical writers lose sight altogether of tests, they fall into ' Legend,' which has been severely condemned as ' la fable convenue.' When the mere critic takes up his dissecting tool we know that he may reduce the heroic to the commonplace, and sometimes glory in leaving no life at all, despite the effects of it which he has under his instrument. For great saints are among the stubborn facts of history ; the superhuman (explain it how you will) throws its splendour across their actions ; and the ' tale agreed upon ' will constantly, in substance, yield a true account of them, while the sceptic by his negative conclusions refutes his own process, enquiring dubiously, ' Was John at all, and did he say he saw ? ' Yet we have the Apocalypse and the Fourth Gospel, which need prophet and evangelist to be their sufficient cause.

Thompson accepts the ' Second Nocturn ' almost, if not quite, as we receive it ; but he sets it in a thoroughly human framework, taking the divine element, like life itself, as ' whole in the whole, and whole in every part.' He comes thus into violent conflict with two writers who have bestowed on Saint Ignatius the only well known and widely circulated drawings of him extant in our tongue ; I mean Macaulay and Carlyle. No one who has read it will easily forget Macaulay's vivid delineation of the Jesuits

and their creator which partly adorns, if it also partly
disfigures, his unique essay on the Popes. Some
portions of it, in their condensed truth and vigour,
might have been dashed down by Gibbon ; they sum-
marise the facts of Ignatius' descent, temper, ambition
and enterprise boldly, yet not without insight, and we
must assent to their general drift. But the Whig
rhetorician was always timid, though always interested,
in presence of the supernatural. He pitied the
visionary saint as, I take it, a more profound psychology would now pity the critic. Ignatius might well
answer him with a question:

> And how shall I assure them ?   Can they share—
> They who have flesh, a veil of youth and strength
> About each spirit, that needs must bide its time—
> With me who hardly am withheld at all,
> But shudderingly, scarce a shred between,
> Lie bare to the universal prick of Light ?

Men are now ceasing to winnow out the phenomena which transgress everyday law from the lives of
spiritual heroes ; we know enough, at least, to decline
making a *caput mortuum*, such as Voltaire gloated over,
by wanton rejection of the incomprehensible whenever we meet it in experience. There is our strong
point ; so, and not otherwise, did the things happen.
If we will go by evidence, let us be faithful to the whole
of it. The ' visions and revelations ' which claim their
place in the biographies, whether of St. Paul or St.
Ignatius, are authentic, attested at first hand by the
subject of them in writing or conversation. They are
facts no less real than the cloak left at Troas, the Book
of the ' Exercises,' the letters despatched to India and
the New World. It is a shallow system which puts all
this on one side as the product of a ' lively imagination.'

o

But we will give Macaulay his due. He admires the Spanish hidalgo, the 'poet and knight-errant of the spouse of Christ.' He has words of high recognition for his enthusiasm ; and he agrees with the Roman pontiffs who saw in him the victorious antagonist of Luther. 'The history of the Order of Jesus,' he maintains, 'is the history of the great Catholic reaction ' ; its triumph he does not deny ; he is even candid enough to ascribe it ' not to the force of arms,' but to ' a great reflux in public opinion,' to a reformation of head and members which cannot be dissociated from the Council of Trent, itself in no small measure the fruit of Jesuit zeal and devotion.

With Carlyle, in his ' Latter Day Pamphlets,' under the heading ' Jesuitism,' we are carried off into the deepest abyss of the ' Inferno.' All he can see in ' Unsaint Ignatius '—we quote him textually with reluctance—is one whose nature abounded in ' audacities and sensualities,' and who ' probably has done more mischief in the earth than any man born since.' The father of a ' black militia,' he has given existence to a ' universe of cant ' ; nay, ' there was in this of Jesuit Ignatius an apotheosis of falsity, a kind of subtle quintessence and deadly virus of lying, the like of which had never been seen before.' I refrain from further extracts, merely remarking that if Luther had been permitted to deal with his Spanish adversary in a last diatribe, he could not much have intensified the venom and vituperation which our Thomas of Chelsea pours forth in a torrent of uncivil speech. Who is under a delusion here ? Is it the author of the ' Spiritual Exercises,' or the author of the ' Latter Day Pamphlets ' ? The decision may be left to any careful reader who will compare them together. From Macaulay we

are able, after some pains, to discover in outline what
Ignatius truly was ; Carlyle evokes a phantom, and
chases him hence with the language of exorcism ; in
his amazing caricature not a line of the original is left.
It is a masterpiece of invective, and nothing more.

Omitting, then, as Sir Thomas Browne would
advise all Christians, ' those improperations and terms
of scurrility betwixt us, which only difference our
affections and not our cause,' I hold that our dead poet
has written a Life exact in statement, beautiful in point
of style, fit to be welcomed by Protestant no less than
Catholic readers on the ground that it presents a determining phase of religion not unworthily.   Such praise
could seldom be given to the biographies of great
churchmen, which are commonly undertaken by writers
without strength of mind or distinction of speech.   It
is a notable addition, if we ought not rather to call it
the beginning of a true English literature, in its own
department.   We have too often endured colourless
renderings from the French and Italian, strangely
foreign to our taste, diffuse and didactic, resembling
neither St. Augustine's ' Confessions,' which is the
supreme type of self-portraiture, nor the ' Flowers of
St. Francis,' which takes us captive by its simplicity
and essential truth.   These are the models a biographer of the saints should keep ever in view ; he
cannot equal them, but if he exchanges for their intimate
manner a tone too abstract, and serves up his living
subject in a category even of supernatural virtues, he
will defeat his aim.   The saints are more than their
virtues, and in this lies the influence which they never
cease to exert.   They are God's men in a world of
fallen humanity ; and if we know them aright we shall
never mistake one for the other.   St. Ignatius could

not have existed before the century in which he played so decisive a part. He was original in his cast of thought, daringly novel from first to last in the conception of his Order. We can hardly imagine a second like him ; and none has appeared. Let us now for a little, in Carlyle's phrase, ' look fixedly at him, till he become a substance and person for us.'

Iñigo, afterwards called Ignatius, and ' Loyola ' *tout court* by a hostile world, was of the Basque race and province, a Spaniard of oldest lineage, without admixture of Jew or Moor in his ascertainable pedigree. He was born in 1491, a year previous to the fall of Granada, and not much more to the discovery of Spain's new continent across the ocean. One era in Christendom was ending, another stood at the doors. In full course the Renaissance was bringing back Hellenic thought, Pagan morals, and the ' reign of the despots.' Mediaeval liberty had been struck down ; the schools of Catholic philosophy were plunged into a quagmire called Nominalism ; and modern nations were emerging from the older system, now hopelessly disjointed, of Pope and Emperor dividing the spiritual and temporal powers between them. Luther was a peasant child of eight, not yet a hermit of St. Augustine's Order, nor learning his classics at Erfurt. Next year, a certain Alexander Borgia would, by simony and other questionable means, be raised to St. Peter's chair, the third Spaniard who had borne a Papal title in that same century. The last sigh of Boabdil the Moor would soon leave Spain one, Catholic, indivisible, with an Inquisition to oversee its *Nuevos Cristianos* and a *Rey neto*, absolute king, who took on himself to be a sort of lay pope, and whose armies would not shrink from besieging Rome itself at his command. There was little or no heresy anywhere ; but in the German, English, and Northern nations generally, a fierce smouldering discontent with the Apostolic Curia, not on grounds chiefly religious, but financial, of the earth earthy. Pass another twenty-seven years, the Teutons would be in revolt ; another thirty-seven, and Henry of England would be soliciting his divorce. The age-long duel between North and South was preparing to take the name of the Reformation. ' In a mighty dust of war and revolt,' says Thompson finely, ' Christendom itself was vanishing.'

Of the thirty years spent by Ignatius in the world prior to his conversion we know very little. He was a soldier, and may have fought under the great captain, Gonsalvo, in Italy, where the Aragonese had conquered and would henceforth rule, not to that ill-fated country's benefit. Or perhaps in Navarre, under his uncle the Viceroy. Our poet describes him from picturés, not contemporary with his younger days, though doubtless a guide to his appearance when he sought renown : ' Short, but well-knit and active, an expert in knightly exercise, with dark and glossy clustering hair and lofty forehead, he has in these portraits something of a Napoleonic countenance, but with an Augustan delicacy of chin that fits ill with the general massiveness of the face. This trait appears in the later and more trustworthy portraits, which show also more unmistakably the considerable aquilinity of the nose. The compelling power of his eyes was memorable ; and like Napoleon as a youth he was a swayer of men.' The ' audacities ' with which Carlyle charges him were surely there ; but of any ' sensualities ' and ' prurient elements ' we have no clear sign.

Ignatius, in the spirit of a troubadour, had chosen some great lady—rumour said Juana, daughter of the Queen Dowager of Naples—to smile on his exploits. To her he dedicated sonnets and even religious poems ; it was the fashion of the time ; but what does that prove ? Not so much as that the fiery Biscayan had a turn for literature, since he never acquired it, writing with strong soldierly precision in the ' Exercises,' with abundance of detail in his correspondence, but leaving no page that would show among the world's classics. He had the genius of action, not of composition. Even as priest and religious he took the soldier's way, the soldier's estimate, driving sheer at the end, too intent upon it to be an artist of words for their own sake. Of metaphysics or theology at this stage he had none. A true Don Quixote, he lost himself in the romances of chivalry, and doated on ' Amadis of Gaul.'

Tenacious as Easterns, the Spaniards do not change. They were little affected, after all, by the Renaissance. They despised the Italians for their frivolity and cowardice ; they were a thousand leagues from suspecting the revolution which was at hand in Germany, the language and character of whose people have ever been to them unknown. Their simple view of life is contained in the famous verse :

Un monarca, un imperio, y una espada.

When Charles V, that ' cold-hearted Fleming,' reigned, their ambition was satisfied. In the crowded sixteenth century three Spaniards prove in divers ways how much could be done with the one sword, of the flesh or the spirit, to maintain the one empire in Church as in State—Cortez, the conqueror of Mexico, Philip II, universal monarch, and Ignatius of Loyola, whose

passion for unity gives the key to all his projects. He
is mediaeval in his crusading zeal ; but modern, and
nowise mediaeval, in his distrust of local differences.
He is neither democratic nor feudal, but absolute and
centralising in the methods of government which he
adopts. The programme of Cardinal Ximenes, aiming
at the political union of the old Spanish kingdoms under
a sovereign whose word was law, and at the expulsion
of Jews and Moors from Catholic soil, throws light on
the movement to which the Ignatian principles furnish,
so to speak, a religious counterpart. Among Germans
a revulsion from the Roman Law in favour of old
Teutonic liberties had been felt. In Spain, freedom
was expiring under the heavy blows of royal ministers ;
the Court rule was establishing itself which lasted down
to the French Revolution. Individually, the Spaniard
was a hero and the King's equal ; but now, in the
mighty empire that bestrode the Atlantic like a colossus,
what had he become ? A courtier who lived or died
at his master's bidding. Loyalty, obedience, was the
password to all noble charges ; the knight-errant
followed his king.

Such were the ideas which Ignatius must have
imbibed from earliest infancy, for they were in the air.
When his hour came, and he lay shattered after the
siege of Pampeluna, having fought but not surrendered,
conversion disclosed to him a higher kingship and
a heavenly ambition, but his mental horizon had not
changed. It never did till his dying day. He put
from him the chivalrous romances and was given the
' Life of Christ,' by the Saxon Carthusian, Ludolph,
instead. The Saints appeared to him as so many
paladins of the Table Round. He was stirred to
emulation. The cry that broke from his lips, ' Isti et

isti, cur non ego ? ' is a soldier's challenge to himself ;
it takes the good cause for granted.   He would have
scorned to consider arguments on the other side.   Delicate or dissolute Humanists were smiling in Italian
palaces at the Christian superstition which fed and
clothed them.   French sceptics would ere long find
a golden mouthpiece in Rabelais, as the Florentines
had found one in Machiavelli.   But this whole view
of things, lying outside the imagination of Ignatius,
never could have detained him.   For a moment he had
looked into Erasmus, neither sceptic nor heretic, but
a delightful mocker of current abuses.   He condemned
that too liberal tone afterwards, and thought it had done
him no good.   The soldier is of a nature too sensitive
to relish ironies which may seem a reflection on the
general staff.   Yet for him was reserved the task of
correcting those very abuses which the ' Praise of
Folly ' satirised.   He was to be the great reformer of
Monasticism—so great indeed that, whatever accusa-
tions have been hurled against his own Society, no man
has ventured to fix upon it the stigma of idleness,
immorality, or ignorance.

His life falls naturally into the secular part,
occupying about thirty years, and the religious, which
covered thirty-five more.   Of these twenty were passed
in the novitiate (where he was truly his own master)
and in founding the Company of Jesus ; the last fifteen
were dedicated to ruling over the provinces that
received these apostles of the Catholic Restoration.
I do not term it simply a ' reaction,' as Macaulay and
Symonds have done ; for reaction carries with it an
idea of fatigue, or the second best, whereas the Church
never displayed more energy, and orthodox minds were
never more active, than during the hundred years

which succeeded the Council of Trent. In this revival
of dogma, discipline and learning the Jesuits led the
van. They took possession at once, says Macaulay
with admiring emphasis, ' of all the strongholds which
command the public mind, of the pulpit, of the press,
of the confessional, of the academies.' Thus it was
that ' literature and science, lately associated with infi-
delity or heresy, now became the allies of orthodoxy.'

To disparage this mighty movement by setting
it down as reaction, is to overlook the original forces
which gave it birth and the newer channels into which it
turned the thoughts of Catholics. It was not so much
a reaction as a development. It bore no likeness to
the Dominican theology, the mysticism of St. Francis,
the homestaying meditation of the Benedictine. This
large innovation upon the past lends to the wandering
years and slowly growing designs of Ignatius a charm
as of some drama gradually unfolded ; rarely to any
saint was the phrase more applicable, ' l'homme s'agite
et Dieu le mène.' He went forth on his knightly
quest, ignorant of what should befall him ; not
dreaming that he was to combat the giants of the North
by a world-wide system of education, to take its sting
from the Renaissance by subduing Latin poets and
Greek philosophers to the yoke of the sanctuary.
Himself unacquainted with classic learning, and at no
time a metaphysician, he was destined to save not only
the faith, but the Humanism which had threatened it
with disaster, from the fanatics who made war on both.

These years of a spiritual Odyssey, in which the
hero became a pilgrim to the Holy Places, a belated
pupil at Spanish universities, a fisher of men in Paris—
years full of adventuring and suffering—give to Francis
Thompson rich matter of fact, to be told as the kind of

epic which it truly was.   Seldom, if ever, has it been
told so well—in English never.   The passionate
naïveté of a Ribadeneira, whom we may look on as the
Saint's Boswell ; the ' reminiscences which Ignatius
from 1553 onwards communicated to Luis Gonzalez ' ;
Bartoli's much-quoted chronicle of the earlier period
of the Society ; and the particulars gleaned from
Polanco, Rodriguez, Lainez, and others, which confirm
Ribadeneira, leave us in no doubt concerning the main
incidents of a career that was enacted in the public light.
For though Ignatius loved and practised solitude like
a Father of the Desert, he moved about among companions who were eager to note his characteristics and
to preserve his sayings.   That he was reticent by
temper, and yet more by determination, appears in all
these narratives ; he had the reserve of a Spanish
gentleman, deepened by his habit of saintly self-control.
A little before his death he burnt all except a few fragments of his spiritual diaries.   This, perhaps, teaches
us more of his governing principles than if we read the
daily account of favours, trials, and practices which he
kept so long.   What he felt we may learn from what
he did.   He was the disciple of no school ; and, once
more, he is best depicted as a crusader who fulfilled
inwardly as well as outwardly the idea of a ' very perfect
gentle knight,' in the service of his Captain, Christ.

He began by cutting off at a stroke the old life with
its trappings, its fopperies, its not ungraceful uses
of the world.   What need to dwell on the picturesque opening of that pilgrimage, the discarded courtly
apparel, the journey to wild Monserrato, high up in the
Pyrenees, the vigil as of a new knighthood and order of
chivalry, on Lady Day, 1522, at the Blessed Virgin's
altar, followed by the retreat to Manresa ?   None, save

that we may recommend a fresh study of it all in the
chapters before us. Every Catholic has been shown
the picture of this new St. Michael preparing to smite
the dragon. From the lonely mountain-cave, where
Ignatius prayed and wrestled during ten most searching
months, he came out a man new made, in his hand the
first rude sketch of the ' Exercises,' in his heart a dim
design which was by and by to ripen into the Company
which our poet names ' the Free Lances of the Church.'
It was now the year 1523, and he set out for Jerusalem,
by way of Barcelona, Gaeta, Rome, and Venice. He
saw in Rome Adrian VI, once Viceroy of Spain, now a
' transient embarrassed ' Pontiff, and took his blessing.
In Venice he slept on the flags of St. Mark's Place, until
a certain Trevisani, afterwards Doge, was warned by
a dream to rise up and give him shelter. He landed
in Jaffa, went on to the Holy City, found that his life-
work did not lie there, and came back to Barcelona,
resolved on learning the elements of education which
he had never been taught. In this heroic drudgery
two years were spent ; and in August 1526 he
removed to Alcalá.

Cisneros, whom we call Ximenes, the great Cardinal, had founded this university, and left means for
the training of poor scholars. Ignatius went thither,
taking three disciples, who forsook him later on ;
he had now (though in a mendicant garb, which led
children to call after him, ' Father Sack ') begun to
catechise in the streets, and to give the ' Spiritual
Exercises.' A layman, he drew priests to listen and
the Inquisition to take notice. Spain, says Thompson,
' appreciated and desired Ignatius on its own terms ;
but of his Order it would have nothing on any terms.
And that was the issue.' The unbending champion

' of forlorn proscriptions and perishing causes,' he continues happily, ' this Oxford among the nations,'
expiated its formalism by ' a Chinese rigour, and arrest
of development.' The Inquisition baffled the Saint.
He was haled to prison, passing on his road the cortège
of the Marquis de Lombay, destined one day to be his
own successor, and St. Francis Borgia in the Church's
calendar. To Figueroa, who charged him with
preaching novelties, he replied, ' I did not think it novel
to speak of Christ to Christians.' Thompson adds,
' his distressing originality was the real offence.' He
was bidden to put on a student's uniform, and to close
his lips about religion till his four years' course of
theology should be over. His teaching had been
declared blameless. But he would not stay.

Moving on to Salamanca, he met with still harder
treatment. He was flung by the same authority,
without anything that could be deemed a trial, into the
common gaol. There, for three weeks, he and his
companion were chained to one another like dogs,
according to the peculiar ideas of arrest and detention
which prevailed all over Europe in that Iron Age.
The procedure makes our blood boil ; Ignatius submitted to it with joy. On being examined, he turned
the hearts of the Inquisitors by his rapt discourse on
the love of God. At last he was absolved from every
charge and let go. He might even preach, but under
conditions. This time the Saint ' entered something
like a protest ' ; he quitted Salamanca and Spain for
ever. The new Order was to come to the birth elsewhere, in the heart of a distracted Christendom, at
Paris, the City of Light and Darkness, the world's
university.

Paris rejoiced in fifty colleges and schools ; it

boasted of its sixteen thousand students, divided into four ' nations ' of the French, Picards, Normans, and Germans. Ignatius, tramping from Barcelona to the great city on foot, entered himself at the Collège Montaigu, where Erasmus, a generation back, had starved and studied. Hitherto, a bad system of endeavouring to follow all branches of learning at once had prevented the distraught mystic from mastering any of them. He would start here afresh with grammar. Thompson aptly remarks on his ' amazing and unflinching thoroughness.' A saint, he was anticipating the methods of science, which does not advance by sudden leaps and bounds, but by infinitely patient observation and experiment. On the whole, such was to be the method of the Society of Jesus ; it reduced individual powers to a common denominator, as Bacon would have made the rules of discovery so level to ordinary sense that any man could employ them. Ignatius never acted in haste. He was now just upon forty ; and what had he done ? He had made himself. In the next six years he would have made, thanks to the ' Exercises,' as many disciples. And then the ' Septem contra Lutherum ' would march to the Holy War.

At no time, perhaps, do we admire the genial handling of our poet-biographer more than now, when he draws in bold strokes the figures of those half-dozen obscure men who were to be captains of hundreds and thousands, leading on the Catholic ' light horse ' in a seemingly forlorn hope. All are renowned with posterity ; two stand among the Blessed whom the Church acclaims—Peter Favre, the shepherd boy of Swiss Villaret, ' room companion ' and tutor to Ignatius at Ste. Barbe ; and Francis Xavier, Spanish but Navarrese, a Basque, who had been lecturing on

Aristotle with applause in the College of Beauvais. From Alcalá came Lainez, the prodigy of learning, and afterwards chief light of the Council of Trent, with Salmeron almost his equal. From near Palencia came Bobadilla (surely of New Christian descent, for his Moorish name bewrayeth him), followed by Simon Rodriguez, ' more Carmelite than Jesuit,' who was to do great things in the Peninsula hereafter. These were all studying in Paris. They had fallen under the spell of a personality which left none indifferent ; they had gone through the ' Exercises ' severally, and in July 1534 they met together for the first time.

Ignatius in their presence took the vows of poverty, chastity, and the mission to Palestine which still haunted him. The others accepted him for their master ; and it was determined to embark at Venice a year hence, or, that proving impossible, to wait yet a second twelve months, then go to Rome and give themselves to the Holy Father. So slowly did the genuine idea of the Society dawn upon its creator's mind ! They were doomed not to sail from Venice, never to see Palestine ; but, instead, to evangelise that Germany of which they knew so little, and to begin the new era of Catholicism. They celebrated the birthday of their Order on our Lady's Assumption, 1534, in the chapel of St. Denis on Montmartre. Three years elapsed. By toilsome ways, amid the clash of armies, they reached Venice in January 1537 ; went on to Rome, and were presented by Ortiz, the Spanish Minister, once an enemy of Ignatius, to Paul III. He had concluded a league against the Turk which would make the seas impassable for pilgrims. ' I do not think,' he said, ' you will go to the Holy Land.' He was a true prophet.

They spent the vowed interval preaching in the cities of Northern Italy ; Ignatius was ordained priest ; and they now took the name of the Company of Jesus. At this period they recall, by their poverty and street preaching, as well as by a certain joyous independence, St. Francis of Assisi and his comrades. Their founder, taking with him Favre and Lainez, set out towards Rome. At the desolate village of La Storta, near the ruins of Veii, once more the heavens opened ; a vision and a voice came to this lowly pilgrim ; he heard the Redeemer say, ' At Rome I will be gracious to thee.' His interpretation was significant of the man and the time ; he understood these words as foreboding martyrdom. Why not ? There were perils manifold in front of him. Paul III, now verging on seventy, had survived after a scandalous youth and a strenuous middle age to become a reforming Pontiff ; but he was always of the Renaissance by his character, his ambition, and his nepotism, to give it no harsher a name. Discerning, nevertheless, what changes were imperatively required, he called about him such able and unlike advisers as Contarini, Caraffa, and Pole. He could never have imagined a combination of enthusiasm and spiritual strategy resembling the Order of Jesus ; but when its rules were submitted to him at Tivoli for approval he cried out, ' The finger of God is here.' After a series of most difficult negotiations the Saint triumphed. In 1540 the Bull ' Regimini militantis Ecclesiae ' came forth, sealing with Apostolic authority the name, the vows, the unique constitution of these ' Clerks Regular,' termed by their founder ' the little Company,' and, possibly first of all by Calvin, the Jesuits. On April 7, 1541, Xavier sailed from Portugal for the East Indies. On the same day in

Rome Ignatius was chosen General of the Society, a life-long office. All the rest had voted for him ; he had refused to vote for anyone—a remarkable circumstance. By his twenty years of extraordinary heroism and consummate wisdom, he was pointed out as the only man who had a claim to that captaincy. At first he declined it, but he must have known that in him the fortunes of the Order were summed up.

'Things won are done, joy's soul lies in the doing.' History shows us a marvellous man and his work, snatched from infinite possibilities ; and we take the sight as something inevitable, as though always there. But once the Society of Jesus was not ; it might never have been ; its idea and its existence are wholly due to this soldier-saint, the wild cave-dweller, the sackcloth witness roaming through Spanish highways, in prisons often, in perils of the deep, begging his bread in London streets and from Flemish merchants, uninstructed till late manhood in prayer as in letters, alone against corrupt living in the Church and heresy outside. Alone, 'Ignatius contra mundum,' if ever a man was. He had to persuade the Roman Curia that a new and unexampled experiment in religious organisation must be made. Only when that was accomplished, in despite of good and bad equally opposed to it, could he begin his warfare on the united hosts of Luther and Calvin. And they were overrunning the world.

Skirmishing had already taken place in Paris. Calvin, who preceded Ignatius at Montaigu and Ste. Barbe, returned when the saint was gaining his first recruits, and himself won to the ' new learning ' Kopp, the Rector of the University. Both were compelled to flee, and the Jesuit band was active in the movement against the Huguenots which followed. Rabelais, too, was on the scene ; but I am not aware of any measures taken, or ascribable to the Society, in criticism of his dissolving and dissolute fantasies. There, too, was Servetus, whom Calvin could not retain as a disciple, but could and did burn as a heretic. No living intellect was broad enough to reflect all the tendencies, or to fix those which were destined to prevail, in that immense confusion of peoples and opinions. It is not to be supposed that Ignatius, unread in the story of the past, no student in the modern sense, had a philosophical idea of what Luther was aiming at, or Calvin was digesting into his ' Institutes ' ; much less would he comprehend the apparently sportive genius who preferred the monks of Thelema to the monks of St. Benedict. And the Socinian, the Unitarian, the Rationalist, lay hid in a doubtful future. Critically, the Spanish mind of Ignatius did not spend itself on these large systems of thought. It moved by another law ; it was bent on a mystic training in which the Christian faith and dogma should be, as we now say, realised. This he undertook, and this he achieved.

He would probably have entered more into the peculiar temperament of Luther than into the firm yet academic reasonings of which Calvin was an accomplished type. Between the noble of Loyola and the miner's son of Eisenach the contrast on every point but one is no less patent than complete. In pedigree, language, humour, what men could be so unlike ? A page of Luther's, violent, unclean, comic, full of old German idioms, or in such Latin as a furious Bearsark would pour forth, is indeed ' half a battle ' ; it appeals to the emotions and is buoyed up on them ; its whole effect is to make friends clap their hands while enemies feel for their swords. Compare any meditation in the

P

' Exercises ' taken at random. There all is deliberate, restrained, solitary ; fancy itself is subdued to a definite end ; religion becomes almost a science. Once more, Luther, although he put his trust in princes who did not fail him, writes as a religious demagogue. He knows how to move the multitude by speech and song ; his very translating of the Bible into German is for their sake. His years of glory were passed as in sight of the whole nation. Thus he was held to be the man of the people, and such among Protestants he remains to this day. Ignatius preached in the public thoroughfares, but he never spoke of himself ; his sermons and catechisings were impersonal. He was raising up a Catholic ' aristocracy of intellect ' ; his disciples read Holy Scripture daily, but they shrank from the profane uses of it which were only too common among the ignorant fanatics who swarmed on all sides. Private judgment, with its eccentricities, quarrellings, sects, and rude caricatures of a sublime creed, was an offence in the eyes of this courtly, sensitive gentleman, to whom the suppression of self was the principle of good manners as well as of religion. In all these ways Luther and Ignatius were opposed.

Yet one thing they had in common ; they were of the temperament which is called melancholy ; and by experience arising out of it they had reached their hostile conclusions. Luther's tormenting scruples made him despair of his own righteousness, from which he took refuge in justification by faith without works. The terrible darkness of spirit into which Ignatius was plunged at Manresa for so long a space drove him upon the virtue of obedience to a director as the only way of salvation. Obedience brought light and comfort ; gloom was the penalty of self-seeking, a sure token that some evil spirit such as afflicted Saul had drawn nigh. Hence those rules for the discernment of states and motives which bear on them a rare stamp of the Saint's intimate trials, while none are more valuable in the ' Exercises.' But during the unparalleled crisis of the Church, when it had lost the nations beyond the Alps and could scarcely maintain itself on the shores of the Mediterranean, what more needful than to make obedience the first article of the creed ?

Moreover, be the cause what it may, who will deny that a deadly gloom has fallen on the Protestant lands, the deeper in proportion as their teachers have receded from Rome ? If melancholy broods over the Saxon, Scottish, and English Puritans ; if it has ever been marked in the Huguenots, the Swiss, the Dutch and American Calvinists, shall we say that climate accounts for it all ? that a stern theology did nothing to modify the dispositions of those who applied it in every walk of life ? Historians do not take this view. But supposing a relation between habits of thought and habits of conduct, we may perceive how the instinct or the grace which impelled Ignatius to look for joy in obedience would react on his ' little Company ' ; how in no long time it would create a school of ethics answering to it ; and how such cheerfulness in meeting evil and conquering vice should be their note to the world, and a rebuke on the lips of their enemies. The sad Puritan virtue took umbrage at most things human, except commerce and conquest. But the Jesuits were emphatically reconcilers, and the education which they freely gave was liberal, intended to produce not only good Catholics but high-minded men of the world.

Luther addressed himself to the populace ; Calvin wrote for scholars and reigned over a strong middle class ; St. Ignatius kept in view the social order from which he had sprung. His ambition was to form these new crusaders from the governing hierarchy ; to deal by means of them with principalities and powers ; to add science to religion, culture to sacerdotal dignity, charm of manner to an edifying life. Themselves bound by a vow of Franciscan poverty, his disciples were to be poor in nothing save worldly goods. The Jesuits may be said to have substituted for the decaying régime of the Middle Ages an alliance between the throne and the altar, with passive obedience so long as kings were loyal to the Holy See—in short, Bossuet's theory of Church and State. Their founder was no more of a democrat than was Shakespeare. True it is that Mariana declaimed until Europe rang with his eloquence on the old Castilian notion of a free people ; and Suarez has been termed (not by Dr. Johnson) the first Whig. But popular rights were not advocated by Ignatius, and did not enter into his scheme.

Neither would he allow national differences to tell in the Society. He had set up a Catholic militia of which the soldier's oath to go anywhere at the Pope's bidding was the very essence. To cut off alien desires and prevent losses he turned the proverbial ' Nolo episcopari ' into a solemn engagement, greatly to the wonder of Roman clerics who beheld rich sees and cardinal's hats rejected by Jesuits in patched garments, —Lainez himself eloping from the Vatican lest he should be forcibly taken into the Sacred College. A discipline, the like of which was unknown to the severest orders, tried all those who would join the Company. It broke and new-made them. Henceforth, detached from country, kindred, and their former selves, they were to do on behalf of religion what the corps of Turkish janissaries had done for the empire of Islam. At the moment when, judging by probabilities, the Roman Church was tottering to her fall, a mighty international power, wielded by a single hand, came to her assistance, and, humanly speaking, saved her.

It is matter of history that the Holy See was deliberating, not to reform the old orders, but to let them die out—a counsel of despair. St. Ignatius came to the rescue, not by travelling on lines already worn, but as creative spirits know how, by interpreting tradition more faithfully while casting it into an original shape. He left the cloister and choral chanting to others ; seized on the school, the hospital, the confessional, which secular as well as regular clergy had neglected ; laid hands on East and West, fulfilling in the sixteenth century a mission like that which St. Paul had struck out for himself in the first. A mission and a revolution we must call both these movements, nor were the leaders dissimilar. St. Ignatius in the last three hundred years occupies a place apart, yet exercises a universal influence upon Catholicism in a manner strictly analogous to the position of St. Paul in the Church of the Apostles. We might illustrate the parallel at length did space permit, but enough has been said for those who will follow it up in detail.

Settled now at S. Maria della Strada, near the Papal residence, acknowledged as defender of the faith by his bitterest opponents, the Saint did not leave Rome more than three times during his last fifteen years. His correspondence was amazing in extent and minuteness of direction. He envied not the miracles but the labours of Francis Xavier, who wrote to the General on his knees, while in the hitherto sealed kingdoms of India, and in the heart of Japan, he approved himself the one Western preacher that has pierced into Oriental reserve or subdued great crowds of the yellow race to Christianity. For an instant it seemed as if the Farther East would be converted. Then Xavier died, overcome by many trials. But the ever memorable chapter of the Jesuit Missions had begun with a splendid page.

In Germany, the Swiss shepherd-boy Favre was restoring with dauntless courage a battle apparently lost. Twenty-one years had gone by since Luther burnt the Pope's Bull at Wittenberg, and still it was not so much disbelief of the Catholic creed as offence taken at the vicious lives of the Catholic clergy that made converts to Lutheranism. So did Favre judge, with indignation but not without hope (see his letter, dated New Year, 1541, from Worms). He would win serious Christians back, thanks to the ' Exercises,' now celebrated for their transforming power. On these and on private conference, far more than the secular arm, he and his companions relied. As yet, however, they preached only in Latin ; but Latin was the common medium of knowledge, everywhere current among the learned. Charles V, politic and temporising, had his own idea of a Council, which the Pope checkmated by announcing the convocation of what afterwards became the Council of Trent. Bobadilla was carried off to Vienna ; Le Jay expounded the Epistle to the Galatians at Ratisbon and gained a footing at Ingolstadt. During a short interval Favre visited Spain, captured St. Francis Borgia, then Viceroy of Catalonia, for the Society ; returned to his German expedition, converted Spire, stayed the advance of heresy in Mainz,

and there made acquisition of Peter Canisius, the chief
of Jesuit apostles in the Fatherland hereafter.

One exploit of this zealous young adherent was to
procure from Charles V the deposition of Hermann,
Archbishop of Cologne, who had driven out the Jesuits
and favoured the new doctrine. It was a significant
victory. The tide, long running furiously in the direction of Protestantism, had begun to turn. What was
now lost to the Reformers they never got back again.
Political intrigues might float men hither and thither,
but once they had been moulded by Catholic principles,
as brought home to them in retreats and spiritual
exposition, they were conquered for all time. Unity
of teaching, and, as Thompson admirably observes,
the 'most eloquent example' of those who gave it,
were telling on all such as dreaded anarchy in thought
and confusion of powers in the State. It was certain,
before the mid-century had been passed, that the Holy
Roman Empire would remain loyal to St. Peter.
Provinces might be torn away, but the Rhine, the
Main, the Danube, would still be Catholic streams.
Even the Thirty Years War, ending one hundred
years after, could not change their destiny.

In France a very ancient quarrel, between the
lawyers and the Holy See, was transmuted into the
attack of the Sorbonne, aided by the Archbishop of
Paris, on this ultramontane and Spanish order claiming
exemption from local authority. The legend of a rule
behind the rule, known as 'Monita Secreta,' began to
make the tour of the world. A party was rising up,
anti-papal, anti-Jesuit, which never henceforward lost
sight of its object, to divorce from Rome the Church
and Crown of France. But it failed in these first
attempts. In 1549 the Cardinal of Lorraine arrived at

the Curia, solicitous for an alliance against Charles V.
Ignatius won him over ; Henry II allowed the Society
a home in Paris ; and the Bishop of Clermont gave
them his town-house, expanded by and by into the
college termed Louis le Grand.   The opposition, however, continued ; there was to be a duel of Jesuits and
Jansenists over the dead body of a Flemish heresiarch,
ending in the ruin which the Parlement of Paris
wrought in 1763.   France would be the grave of the
Order, when it died to rise again from its ashes.

Out of Spain the Saint had been forced to retire.
He now came back in his lieutenants, Favre, Villa-
nueva, Simon Rodriguez, who carried all before them.
Colleges, which grew into Jesuit strongholds, were set
up in Alcalá, Coimbra, Salamanca ; royal bequests and
public favours made atonement for the slights once
inflicted on a great Saint by a purblind Inquisition.
But the time would fail us to speak of these and other
enterprises, mostly successful, ever displaying the
indomitable spirit which had now breathed fresh life
into Catholics in Ireland, Belgium, Italy, Sicily.   ' Go,
set all on fire,' was the parting admonition of Ignatius
to his envoys.   Among them none showed more zeal
than the heroic scapegrace, Ribadeneira, who held the
keys of his General's heart, and whose doings throw
a welcome ray of comedy, of human feeling, over these
all-daring expeditions.   In ten years the Company had
revolutionised the tactics of the Church.   From a timid
and embarrassed defence, they had become boldly
aggressive.   But Favre, the one successor whom his
chief would perhaps have chosen, died in 1546.
Francis Xavier was taken away in 1552.   What men
would continue the work ?

That question was decided by the entrance of

Francis Borgia into the Company, though for a while he kept his great place in the world, and by the extraordinary triumphs of Lainez and Salmeron at the Council of Trent. Between the Reformers and the Jesuits a gulf was now fixed which all the attempts at reconciliation have not succeeded in filling up. On one side, justification by faith alone was opposed to the objective and sanctifying virtue of the Sacraments, on the other. Private judgment read the Scriptures by its own light ; Catholic consent would not allow men to depart from the tradition of the Fathers. The Mass involved the priesthood ; its denial reduced the ministry to the office of preaching. These differences were vital, and the Pope's authority protecting the old creed made the dogmas of Trent a foregone conclusion. It signified little whether Protestants came or stayed away. The embittered controversies of thirty years which led up to the Council had already shaped it. No reconciling influences survived. Moderate leaders, Contarini or Pole, who saw the beginnings of the Reformation, did not, perhaps, understand how stern was the logic, how imperious the alternative, of ' priest or no priest,' which lay beneath the entangled quarrels of their time. But Luther did, and so did Lainez. Each of these mighty minds grasped its own position, dwelt on principles, and drew out consequences unflinchingly. The types were not to be assimilated.

And each remained a victor in the field he had chosen. The priest gave way to the layman in all countries where Reform got the upper hand. In Catholic nations the power of the Pope, weakened by two centuries of strife and degradation, recovered much of its vitality. Not only the articles of belief which Trent had published, but its decrees on discipline, found apt instruments in the Jesuit teachers and confessors, who enforced them wherever the Society spread. St. Ignatius had petitioned for the Council ; his sons had appeared in it as theologians sent by the Pope or delegated by princes. The amazing memory, eloquence, piety, of Lainez had given him a place among the Fathers like that of the deacon Athanasius at Nicaea. When he fell ill, the Council waited for his days of convalescence. Hardly a shadow now haunts the reformed churches of Luther's doctrine ; but the interpretation which was declared at Trent, largely under Jesuit guidance, to be orthodox Christianity, has filtered into Anglican and even Dissenting pulpits. Calvinism has provoked a violent reaction, lapsing into unbelief generally, but sometimes impelling the children of Huguenots to embrace the ancient faith. Of Protestant creeds how small a portion is left ! But Trent, which was the prelude to the Council of the Vatican, abides every Christian challenge, and though Luther be the name best known, Lainez accomplished the more enduring feat.

In this way, undreamt of when he set out, has Ignatius the Basque, to be called Loyola by myriads that hate and admire him, fulfilled his vocation. Wearing neither tiara nor mitre, he has become the general of the Catholic army, his light horse scouring all regions, pushing back the hosts of Apollyon the destroyer, encamped lately under the walls of Rome. Discipline is tightened, the faith crystallised into adamantine propositions, the Papacy itself (shall we dare to utter the word ?) reformed. A layman has conceived the plan, a layman written the book of meditations, second only to the ' Following of Christ,' by which the miraculous change is effected.

An enthusiast, if you will, a saint according to Catholic uses and principles, has been given in the very crisis of her fate to the Roman Church, and after doubts, amid conflicting voices, she has recognised her heaven-sent champion. From now onwards, starting with Melchior Cano the Dominican, that suspicion and dislike which Thompson hits off in a sentence, ' the convinced hostility of honourable men,' will never be wanting to the new Templars. ' If these Religious Orders go on as they have begun,' said Cano, ' God forbid that a time should come when kings shall desire to withstand them and find it impossible.' The time did come ; it is not yet ended.

But Ignatius enjoyed, in his deep silent way, the felicity seldom granted to mortals, of beholding, ere he had reached his sixtieth year, the enterprise successful and acknowledged, that little by little had been revealed to him. Continually retouching the ' Exercises,' proving and revising the ' Constitutions,' he laid sure bases for the future. With exquisite suavity, there was no judgment of any of those around him which he did not consult ; but the master-mind, or, as he humbly said, the vision shown him at Manresa, prevailed over all. Attempts, neither exact in details nor betraying much critical acumen, have been made to rob him of those ' Exercises,' on the ground that he borrowed them from Cisneros. We might as well take his plays from Shakespeare because they are founded on history. The system and spirit of that wonderful text-book, which has taught generations how to pray, did not exist before Ignatius ; they are utterly original, yet beyond suspicion orthodox.

Equally without precedent are the rules and ordering of the Company itself ; so much so that strong exception has been taken to them, and to this day is not unknown, by contemplatives who love the cloister, choristers who delight in the Liturgy, men of spontaneous instinct who prefer freedom to so stern a discipline, and praisers of old time who miss in their stricter practical directions the poetry that cast a gleam over the age of the Fathers and mediaeval Christendom. Every several Order appears to have found its own text, a motto and an inspiration, in Holy Writ. The Benedictine murmurs 'Pax,' the Franciscan 'Beati pauperes,' the Friars Preachers would cry 'Dominus illuminatio mea.' What of the paladins of St. Ignatius ? For them this word is enough, 'Obedite praepositis vestris.' Obedience amid surrounding anarchy is the virtue they prize. Much as they have cultivated science and taught classic literature, it is to military Rome or disciplined Sparta that we look for their model, rather than to the Athens of Pericles.

A year before he died, the General handed over his government of the Society to three men, one of them Polanco, long his secretary, a Jew by descent, but to Ignatius, as it were, 'hands and feet.' St. Francis Borgia was greatly increasing the Jesuit influence among Spaniards. In Rome the College of the German nation was opened. The illustrious Roman College, afterwards made the Gregorian University, belongs to the same period. The new and fruitful idea of training clerics from every part under the shadow of St. Peter was acted on. From Goa to Mexico the movement was spreading which united scholarship with piety, and sanctified the secular life by devotion to the inward spirit. Ignatius himself had carried on an administration equal to that of a kingdom ;

yet no day passed on which he did not give hours to prayer. His 'singular dignity and recollection' were due to this waiting on the Divine presence for light. In all things deliberate, he, like Lord Burghley, set down the reasons for and against every measure with a fullness that seemed to belie his gift of intuition ; but his counsel was eagerly sought, and the Spanish envoy remarked that to follow it was to succeed, to oppose it disaster.

Always courteous, moderate in speech and tone, a ' fountain of oil ' to his brethren so long as they acted in the spirit of the Society, avoiding preferences, or betraying them only by the heavier burdens he laid on those whom he could not help liking, the Saint lived and died ' alone with the Alone.' His natural disposition did not run counter to the view which he adopted of a life hidden in God. We cannot pretend to know him as we know his friend and admirer, St. Philip Neri, whose gaiety and charming eccentricities may have brought a smile to those resolutely silent lips. There was even in the Basque temperament a somewhat saturnine humour, a flash of lightning that made short work of opposition. Ignatius could be patient with strong, impetuous characters, such as had been his in the days of youth. He would not brook self-will in another, unqualified by heroism ; he was never cruel, but on occasion severe. In dealing with great persons, with worldly-minded churchmen, still bearing on their purple some taint of the Renaissance, he considered the good which might be gained through them in an evil hour. He rebuked Bobadilla, who had censured Charles V for his device of the ' Interim ' too loudly. Towards cardinals like Alessandro Farnese his conduct was determined by their ostensible claims on respect.

In a court where nepotism flourished, what else could be done ? His mild wisdom overcame the long pre-possession against him of the Neapolitan Caraffa, who could not but detest all Spaniards, and who, as Paul IV, provoked King Philip into a war which brought Alva to the gates of Rome. One may say that it was impossible to make an enemy of Ignatius, chiefly because he had learnt his own lesson touching ' the use of creatures,' and he was a friend on the same rule of detachment or philosophy, whichever we define it to be. Altogether, we may see in him the hermit turned states-man, who, from within a magic circle that none dared to cross, controlled not his Order alone but the policy of Popes and the legislation of Councils, towards an end of which he never lost sight.

That end was the triumph of a Catholicism strong at the centre, ruling from Rome as in the days of St. Gregory VII, with his own Company for its picked militia, and all the kingdoms of the world obedient to St. Peter's Chair. In one word, his governing idea was Theocracy. And a Papal Theocracy, for what other could there be ? In the sixteenth century abso-lute, government held sway, not only in fact but in theory ; between the fall of feudalism and the rise of democracy no politician could have suggested any more liberal system with a chance of establishing it. Again we must remark that each Religious Order bears the stamp of the times and circumstances under which it arose. The Company of Jesus sprang up in a period of revolt and reaction. It is a product of the Renais-sance, and it took over the absolute politics as well as the art and literature which it found in esteem but did not create. Its Latin style, correct but seldom charac-teristic, was derived from the Humanists. It has never felt in sympathy with the strong, rude, but heart-stirring romance of the Middle Ages, whether in prose or in verse. Its poet is Vida, not Dante ; its theologian Suarez or Molina, elegant and acute, but exponents of a system which St. Thomas Aquinas would not have signed all through. Its tendencies were not at all towards Platonism ; and in physics as well as metaphysics it has pursued a line of its own. Those who indulge in analogies, fantastical but sometimes not wholly false, may be tempted to consider that St. Ignatius in the ' Exercises' did for religion what Descartes in his ' Discourse on Method' did for philosophy. In both, at all events, the individual starting from clear principles, as if alone in the universe, arrives by introspection at a sure belief in spiritual realities and a law of duty. But enough of these speculations.

On July 31, 1556, Ignatius died in Rome of malarial fever. His last moments were solitary. There is nothing to record of them except the perfect patience with which he passed out of a troubled scene. If the Catholic religion were all that its enemies charge upon it, then had Loyola been ' the most offending soul alive,' for he shaped its policy in a fashion that not only secured it from the fate of pagan Rome, but in less than half a century defeated the most formidable enemies it had ever encountered. That he should be raised upon its altars was a recognition of his unmatched and unexhausted merits. St. Augustine had bestowed on its teachers a philosophy ; the poor man of Assisi had, by renewing the Gospel in a tumultuous age, brought back to it the common people ; St. Dominic had won the Universities. But St. Ignatius, when culture and religion, as it seemed, were banding themselves against

the decadent Papacy, had in his single heart discovered
how culture might be made Christian and religion
proved still to be Catholic. Education, missionary
enterprise, works of charity, spiritual direction—he
seized on all these ways of creating an orthodox and
civilised world in which the successor of the Apostle
should rule supreme. His own life was a page of some
chivalrous tale ; let him be called Don Quixote, so
long as we render to the story its nobler meaning and
see the knight-errant victorious in his quest. The
world changes ; absolute rule is dead ; shoreless
democracy is sweeping in ; the word, let us hope the
reality, of the days to come will be freedom. But the
Church needed saving four hundred years ago by other
means, and the man chosen on high was Ignatius.
A poet, marked with the sign of the cross, imaginative,
true to fact, splendid in delineation, has taken the
tongue of Shakespeare, Ralegh, Milton, and in words
of flame has depicted the heroic figure. It is a tribute
and a trophy. I congratulate English Catholics on
this superb achievement ; but the irony and the pity
of it are worthy of tears.

IX

CATHOLICISM AND THE SPIRIT
OF THE EAST [1]

THIS year (1911) Italy is keeping festival in remembrance of the battles, sieges and votings by which, half a century ago, she began her career as a kingdom, one and indivisible. In the same rejoicings are caught up a series of strange events which made Rome her capital and a modern city. On the other hand, Catholics, of whatever nation, have marked September 20, 1870, as a *dies nefastus* in their calendar. It was the day when those new Lombards, under leadership from the House of Savoy, broke through the Roman walls, and the Holy Father entered on a captivity that has lasted forty years. Ever since the drama has gone forward without pause which sets the King over against the Pope, divides the Quirinal from the Vatican, and throws between them a Parliament at Monte Citorio. The ' sacred and immemorial throne,' as Disraeli with his large imagination called it, whence Europe was taught and ruled, has fallen. The ' new civilisation ' reigns in its stead. Hence the everlasting quarrel, the two Romes, and the strongly opposed characters given to this memorial year by the victors and the vanquished of 1870.

We are looking on, in truth, at a world's debate,

[1] *Marc-Aurèle et la Fin du Monde Antique.* Par Ernest Renan. Neuvième édition. Paris : 1903.

Q

to the vast implications and issues of which Italians brought up in the school of Machiavelli pay little heed. Astute politicians, they are seldom philosophers ; their mind dwells in the concrete, the local, the lines and forms to which they have been accustomed. They cannot see that Rome belongs to mankind. Rome which like Jerusalem, like Athens, is the ' city of the soul,' the place where all histories meet, these narrow-minded imitators of French-English constitutions would transform to a second-rate Paris, with its boule-vards, cafés chantants, debating clubs, parliamentary cliques and the other adornments of latter-day civilisa-tion. Rome, the capital of Italy, is no longer to be Rome, the capital of Christendom. For to the intellect fashioned by Machiavelli Christendom is an exploded idea. It has had it day. Under many names, and after vicissitudes which fill the last four centuries, that view of life discovered at the Renaissance now inspires literature, shapes the laws, dominates the school, the university, the newspaper. It colours the whole horizon. It has made to itself eyes, hands and feet in ten thousand ministers who do its will. Regarded as culture its admirers term it Humanism ; as a theory of government it is liberal and democratic ; when it touches religion it professes ignorance and toleration, but its very silence is denial and its outcome hatred of the supernatural in every form. Wherever it holds power, and in whatever degree, the Catholic faith suffers. As we might expect, its presence and its policy reveal themselves in the Latin world with a peculiar distinctness of outline. This idea it is which entered Rome in triumph with the Italian army, which has shut up the Holy Father in the Vatican, and which keeps its royal jubilee in the year now passing over us.

What, then, is the power, certainly neither tangible nor visible, that traces round the Pope a magic ring within which he is safe, which his enemies dare not cross and which has enabled him to live in their sight when other dispossessed sovereigns have gone into exile ?   Temporal dominion beyond the Vatican garden he has none.   Guarantees from the governments of Europe, though talked about, were never given to him and do not exist.   He is quite helpless.   To be elected successor of St. Peter is to share St. Peter's prison. Three of the Roman pontiffs have thus lived a secluded life, which to the generation born since the breach of Porta Pia must seem to be their natural condition. If we were not used to it, should we not think it altogether the contrary, a miracle of Providence or an outrage inflicted by men and not to be endured ?   There is no other sovereign in the world at once so absolute and so feeble.   What is the account of it ?   On every line of assault by arms and diplomacy the Pope has undergone defeat after defeat.   Humanly speaking, he has lost all he ever had, during the ill-starred eighty years that separate Pius X from the accession of Gregory XVI.   Yet he neither leaves Rome nor surrenders nor dies.   He disposes by unquestioned fiat of the fortunes and possessions of the Church in France ; he puts down Modernism ;   he creates a world-wide legislation ;   he is a name and an influence which no State can afford to overlook.   If he were only a King, he might be deposed ;   if but a man of genius and nothing more he would have to charm or persuade before winning followers.   What is he, then, that he should remain alive and invulnerable after all these strokes ?

We reply that he is the embodiment of Eastern

religion in an imperial Western power. He sums up in his own person and expands into all his institutions an idea distinct from the ideas of the West, self-sustained, aboriginal, the expression of realities that modern civilisation did not call into being and is impotent to destroy. Because the Pope holds of the East he can defy the West. Because he is throned in the West he can evangelise the East. Rome is the centre, therefore it never will sink to be merely the capital of Italy. By position, by history, by outlook, by aspiration, these ecumenical attributes of the Papacy are justified. Even the shadows which at a remote distance fall from the unity of ancient Christendom, founders of sects, generals of Salvation Armies, prophets and prophetesses after whom the ignorant crowd dances and runs mad, would never have known how to conjure up a free Church, had the spiritual might of Rome not shown them the way. It is discipline, cries one ; or the gift of exploiting enthusiasm, answers another ; it is Jesuit cunning, say many more ; it is shameless self-affirmation, pretended miracles, age-long establishment. But a simpler, deeper philosophy would bid us consider if it be not something elemental, mysterious, perhaps divine—the secret which was revealed to man (primitive and not yet civilised), never utterly forgotten in the East, a living energy whereby we attain to union with the Everlasting. And this not private ecstasy but public communion. What we perceive as the outward tangible form of Catholicism we may fix in the word hierarchy ; but the inward essence that gives it life is the vision of faith ; and if the form be Roman, the spirit is Eastern. Combining these elements as the course of ages exhibits them, we find ourselves face to face with a Theocracy.

Theocracy in modern, scientific, democratised
Europe and America, that is the wonder.   On that,
and on nothing else, the debate, whether by argument
or force of arms, will surely be seen to turn, if we do
not confuse our minds by a multitude of side issues.
The claim is a challenge to every power in the world.
It cannot be given up ; it survives the individual Pontiff ; and it is strong in possessing a local habitation
and a name more august than the cities of men dare
question.   For they are but secular capitals while
Rome is sacred.   In the apologetics of an older stamp
weight was laid on the ' undesigned coincidences ' to
be met with in Holy Scripture.   A fruitful theme
would be the designed or Providential coincidences of
history, and ' Roma Sacra ' points the most significant
among them.   We have already dwelt upon it ; but
our train of thought demands that we should here in
a few strokes sum up the remarkable story.[1]   Let our
drift be indicated beyond mistake.   As we are now
considering those facts which determine the fortunes
of religion, Rome and Jerusalem are, so to speak, the
vital centres, the foci, of that orbit along whose path
Christianity moves.   Jerusalem leads up to Rome ;
and in Rome the idea which lay at the heart of Israel
finds its universal expression, its fulcrum, and its law.
Rome is the Western Israel.   Or, as on an earlier
occasion we ventured to phrase it, St. Peter has become
the Pontifex Maximus.   In taking over that title,
which antedates the New Testament, St. Peter's successor absorbs Rome.   He does more.   He seems
to tell the nations that Rome was waiting for him.
The Lateran is thereby exalted above the Capitol, and
in Dantean language ' has ascended beyond mortal

[1] See *Dublin Review*, July 1907, ' Roma Sacra.'

things.' To the poet and the philosopher, bent on
' contemplation of the high effect,' it seemed clear that
Aeneas, the pilgrim of eternity according to Virgil,
came into the line of prophetic forecast:

> Since he of Rome, and of Rome's empire wide,
> In heaven's empyreal height was chosen sire ;
> Both which, if truth be spoken, were ordained
> And 'stablished for the Holy Place, where sits
> Who to great Peter's sacred chair succeeds.[1]

This origin of Rome from the East, not as we
might well imagine from the colonies that brought into
Magna Graecia the arts and culture of Hellas, proved
to be the turning-point in human events. It is a
legend made beautiful by Virgilian enchantment ; we
may also hold it true, since the Greeks never established
their claim to a foundation by the Tiber. And while
tradition spoke without wavering of an old descent
from Lydia to which the Etruscans traced their pedigree, the Romans themselves venerated Troy as their
Alma Mater. The argument runs thus : if Rome was
not an Hellenic outpost (and it never was), the peculiar
hieratic style which always clung to it, and which is
equally discernible in Cicero, in Virgil, in Livy, otherwise so unlike as writers, can be accounted for only by
taking as well founded the Oriental ancestry this proud
people accepted. Phrygian or Lydian, its affinities
were of a deeply religious character. The first King
of Rome was made the god Quirinus ; the first
Emperor, Augustus, was deified while yet living. On
these facts and all they imply as regards ' sacred Rome '
we need not enlarge a second time. But there is an
inference of moment to be drawn from the vicissitudes
which Roman policy underwent in its long struggle

[1] *Inf.* ii. 20.

with invading Eastern cults.   It cast them out again
and again ; nevertheless, they conquered in the end.
Greek letters and Greek art have taken up their abode
more than once on the Palatine or the Vatican ; but
among the Seven Hills no Greek was ever quite at
home.   Dilettante or parasite, the true Hellene
brought thither waited on his master's pleasures ; he
served, he did not reign.   It was the Oriental who dictated his religion to Greek and Roman, the strange
unearthly mystic and initiate from beyond the pale
of the Forum and the Schools, not Epicurean or Stoic
or Lawyer, whom Clement of Alexandria and Tatian
call the Barbarian.   We employ this term with later
chroniclers to designate the tribes of the North.   But
in Clement it signifies the everlasting opposition between Greeks who argue and Easterns who meditate.
Rome despised the Greeks but yielded submissively at
length to the yoke of these Barbarians.

Not, we say, until after a struggle, and that lasting,
perhaps, five hundred years.   Rome as a divine yet
military State held, like all other associations of the
same type, to its First Commandment, which ran,
' Thou shalt not have strange gods before me.'   These
foreign (exotic) deities were to the colleges of pontiffs
and augurs anathema, save when brought home to the
Capitol from vanquished cities.   Any worship alien
from the rites and traditions of the tribes dwelling
within the consecrated bounds of the Pomoerium was
high treason as well as sacrilege.   Church and State
were one.   The Kings might be driven out ; the
priesthood remained.   It could not perish, for ' the
great immortals known as gods,' whom it represented
and propitiated, were themselves rulers over Rome.
We have elsewhere observed that when Virgil speaks

of the ' Pater Romanus,' it is impossible to say whether
he has in mind Mars who begot Romulus, or Romulus
who dedicated the city for Mars, or Augustus who had
become their living image and their vicar. If he
meant all three it would be in accordance with patriotic
feeling. This identification ran its natural course, ever
widening in scope and attributes, as the city on the
Tiber grew to be the capital of the civilised world.
Rome was the great goddess ; the Emperor enjoyed
divine honours ; his home on the Palatine had all
the sanctity of a temple ; and the Pontifex Maximus
reigned from the Euphrates to the Atlantic.[1] Modern
historians, knowing all this in detail, have seldom
allowed the hieratic figure of Rome to occupy their
pages. To them religion is but the accessory or the
background of political movements, and the Emperor
a mere prince of this world. But ancient history cannot be understood by casting it into secular moulds.
Before all things, it is the record of a conflict between
various ideas and institutions which aimed at controlling divine mysteries.

Be it observed that no exclusive truth, in the sense
which is familiar to us, no dogma, entered into the conception of the old religious City-State. Intolerance
there was, but it regarded the violation of caste by
taking part in foreign rites with which as a native
citizen one had no concern. These imported and
often secret ceremonies were condemned as infamous
crimes, detestably wicked and unclean. The language
employed, for example, by Livy touching the Bacchic
assemblies on their first introduction at Rome, is full
of a shuddering disgust ; and it has not, perhaps, been

---

[1] Ovid (*Fasti*, iv. 949) says the House of the Pontifex on the Palatine
was shared by three gods, Apollo, Vesta, Augustus.

remarked how closely resembling it are the words of
Tacitus when he describes Christianity and almost
apologises for Nero, as putting down a horrible superstition.   In Tacitus we read, ' quos per flagitia invisos
vulgus Christianos appellabat ' ; and he explains the
presence of these wretches in the city as a place ' quo
cuncta undique atrocia aut pudenda confluunt cele-
branturque.'   Where crime abounded Christians were
likely to flourish.   Livy reports of the Bacchanalians,
' nihil nefas ducere, hanc summam inter eos religionem
esse.'   Entirely germane to our subject is the consul's
declaration made in public on this critical juncture ;
' How often,' he exclaims, ' have not the magistrates
been commissioned to forbid exotic rites, to drive out
of the Forum, the circus, the city, strange priests and
soothsayers, to search after and to burn their books of
prophecy, and to abolish utterly whatsoever form of
sacrifice differed from the Roman ? '   For, he goes on
to conclude, ' the wisest among lawyers and divines are
agreed that nothing is so apt to destroy religion as
offering sacrifice in a foreign way and not as our fathers
have bidden us.'   The lists were open ; persecution
(so we should call it now) had begun.   Such numbers
were guilty or in danger that Rome put on the likeness
of a solitude.   The Senate decreed that no Bacchana-
lian festivities should be held in the city or in Italy.[1]

We may, nevertheless, reckon from this year,
186 B.C., to the year of Christ 313, as a period during
which the ancient rites were yielding little by little
to Eastern influences, until with Constantine's edict
they acknowledged their defeat.   Bacchus returned in

[1] Compare the pregnant phrase in Tacitus, about Jewish proselytes
(*Hist.* v. 5), ' Pessimus quisque spretis religionibus patriis.'   The other
references are to Tacitus, *Annals*, xv. 44 ; Livy, xxxix. 13, 16.

triumph ; Isis followed ; the Idaean mother, Cybele, herself a Phrygian goddess, took possession of the Palatine under Augustus (see the inscription of Ancyra). Gods from every land might now be harboured in the city, which grew more and more indifferent to the rude old ceremonies and unintelligible chants (*carmina*) so long deemed the safeguard of its power. The names and offices continued, but they had lost their significance. The civil wars had bled even to the white those genuine Roman families, patrician and plebeian, to whose inbred piety the religion of Numa might appeal. Eclectic and decadent, Roman society found exciting pleasures, as well as a vague sense of the sublime and perhaps of comfort, in the mysteries, Egyptian, Syrian, Persian, to which men and women thronged, after Augustus had for a brief season restored the prestige of Italian devotions. But whereas in their aggressive time, the Roman people found their god a tower of strength, now who was there that believed in Mars Gradivus, in ' high Jove ' himself ? No suggestion of the infinite or the eternal breathed from these dumb idols. Crude and gross, magnified men of an epoch which dealt not in philosophy, and which identified the soul with blood or ghost or vapour, of all divinities worshipped by mortals the native Roman were least divine.

Moreover, a new mental atmosphere was making itself felt among the vast population, whether of slaves or free men, but certainly drawn by the thousand from Oriental provinces to Rome, who cared as little about the indigenous gods as Russian Jews in America may be supposed to care about Puritanism. Thus a twofold movement meets the historian's gaze when he looks upon the Imperial centuries as a whole. There is always a Pontifex Maximus on the throne, with colleges of priests and augurs complete ; but with religion, inward or spiritual, they have nothing in common. Beneath and around this hierarchy a current of life is flowing which seems to issue forth from the unseen and to return thither. Old Rome was mighty as an armed State. The new Rome, struggling towards the light of day, has no weapon but the promise to all who will take it, of regeneration. Isis or Mithras, not so much pitted against Divus Caesar as transcending him by a mystical philosophy, win adepts from all sides. What is to be the fate of the Eternal City ?

Marcus Aurelius, the Stoic saint and philosopher-king, might have seemed more likely than Augustus to preserve the old hieratic mythology from decay. But even Marcus restored the solemnities of Isis which Augustus had forbidden, and he was devoted to the ' new gods.' Fusion, or syncretism, while resolving the distinct personalities which had once created legends into vague (one had almost said Ossianic) forms, led on to the more intimate, ecstasy-provoking and secret ritual, in which the State had no part at all. These religions foreshadowed the Catholic idea ; they were at once universal and individual ; whoever joined them passed within the veil. We may compare them to a widespread Freemasonry ; and it is clear that on certain points they suggest as in a confused dream observances not unlike the vows and self-mortifications which a purer faith was to consecrate. Too often they may have been but the ' epitome of the Pagan world,' showing ' the depth of its corruption and its perfection of form.' It will ever astonish and perplex the historian that Marcus, perfect in his lofty kind, should have passed away leaving no trace on the Roman conscience ; and that an effeminate Syrian boy, a priest from the Lebanon, should have seated himself in fantastic vestments over against Capitoline Jove, on the Palatine, to which he ' attempted to remove,' says Gibbon, ' the ancilia, the Palladium, and all the sacred pledges of the faith of Numa.' Yet, as the same acute writer observes, ' this holy vocation '—the priesthood of the Sun—' embraced either from prudence or superstition, contributed to raise the Syrian youth to the Empire of Rome.' Thus the City-State, forsaking its guardian gods, and under Caracalla granting its right of citizenship to all who would buy it from the exchequer, had abdicated. Henceforth Rome is the prey of the strong hand ; the West awaits a master and a religion.

Meanwhile, in the words of Suetonius, who quotes them as a prophecy, ' men issuing from Judaea ' had appeared in the world's centre, and by preaching and martyrdom had made good their claim to it. Nero burnt Rome and crucified St. Peter. That day, possibly August 1, in the year 64, when the Vatican circus blazed with living victims and the Prince of the Apostles died there, was, after the day of Calvary itself, says Renan, ' the most solemn in Christian history.' No reflecting mind will deny that when Peter and Paul succeeded in popular imagination to Romulus and Remus a new Rome came into sight. Within thirty years from the Apostles' death we are listening to the accents of a new lawgiver in St. Clement's Letter to the Corinthians. This venerable document strikes the keynote of all future encyclicals, sober, judicial, authoritative, a judgment rather than a pleading. It indulges in no Greek subtleties of argument ; it avoids esoteric jargon ; it has the majesty and the grace of a

Senatus-Consultum marked with the sign of the cross. There, we say on reading it, speaks the Roman genius, but converted and baptised.   St. Clement's Letter is the happiest fusion of a spiritual creed with sacerdotal forms.

But now the Roman Christian, like his predecessor in the pages of Livy, had this recurring problem to solve —how should he deal with Eastern mystics, fanatics, Gnostics ? with Illuminati who took their inspiration, or at least their point of departure, from the Gospel or St. Paul ? If we would measure the extent and the perils of such an enterprise, thrust upon a Church always liable to persecution even from mild officials like the younger Pliny, we may glance over the scene of bewilderment sketched, when things had a little calmed down, by St. Irenaeus, himself an Asiatic and Bishop of Lyons.   From about A.D. 120, when Hadrian was Emperor, crisis followed upon crisis, associated with leading men who, if not so much thinkers as dreamers, knew how to entrance multitudes. Such were Basilides, Valentinus, Marcion, Saturninus, Montanus, prophets wild and austere, sometimes perhaps giving just grounds of scandal to their enemies, but without exception transforming the faith to romantic systems in which it was utterly ruined, or corrupting the Scriptures, or else throwing open the creed to every vagary of private judgment.   All these sects ' had in common a tendency towards moral indifference,' says Renan, ' a dangerous quietism.'   And he continues, ' their stiffnecked docetism, their attribution of the Old and New Testaments to contrary gods, their aversion to marriage, their denial of the Resurrection and the Last Day, shut them out from a Church whose rulers observed moderation and shunned extravagance.   It was on the rock of ecclesiastical discipline, represented by the Bishops, that all these movements of disorder were dashed in pieces.'[1]

At Rome, very early, or perhaps first of all, the name of the Catholic Church was uttered. By the time of Anicetus and Soter a visible centre of the hierarchy is not to be mistaken, shown by the Pope's large correspondence with other Churches, by his world-wide charities, by the pilgrimages and appeals to the ' most ancient Church,' as Irenaeus terms it, of orthodox and heterodox, for we find the most opposite of combatants hastening to plead their cause before the Apostle's shrine. Catholics, again says Renan with profound insight, ' took the Church as it was ' ; they turned away from the heresiarchs who had fallen in love with their own chimeras. Rome might be dogmatic, in the sense of maintaining tradition unaltered ; but Rome never was speculative, or fanciful, or subject to attacks of mere enthusiasm. Her apologists had reason on their side as well as the traditional understanding of the Gospels. If proconsular Asia and Roman Africa were the chief battlefields where Gnostics and Montanists fought for their unwholesome reveries, in those very regions the hierarchy was united and strong, while Rome sustained it with an unfaltering hand. Dogma set bounds to Greek-Oriental theorising ; the exclusive administration of the Sacraments by an ordained clergy saved Christian grace from degenerating into the convulsions which prophets and prophetesses imagined to be signs of a heavenly presence. The Papacy and the sacramental system had by the reign of Callistus, say in 220, won their triumph over anarchy.

[1] *Marc-Aurèle*, p. 137.

Great problems lay in the future unresolved ; but the Roman method of dealing with them was now firmly established.   A new Pontifex Maximus, according to the gibe of Tertullian, had appeared.   The Empire could not survive upon its ancient lines ; the West fell into divisions which portended nationalities yet to be born ; the East was no longer well read in Greek philosophy and was forgetting Greek literature. In the Papacy alone did the true Roman valour, the practical wisdom, which had been the secret of Roman conquest, display its force.   Catholicism was already in idea bound to the Chair of St. Peter.   When St. Cyprian wrote ' De Unitate Ecclesiae,' manifestly his arguments might be turned to advantage by Rome. Not private inspiration nor abstract ideas were to govern the rising Christendom, but a power deep-rooted in history, true to its trust, a Practical Reason deciding with authority what it could accept and what it must reject in order to preserve the creed.[1]   Its method was judicial and moved by precedent ; its acts illustrated the reign of law.   The Pope did not profess to be an original thinker, but the guardian of a treasure confided to him.   With Hellenic systems he had no direct concern ; yet he was free to pass his verdict upon them so far as they expressed or traversed the doctrines of Catholicism.   In like manner he sifted the religious experiences submitted to his view by Orientals without becoming an Eastern.   But his rule was already distinguished as theocratic, and St. Peter's commission was its charter.

Rome had, therefore, to provide against the analytic or rationalising tendencies of the Greek, who was bent on making of Christian truths a mere abstract scheme.

[1] ' Cette belle autorité raisonnable,' Renan, *Marc-Aurèle*, p. 633.

But it was just as much her duty not to suffer the mystic—Egyptian, Phrygian, Syrian, perhaps even the far-off disciple of Buddha—to indulge his wild fancies, to be secret and, as was all too likely, antinomian. Reason must be the handmaid of Revelation ; spiritual gifts must submit to be tested by authority. St. Ignatius of Antioch had insisted on the Bishop's rule as the rule of faith almost within St. John's lifetime. The local hierarchies condemned and cast out dissenters, Ebionite and Gnostic, Montanist and Donatist. Consider what would have been the fate of religion had Papal Rome blessed any one of these widely ranging sects. But Rome invariably rejected them, and by a simple axiom, ' Nihil innovetur.' St. Irenaeus found in Catholic consent and episcopal union the only safeguard against contrary but destructive systems, both of which aimed at supplanting the Gospel ; we may not unfairly describe them as Illuminism and Rationalism. The Cathedra Petri was from the beginning destined to make war on such aberrations of sentiment and intellect with a success equal to its vigour.

To the Greeks we owe heresies, councils, dogmatically worded creeds, the Byzantine Emperors, and the schism of Photius. To the Orientals we owe monasticism on the one side and the victory of Islam on the other. Greeks in their hatred of mystery, trained by Aristotle to logic and its demand for plain terms with conclusions intelligible to the average mind, were led by Arius and Nestorius to deny Christ as He is revealed in the New Testament. Alexandria, that is to say Egypt, became monophysite in its passion for ecstatic enjoyment of God. These two forces, not controlled by the sense of Catholic brotherhood, rent asunder the great civilised realm which extended from

Illyria to Armenia, and from Thrace to the Libyan desert. They made not for unity, but for disruption ; with what sad consequences let the Saracen and the Turk declare. Rome, as in previous troubles, knew how to hold firm, how to discriminate between parties which only a hair seemed to divide, and which were yet irreconcilable. No praise can exhaust the wisdom that upheld St. Athanasius against the Eusebians, and restored the good name of St. John Chrysostom. If, as Catholics believe, a more than human sagacity was guiding the Holy See in these judgments, it is at any rate sure that history has ratified them. We need not expect in a system putting forth its first essays towards ecumenical action the style or the procedure it was hereafter to adopt. Enough that a law of tendency is visible ; that instances fall into line ; that, while the East is breaking up, the West is coming by force even of its utter desolation to rely on St. Peter as holding the keys of faith and culture.

But the last great gift which Orientals bestowed on the Latin world was brought to the Tiber and the Rhine by St. Athanasius. An exile, yet welcome in Rome, he spread abroad the knowledge of monasticism among Westerns. It encountered opposition, it underwent significant changes. The clergy did not always heartily approve of this Vita Nova, with its severe practices. Priscillian, the Spaniard, made asceticism a cloak for Gnostic delusions and paid the penalty on the scaffold. Yet men so typically Roman as Pope Damasus and the ever memorable Saints, Ambrose, Augustine and Jerome, did all that in them lay to favour the monks. With St. Benedict their future is assured. When we speak of religion during the Middle Ages we cannot but mean a theocracy the head

R

of which was the Pope and its chief stay the religious orders. St. Gregory the Great begins a restoration which St. Gregory VII completes of the Roman power, informed by the spirit of the East.

These unquestioned facts bring us to a remarkable conclusion. Papal Rome has never changed its attitude towards philosophy, towards the friends of the Inner Light, towards monastic ideals, towards secular governments. Surely, it never will. And that is the world's quarrel with it. Whenever the Latin State rebels against Christian truth, its policy falls into the same track. It breaks off diplomatic relations with Rome and proceeds to suppress the monasteries. What is called in France ' anticlericalism ' we may learn to understand if we will hear it described by M. Faguet; but, however shaped or disguised, it starts up in its genuine form when confronted with the Pope or the monks. For it aims at unlimited sovereignty, and it cannot endure to be told of righteousness, temperance and judgment to come. Monastic life throws into the strongest opposition East against West ; it affirms the transcendent, the supernatural, not by rhetoric such as delighted the literary imagination of Seneca, but by acts, by renouncements, by an expressive silence, by a most trying obedience, by simply going out of the world and refusing to continue in it. There is the scandal which provoked men like Nietzsche to brand and scourge Christianity as the religion of slaves, as decadence reduced to a science, as the death of art, freedom, manliness. The monk in this view is a low-caste horror, and his Church the congregation of the unclean. He is the vilest of democrats, an insult and a menace to life at its best. And the Pope is the monk's champion. In outward seeming the Vatican is a palace, a library, a museum of beautiful antiques ; but inwardly it is a convent and the Pontifex Maximus a friar. He wears the white wool of St. Dominic ; he lives in retreat ; he is a King who says Mass ; and he never dies. How is the modern State to cope with him ?

The modern State ! Few Englishmen have so much as made an attempt to grasp what that State is, especially in countries which, modelled on the Code Napoléon, are still governed by the Imperial Roman Law. The Code or the Law, whichever we choose to name it, is a lay institution, affecting unlimited power. It recognises no god but itself, and it would fain be the City-State, now no longer believing in Jupiter Optimus Maximus. No rights, individual or collective, exist for such a government except those which it has distinctly granted. Secular education is its chief instrument whereby to create in all citizens a type of mind corresponding to the ideals, of the earth earthy, which it sets up in stern opposition to the ' other-world ' notions entertained by Christians. It exacts obedience to its slightest commands ; but it leaves the will undisciplined, the conscience a blank, and the character wanting in self-control. It can teach nothing beyond words and civic ceremonies. Consequently it leaves the mind of youth a chaos, without light or law. The morality of laicism, resting on self-interest but professing devotion to the commonweal, is hypocrisy made perfect. The State decrees to itself divine honours ; but who will pay them except in lip-worship and hollow platitudes ? This loudly acclaimed patriotism, as a substitute for Christianity, cannot but make us smile. Men have known greater gods ; they will not stoop except in mockery to adore the Lares and Penates of a parliamentary régime.

But the State is resolved to be absolute. What, then, will it answer when the Pope declines its jurisdiction ? It allows no other society a free existence ; the Catholic Church claims to be independent by divine right. Education is to be a State monopoly ; but Catholic teachers obey their own code, which includes a philosophy of life and action not consistent with ' lay ' ethics ; how can they be silenced ? The State is really a Church in disguise, the Church of unbelief, with dogmas of its own, though negatively expressed. And ' vulgar rationalism ' in France or Italy destroys but cannot build up. It is neither honest nor serious ; it brings no comfort ; it has long ceased to shine by wit or to stir by the poetry of revolution. The State, says M. Faguet, speaking of the Third Republic, cultivates anticlericalism that it may not be devoured by Socialist agitators. It has indeed law on its side and the public resources ; the common school is its preserve, the university its enclosed garden. Officials are its slaves and voters dare not oppose it. Scandals and abuses leave it intact. Civilisation appears to be in its keeping. And is not Theocracy, as was said, an exploded idea ? [1]

So we have travelled round to the beginning. Renaissance and Revelation, the powers of the world that now is and the powers of the world to come, are seen struggling at every point in the vast orbit of civilisation. If Humanism, if science, can satisfy the whole man, building up his life in reason and equity, kindling his imagination with lofty dreams and spurring him on to realise them, no doubt the West will have conquered the East for evermore. The West, reinforced by the North, or in terms of race, the Greeks

[1] Renan, *Marc-Aurèle*, p. 587.

and the Teutons, who together furnish all that thinks
and all that acts in the State, so far as it is not Christian.
It may be objected, ' But is not the Roman Church
permeated with Greek and Teuton elements also ?
How, then, do they constitute a specific difference
outside it ? ' The answer is simple and momentous.
Forces are differentiated by forms (to use the language
of St. Thomas) ; or, as we now speak, the spirit of
a system determines its nature and efficacy. The
Roman Church embodies for all civilised peoples—
such is our contention—that mysterious tendency in the
soul which we designate the spirit of the East ; and its
form is the supernatural. But whereas the prophet
standing alone, remains a visionary or degenerates into
a fanatic, Rome offers him a place in her order among
priests and rulers of men. Israel had the Book ; Rome
has the Chair—the Chair which protects altar, cloister,
Scripture, Revelation. It needs not fertility in new
ideas but the genius of discernment. To select, to
adapt, to transmit from the boundless achievements of
humanity whatsoever will fit in with Catholic tradition
is the task laid upon St. Peter's dynasty.

But these elements are subordinate ; they never
can be sovereign over a world which they have not
created, and which would last on though they came to
naught. Revelation found its origin elsewhere than in
philosophy. It borrows nothing but a few technical
terms and certain illustrations from Aristotle or Plato.
In essence it is Hebrew, and that not only by its gospel
of righteousness (as Arnold thought) but even more by
its Messianic hopes, their fulfilment and their future.
Its heart is not morality but the Incarnation, the wisdom of God made man. Therefore it is committed
to sacred persons speaking with authority, not to the

individual and his arguments. When the Reformation stepped down from this height its Christianity sank to be one among the sects of philosophers ; the vital form became a ruin and dissolution followed. The analogy between Protestant and Gnostic is the plain refutation of both.

There remains the lay or secular State, throned in many capitals and making holiday in Rome itself, a foe that has outlived Luther. When we view it as a system of laws, we seem to be gazing on the mighty Empire, governed by Marcus Aurelius with his wise men, which had no need of Revelation, so these jurisconsults and Stoics held, but was framed altogether on reason. The Christian, so far from enjoying any rights, bore an illegal name ; his religion was *lèse-majesté* ; fire and sword were the benefits which that humane common law bestowed on him. The martyrs of Lyons write in their blood an eloquent commentary on such law, becoming by force of toleration intolerant. Modern France and Roman Gaul teach the same lesson ; alike they tell Catholics ' Non licet esse vos,' a hackneyed but wonder-working phrase which is to justify the exile, and proscription of men and women admittedly culpable of no crime but their faith. Of all Catholics, indeed, from the Pope downwards, it may be said that modern legislation puts them outside the law. To confiscate Church property is a duty in the eyes of Continental ' Liberals.' To suppress the religious orders, we are assured, is incumbent on civilised society. The temporal dominions of the Holy See were annexed to Piedmont, not because they had been ill-governed but because the Church owned them. The Pope is virtually a prisoner because he declines to be a subject. The Martyr-Church and the persecuting State of the

second century come back in the twentieth, expanded
to world-wide dimensions but unchanged.

Why, now, did Christian Rome prove stronger
than the Rome of Marcus Aurelius ? It was because
philosophers could not give the people a religion ; nor
the Stoics do away with superstition ; nor the law
create morality ; nor art and culture satisfy the soul ;
nor Fronto charm with his reasoning as Apuleius did
with his worship of Isis ; nor the Emperor's ' Meditations ' bring men strength and joy like the Gospel.
Before that exquisite and stately vision of things human,
when the Empire was at rest, Marcus himself felt
weary.   It seemed a reminiscence, an autumnal scene,
bearing no promise of spring.   It vanished amid the
confusions of the succeeding age ; Diocletian and
Julian, the last who may be thought in any sense
disciples of the Antonines, could not revive their glory.
Pagan Rome was dead.   Humanism had no power to
save it.   But into its hollow moulds and decrepit language and empty shrines the Church of the Martyrs
poured a new life.   Rome was born again at the
Confession of St. Peter.

Our last word is a hope and an aspiration.   From
no quarter of the sky does one gleam appear which
might herald the dawn of a religion more human or
more spiritual than the Roman faith.   New theologies
are shown to be old Eastern fancies, wanting the secret
of the Incarnation, and therefore as inhuman as the
dreams of Valentinus.   That curious aberration, at
once Gnostic and Agnostic, which ' overcame us like
a summer-cloud ' and was called Modernism, did not
even pretend to set up a Church.   It was conceived in
the very spirit of dissolution ; at its touch the Sacraments, the Bible, and all that Revelation contains, were

melted into vapour, soon to leave not a rack behind. As for the lay State its impotence to frame philosophy of life would be pitiable were it not something worse. We conclude that civilised nations cannot hope to survive, any more than the Roman Empire of seventeen hundred years ago, by relying on law, culture, art, material wealth, or even ethical philosophy, without religion. The West cannot live as it ought unless it bows to the wisdom of the East. And our hope is that every spirit touched to fine issues, desirous that civilisation shall be more than a painted surface, will recognise in the Papacy its guardian and defence. When the Holy Father comes forth from the Vatican to celebrate the feast of reconciliation with a repentant Italy, the third Rome, Catholic and modern, may keep its birthday.

INDEX

DATE DUE

DEC 0 8 1997		
APR 1 6 2002		